EVALUATING RESEARCH ARTICLES FROM START TO FINISH

Ellen R. Girden

 **SAGE** Publications
International Educational and Professional Publisher
Thousand Oaks   London   New Delhi

Copyright © 1996 by Sage Publications, Inc.

For information address:

 SAGE Publications, Inc.
2455 Teller Road
Thousand Oaks, California 91320
E-mail: order@sagepub.com

SAGE Publications Ltd.
6 Bonhill Street
London EC2A 4PU
United Kingdom

SAGE Publications India Pvt. Ltd.
M-32 Market
Greater Kailash I
New Delhi 110 048 India

Printed in the United States of America

Library of Congress Cataloging-in-Publication Data

Girden, Ellen R.
  Evaluating research articles from start to finish / Ellen R.
Girden.
    p.   cm.
  Includes bibliographical references.
  ISBN 0-7619-0445-X (cloth : acid-free paper). — ISBN
0-7619-0446-8 (pbk. : acid-free paper)
  1. Research—Evaluation. 2. Research—Statistical methods.
3. Research design.   I. Title.
Q180.55.E9G57   1996
001.4—dc20   96-10033

        98 99 00 01 02 03 10 9 8 7 6 5

Production Editor: Vicki Baker
Copy Editor: Joyce Kuhn
Typesetter/Designer: Janelle LeMaster

CONTENTS

PREFACE

This book was written to fulfill a need of potential consumers of research as well as of eventual researchers. Whereas research design courses emphasize designs and appropriate statistical analyses, the stress is on *constructing* good designs. As a result, students may be able to apply their knowledge to originating research. But most consumers of research read articles based on original research and may be unable to apply that same knowledge to evaluating the article in terms of soundness of the design and appropriateness of the statistical analyses. These are crucial for practitioners who might consider adapting methods based on results to their practice, whether it be education, sociology, psychology, medicine, dentistry, or any other field. The goal of this book is to fill the void.

This is intended to be a supplement to more intensive text-books rather than a book that teaches design and statistics. As such, the intended audience is assumed to be familiar with elementary research design and have at least a knowledge of intermediate-level statistics.

Whereas previous evaluation books have emphasized well-designed studies and presented statistical analyses in separate sections, this book includes flawed studies and introduces interpretation and evaluation of appropriateness of the statistical analyses as they appear in the article. Evaluative questions are grouped into four categories: the rationale and purpose of the study, design of the study, statistical analyses of the data, and the conclusions reached by the author(s). You read an article by sections, and so evaluations are presented in that order. If, after studying this book, you read your selected articles with skepticism, I will have accomplished my goal.

ACKNOWLEDGMENTS

I am very grateful for the helpful suggestions made by the reviewers of the original manuscript: John Brewer, Trinity College, Hartford, CT; Susan Dutch, Westfield College, Westfield, MA; Dale Shaw, University of Northern Colorado, Greeley, CO; and Paul E. Spector, University of South Florida, Tampa, FL. I also extend thanks to the staff at Sage for their cooperation and patience. And I especially thank the editor, C. Deborah Laughton, for her guidance, support, and above all, confidence in me.

I would like to thank the following individuals for granting permission to use their articles:

Dr. A. Ben-Ari	Dr. G. B. Martin
Dr. J. G. Corazzini	Dr. J. M. O'Connell
Dr. D. J. Cox	Dr. R. Pasnak
Dr. M. S. Goldman	Dr. E. D. Rie
Dr. C. L. Hanson	Dr. S. Sevush
Dr. S. B. Johnson	Dr. M. S. Singer
Dr. G. E. Jones	Dr. D. J. Woehr
Dr. J. H. Kirshner	Dr. L. D. Zaichkowsky
Dr. S. Landau	

1

INTRODUCTION

The purpose of this book is to train students—potential consumers of research and researchers—to critically read a research article from start to finish. You will grow to understand an introduction, which sets the stage by describing the rationale for the study (i.e., what led to it) as well as the purpose of it (i.e., what the study hopes to accomplish). You will learn how to "dissect" the method section so that you can decide whether precautions were taken to guard against threats to internal validity, in terms of assignment of participants to the various conditions of the study and use of control procedures and groups. You will become more familiar with interpreting results and even with performing additional calculations or checking a particular result. Finally, you will evaluate the experimenter's discussion of the results in terms of the extent to which the conclusion is justified, can be generalized, and has limitations.

Studies are presented in order of increasing complexity. Each is prefaced with a brief introduction that describes the basic design and statistical analysis. Every effort has been made to locate examples of good as well as flawed studies in each of the categories, ones that performed statistical analyses that are commonly taught at an intermediate and advanced level. When it is feasible, articles are presented verbatim (even their own table numbers have been preserved). For the most part, however, sections have been excerpted and/or revised for clarity. Revisions or synopses are indented from the margins and always appear in italics. Many of the chapters contain one example of studies that employed a particular design. In these instances, the study is evaluated by you (with my help). Copious notes are added to alert you about potential flaws or good aspects of the design. When two examples are presented, most often only the first is evaluated by you and me; the second article is reproduced or excerpted without notes, followed by a series of critical guide questions, the answers to which are found in a separate section immediately after the questions.

When we evaluate articles together, the excerpts are indented. Questions and answers are not indented and are shaded to make them distinct. Exercise articles, with no comments, are not indented.

The remainder of this chapter presents a review of potential troublespots that can invalidate a conclusion about the effectiveness of an independent variable.

Threats to Internal Validity

To evaluate the soundness of each design you need to keep in mind potential sources of confounds or other explanations of results. These are variables that may be operating in conjunction with the manipulated independent variable that make it impossible to determine whether observed changes or differences in the dependent variable are due to the manipulation, the confound, or a combination of the two. Because these potential confounds may threaten the extent to which the conclusion is valid or justified (i.e., internal validity of the study), they are called threats to internal validity. Briefly, the threats include those that operate when the study entails a pretest and posttest or any other situation with or without a pretest and posttest.

Studies With Pretests and Posttests

History. This refers to any event occurring in the interim that directly or indirectly could affect the behavior being measured and therefore also could account for the results.

Maturation. This refers to any change within the participant that occurs during the interim and can just as easily account for posttest performance.

Instrumentation. This refers to any change in the measuring instrument and/or evaluator from pre- to posttest that can just as easily explain a change in scores.

Initial testing. This refers to a change in posttest performance that results from pretest experience.

Regression toward the mean. This is a predicted shift in posttest scores when participants were specifically selected because their pretest scores were extremely high or low. Posttest scores are predicted to be less extreme, regardless of treatment effects.

Other Research Situations
With or Without Pre- and Posttests

Selection bias. This refers to the assignment of participants to the various test conditions on a nonrandom basis. Differences in performance may be associated with a participant characteristic instead of, or along with, the independent variable.

Selective loss (mortality; attrition). This is the loss of particular participants from a group (or groups) in such a way that remaining participants no longer can be considered to be initially equivalent with respect to the dependent variable.

Diffusion of treatment. This is the unintentional administration of treatment to a control group (or groups) that results in a smaller difference among group performances at posttreatment assessment.

Compensatory equalization. This refers to the administration of some treatment to a control group to compensate for its lack of the beneficial treatment being received by an experimental group. This reduces differences between posttreatment means of the groups.

Compensatory rivalry. This refers to behavior of a control group such that participants attempt to exceed performance of an experimental group because they are not receiving equal treatment. This reduces posttreatment differences between groups.

Resentful demoralization. This is a lowered level of performance by a control group because participants resent the lack of experimental treatment. This increases the differences between posttreatment group means.

Interaction effects. These refer to threats that operate on a select group of individuals that could also account for observed results (e.g., a historic event that affects one particular group of participants).

Experimenter expectancy. This refers to a characteristic of the individual who is collecting the data. When a researcher (author of the article) tests the participants, his or her expectations for certain results may unintentionally affect participants so that they behave in accordance with the hypotheses. Concomitantly, recording errors may be made, also in the direction of a hypothesis.

Threats to Statistical Conclusion Validity

In most instances of experimentation, the conclusions reached by the researcher are based on the outcomes of statistical analyses. Typically, this involves rejection or retention of a null hypothesis. When the null hypothesis is retained, the researcher concludes that there is insufficient evidence for a difference between group means (or whatever statistic is being evaluated). If treatment truly was ineffective, the conclusion is correct. However, if treatment effectiveness simply was not evident in the statistical analysis, the conclusion is erroneous, a Type II error. When the null hypothesis is rejected, the researcher concludes that there was evidence for a difference between group means, that the independent variable was effective. If this is so, the conclusion is correct. However, if treatment actually was ineffective, then the researcher's conclusion is erroneous. A Type I error has been committed. Any factor that leads to a Type I or Type II error is a threat to validity of the statistical conclusion. Briefly, these threats include the following:

- *Insufficient power of statistical test.* This is one of the most prevalent causes of a Type II error. Power refers to the likelihood of rejecting a null hypothesis that is false, or correctly declaring a difference in some statistic significant. Assuming that a difference of a particular size is anticipated, sample sizes have to be large enough to detect that difference. Often, because of research constraints, an insufficient number of participants are tested, not enough to reveal the effect of an independent variable, particularly one whose effect is weak. Had the sample been large enough, and/or the significance level of the statistical test been less stringent, the effect would have been detected. Better studies include a prior analysis of the sample size required, at a certain significance level, to obtain a significant difference.
- *Unreliable instrument.* If the measuring instrument is not reliable (does not measure consistently), performances will be variable, the error term of the statistical test will be inflated, and a true difference between means may not be evident.
- *Varied test conditions.* If testing conditions are not uniform, performances will be variable and a true difference between means may not be evident.
- *Varied participant characteristics.* If participants differ in age, gender, intelligence, and so forth, performances will be variable and a true difference between means may not be evident.

- *Violation of statistical assumptions.* All statistical tests have underlying assumptions. If at least one is seriously violated, the analyses may fail to reveal a difference that truly exists or may reveal a difference that is really due to chance.
- *Fishing.* When an unreasonable number of statistical tests is conducted on the same data, by chance alone one may reveal what appears to be a significant difference.

Although there are also threats to construct and external validity, we can address the issues as they arise. These relate to the extent to which the intended construct (e.g., intelligence, stress) has been manipulated and/or measured by a reliable and valid test and to the extent to which obtained results can be generalized.

Plan of the Critiques

Questions within or after each article are designed to guide you step by step as you read. Questions also appear throughout the articles being evaluated with you. These are repeated because they are questions that you should be asking yourself while reading an article. Two parts of an article are not addressed: the Abstract—a concise summary of the study—and References. You start with the **rationale** for the study. This lets you know what, in the past literature, aroused the investigator's interest in the subject matter to begin with: inconsistent or contradictory findings, a possible confound in earlier studies, curiosity, a logical deduction from a theory that could be tested, and so forth. Always ask yourself: What was the rationale for the study? Next, you move on to the **purpose** of the study. This lets you know exactly what the investigators intended to accomplish. Often, it is in terms of testing particular hypotheses. Sometimes, it is in terms of what they wanted to demonstrate or determine. Always ask yourself: What was the purpose or reason for conducting this study? The **method** section is next. You focus on participants first. You want to know who were tested, how they were recruited, whether participants were randomly selected or assigned, matched, lost because of attrition, and so on. Here is where you want to consider that groups may not have been initially equivalent. Next, you might want to look at tests that were used. If they are not well known, you want assurance that they are reliable and valid and always consider the possibility that they might not be so. If more than one is included, you want assurance that they were presented in counterbalanced order. Finally, the rationales given for using the particular tests should indicate that they are appropriate for fulfilling the purpose of the study.

The procedure section focuses on what was done. A question about **general procedure** tests your basic understanding of what was done to the participants or what they were required to do. Specific questions alert you to possible sources of confounds (e.g., a shift in testing conditions, a failure to assess a manipulation, or testing performed by the researcher rather than by a naive experimenter).

The questions relating to **results** of the study focus on appropriate analyses of the data. Readers always assume that no mistakes have been made and that assumptions underlying all tests have been met. This is not always true, and the outcome can be serious: A mistake in calculations can change the conclusion reached by the investigators. Hopefully, you will remember enough statistics to check on the accuracy of degrees of freedom for independent and dependent t tests and analysis of variance, as well as the appropriateness of the alpha levels used, especially for planned and post hoc comparisons. These points are reviewed in the introduction to the article. Specific questions address these issues. Consider them as quick checks. If they are correct, hopefully the calculations are accurate. Unfortunately, this will not tell you whether the statistical test is appropriate nor if basic assumptions have been met. But even here, quick checks are possible. If standard deviations are given, you can square the values to obtain variances and form simple ratios of the largest to the smallest to see whether there is homogeneity of variance. If the study involves repeated measures, you can check the significance of F ratios with $df = 1$ and $N - 1$ to see whether they are still significant. This checks the validity of statistical conclusions if lack of circularity—equality of variances of differences—has not been considered. If F ratios still are significant, results (at least statistical) are valid. If not, conclusions about means differences may not be warranted. Again, each is reviewed with the relevant article.

The final section of the report is the **discussion**. It is here that the researchers reach some conclusion regarding the outcome of their manipulation—for example, its effectiveness. It is here that questions deal with the validity of the conclusion. You will be asked to consider that threats to internal validity might not have been eliminated, rendering the conclusion unjustified. And because the intent of the study is to generalize the results, you may be asked to consider issues related to external validity (i.e., limitations in the extent to which results will generalize).

Two Sample Studies

Before beginning our detailed analyses, let's consider two studies in abbreviated form, both of which use the same basic design but differ in the extent to which valid conclusions can be drawn. The design is a simple within-group one, in which both sets of scores usually are obtained from the same participants. When the manipulation involves a factor other than time or trials, the levels are presented in counterbalanced order to control for the effects of practice and fatigue as alternate explanations of results. That is, with two levels, A and B, half the trials are presented as AB and the other half as BA. This procedure assures that each level appears equally often at each stage of practice. It also controls for a carryover effect by assuring that each level precedes and follows every other level an equal number of times. Any differences between performances under A or B, therefore, cannot be explained by the cumulative effects of practice and fatigue or by a carryover effect of going from A to B or B to A. If there is a greater effect of going from A to B or B to A, one resolution is to have half the participants start with A and go on to B and the other half start with B and go on to A.

STUDY EXAMPLE 1.1

The present study attempted to determine whether Ritalin has a beneficial effect on achievement test performance over a 2-day span as well as on retention of a story after 2 hours versus 2 days.

The Study

- Rie, E. D., & Rie, H. E. Recall, retention, and Ritalin. *Journal of Consulting and Clinical Psychology, 45*(6), 976-972. Copyright © 1977 by the American Psychological Association. Adapted with permission.

    Ritalin has been prescribed for hyperactive children and is effective in increasing attentiveness. Whereas teachers have noted improvement in school performance on short tests, no long-term effect on achievement has been noted. The purpose of this study was to reconcile the differences between immediate improvement in performance noted in the classroom and lack of long-term effects, as measured by standardized achievement tests, by observing drug effects on recall at two time intervals, and to determine whether drug affects achievement without the passage of time.

Method

First, in the study of recall as a function of Ritalin, children learned a story to criterion. Two hours later and again 2 days later, recall was tested in the absence of further instruction and without drug administration.

Thereafter, Ritalin was prescribed, and some 15 weeks later, while medicated, the children underwent the same procedures with an alternate story of comparable difficulty. . . .

Second, in the study of test performance as a function of the drug, using the Reading subtest of the WRAT and the Word Analysis subtest of the Iowa, children took both tests off Ritalin and 2 days later on Ritalin. The intervention time obviously was inadequate to permit significant skill acquisition to occur.

Subjects

Sixteen males and four females served as participants. They had a mean age of 8.35 years and mean I.Q. of 105.8. All were underachievers, showed behaviors usually responsive to Ritalin, were not taking any other medication, had no neurological impairments, had at least a 6-month reading deficit, and had not been previously medicated.

Procedure

Each child was seen initially at school.

Story items from the Stanford-Binet test were read to the child until all questions about them were answered correctly.

. . . The number of trials required to achieve this criterion was recorded. Two hours later, the questions (only) were repeated to determine retention of the story.

(Note that the initial tests for retention, without medication, were made at school.)

Two days later, on a clinic visit, the children were once again tested for retention without additional repetition of the story. *To this point, the procedure involved no medication.*

(Note that the 2-day test for retention was made in a different environment, at the clinic.)

Medication was then prescribed. . . . Approximately 12-13 weeks later, the story recall procedures were repeated with the same (2-hour and 2-day) intervals for recall while the children were treated with Ritalin.

(Note that both tests under Ritalin were given in the same place, at the clinic.)

To avoid practice effects from the predrug procedures, alternate stories of comparable difficulty were used. The story recall task therefore yielded four measures: (a) initial number of correct responses; (b) number of trials required to criterion; (c) 2-hour recall scores; and (d) 2-day recall scores, both without drug treatment and with drug treatment.

For the study of the drug on test performance, the Reading subtest of the WRAT and the Word Analysis subtest of the Iowa Test of Basic Skills were administered during the initial visit to the child's school. . . . This test administration occurred during the 2-hour period between the story recall administration and the test of story retention.

> *(Note that this test was given before the 2-hour recall test and could have interfered with recall. Moreover, there is no report that the two subtests were given in counterbalanced order.)*

During the noted clinic visit (following the predrug test of story retention) 2 days later, each child was given a uniform single dose of 10 mg of Ritalin orally. . . . One hour after the drug administration, the WRAT and the Word Analysis subtest were administered again.

> *(Note that this second test, under Ritalin, was administered before the retention procedure was begun.)*

Consequently, both of these measures were obtained off drug (during the initial school visit) and on drug (during the clinic visit) with an interval of only 2 days.

> *(Again note that the first test occurred at school and the second test occurred at the clinic.)*

Finally, to determine probable practice effects of test repetition after so short a time, a control group of 30 children was also given the WRAT at 2-day intervals in the absence of the drug. The children were matched to the experimental group by grade and socioeconomic status.

> *(Note that this group of control children was matched with experimental children who were reported to be underachiev-*

Table 1   *Drug-related Changes in Story Recall*

Variable	M		t
	Drug	No drug	
Initial score	2.80	2.85	.128
No. trials to criterion	2.80	2.95	.440
2-hour recall	4.10	3.55	1.770*
2-day recall	3.60	3.50	.288
2-hour recall minus initial score	1.30	.70	1.842*
2-day recall minus 2-hour recall	−.50	−.05	1.966*

*$p < .05$.

ers, with some held back. Therefore, controls could have been younger and more intelligent than the experimental children.)

Results

With respect to the Story Recall task, the basic findings . . . represented in . . . Table 1 indicate no difference between drug and no-drug conditions in initial number of correct responses or in number of trials required to criterion. Recall of the story 2 hours after it was learned under both conditions was clearly greater under the drug condition ($t = 1.77$, $p < .05$). Two days later, recall proved to be no different under the two conditions, with almost identical means for both. The initial (i.e., 2 hours) enhanced performance on Ritalin was not sustained, even for 2 days. . . . A comparison of the changes under the two treatment conditions shows that the gain from the initial number of correct responses to 2-hour recall was significantly greater on Ritalin ($t = 1.84$, $p < .05$) as was the **loss** from 2-hour recall to 2-day recall ($t = 1.97$, $p < .05$).

A difference of .39 grade equivalent was obtained on the WRAT between predrug and "on-drug" test administrations 2 days apart (see Table 2). This increase is significantly greater than the zero change that would be expected in the absence of time for skill acquisition ($t = 3.5$, $p < .005$)

Table 2   *Drug-related Changes in the Wide Range Achievement Test and the Word Analysis Subtest of the Iowa Test of Basic Skills*

	Difference	
	Postdrug (Day 3)	
Test	minus predrug (Day 1)	t
Wide Range Achievement Test		
Total	.39**	3.50
Practice	.20	
Residual	.19*	2.51
Word Analysis Subtest		
Total	.41***	4.28

Note. *t* values were calculated for predrug to postdrug change relative to the expected change of zero.
*$p < .01$; **$p < .005$; ***$p < .0005$.

. . . reflects practice effects as well as changed test "performance" attributable to drug. The magnitude of such practice effects was determined by administration of the test to a control group 2 days apart, without the use of medication. A 2-day "gain" of .20 grade equivalent was obtained with the control group. The difference of .19 grade equivalent between the total 2-day gain and the .20 gain attributable to practice represents the change in test performance attributable to the drug.

(Note the basic assumption that the gain due to practice shown by the control group would be the same gain shown by the experimental participants.)

This immediate drug effect differs significantly from the zero change expected in 2 days ($t = 2.51$, $p < .01$). . . .

A difference of .41 grade equivalent was obtained on the Word subtest of the Iowa Test of Basic Skills between predrug and on-drug test administration 2 days apart (see Table 2). This increase is also significantly greater than the zero change that would be expected in the absence of time for skill acquisition ($t = 4.28$, $p < .0005$). . . .

(Note that gains in recall (number of correct responses) were greater for the 2-hour test (versus the initial test) under Ritalin as opposed to the no-drug condition. One possibility for this finding is the effectiveness of Ritalin, as the authors suggest. Another possibility is that the achievement test, given before the 2-hour recall test at school may have interfered with that recall, whereas such an interfering effect could not have occurred when the 2-hour recall test was taken under Ritalin at the clinic. However, loss in retention from the 2-hour to the 2-day test was greater under the drug than the no-drug condition. This finding eliminates the possibility that no-drug scores were confounded by an environmental variable. The 2-hour test taken initially was at the school and the 2-day test was taken at the clinic. This change in environment might have reduced scores, but it did not.)

Discussion

The issue in the present study was not the effect of Ritalin on scholastic achievement . . . the focus was on the apparent disparity between our previous findings and the impressions of teachers and parents that treatment with Ritalin enhances scholastic performance.

The story recall findings are relevant to this issue. Short-term memory of this kind of age-appropriate material is indeed enhanced by treatment with Ritalin. . . . Consistent with our earlier findings, however, eventual recall (even after only 2 days) was no different under the two treatment conditions. . . . [T]hese effects . . . lend no credence to the assumption that Ritalin facilitates scholastic achievement.

The findings obtained with the WRAT and Word Analysis subtest similarly demonstrate immediately enhanced test performance . . . gains were measured as a function of drug treatment rather than as a function of time during which skill acquisition could have occurred. . . .

(Note that the basic conclusions are that Ritalin enhances immediate recall but not long-term recall. There is no evidence for long-term improvement in scholastic achievement. However, the conclusion regarding long-term recall may not be com-

pletely justified because the achievement test, given prior to the no-drug 2-hour recall test, may have confounded results.)

STUDY EXAMPLE 1.2

This study is taken from the education field. It makes use of two classes of students, each of which participates in both parts of the study. Therefore, there is really only one group, with half using one order of the conditions and the other half using the other order. Ideally, each order would be randomly assigned to each participant, but this would have been very impractical because one of the conditions was the equivalent of an examination, which could not be administered to only half the class. The intent was to evaluate the quality of student essays when they addressed two different audiences. The basic statistical test applied was the *t* test for correlated samples.

The Study

- Cohen, M., & Riel, M. (1989). The effect of distant audiences on students' writing. *American Educational Research Journal, 26*(2), 143-159. Copyright 1989 by the American Educational Research Association. Adapted by permission of the publisher.

  The authors note that student writing is teacher bound to fulfill assignments rather than to communicate. Therefore, they do not demonstrate their skills in writing to an audience. The purpose of the study was to compare quality of student writing in an evaluation situation (for a grade) and communication situation (to a peer in another country). There was interest also in whether writing would differ in the two audience conditions.

Method

The subjects in this study were students in two seventh-grade classrooms in a school in Jerusalem. There were 22 students in each class. The students wrote two compositions in Hebrew. One of these compositions was required by the students' teacher as a regular midterm examination; the other was addressed to peers in other countries after students learned that they would soon be participating on the InterCultural Learning Network. . . .

This study was explicitly designed to test the effect of writing to communicate ideas with peer audiences on students' writing *before* they learned to use the computer for writing. . . . Therefore, all compositions in this study were written with pencil and paper under two conditions that were counterbalanced for order across the two classrooms.

Condition 1: Writing to the Teacher to Demonstrate Skill

At the end of each semester, students were required to write a paper that was used to determine their semester grade. The teacher assigned a list of topics and the students were required to choose one topic and write their essay during the class period. Students were asked to describe and discuss one of the following topics: (a) a recent sports game, (b) a major power or water supply failure, (c) increase in costs due to inflation, or (d) military reserve duty of fathers.

Condition 2: Writing to Peers to Communicate Ideas

Students wrote to peers on the InterCultural Learning Network to share information about themselves and their culture. The International Newswire Service project was explained. They were told that their writing would be translated and retyped into the computer and sent over the wire . . . to an electronic mailbox located in Virginia, USA. . . . The students were asked to write on one of the four topics listed above.

In classroom 1, the seventh-grade students were told about their participation in the InterCultural Learning Network one week **before** their semester exam. Therefore, their first compositions were written to communicate with students in other countries. For their exam, they were asked to write on the same topic they had selected in writing to the network. In classroom 2, the seventh-grade students were given the routine semester exam. One week *after* the exam they were told about the InterCultural Learning Network. They were asked to write on the same topic that they had selected for their exam. The students had not received any feedback on their exams. Most students (71%) wrote on the same topic in both conditions. The change in topics among the other students did not indicate any systematic preference or avoidance of a topic in either of the writing situations.

(Notice that order of the two conditions was counterbalanced between the two groups. This allows students to serve as their own controls for such factors as intelligence and writing skill while controlling for effects of fatigue, practice, and carryover.)

Assessment of the Papers

The researcher collected each set of compositions from the classroom teacher at the end of conditions 1 and 2. The compositions for each classroom were marked by the researcher with a code so that the classroom teacher could grade the papers without knowledge of the audience condition. All 44 papers from each classroom were scored by the classroom teacher. . . .

Then the pair of compositions written by a single student were typed without teacher comments and given to two independent raters who scored each of the compositions using a guide based on the Composition Profile Method. . . .

The papers each received a 1 (*low*) to 4 (*high*) rating on each of five aspects of composition: content, organization, vocabulary, language use, and mechanics. Interrater reliability ranged between .69 to .93 for the five aspects. After reliability computations, discrepancies on grading were identified and discussed so that the final rating was a consensus score from the two raters.

Table 1   *Mean Scores of Students' Compositions*

Aspects of composition	Condition 1: Teacher evaluation n = 44	Condition 2: Peer communication n = 44	t test
Content			
M	2.14	2.65	4.37**
SD	.64	.92	
Organization			
M	2.09	2.74	4.91**
SD	.75	.93	
Vocabulary			
M	2.14	2.26	2.35*
SD	.77	.82	
Language use			
M	1.93	2.35	4.14**
SD	.70	.90	
Mechanics			
M	2.30	2.44	2.22*
SD	.74	.77	
Total score			
M	10.60	12.44	5.04**
SD	3.09	3.89	

Note. Mean scores are based on a 1-4 point scale with 4 being highest.
$*p < .05$; $**p < .001$.

(Note several other good features of this design. Teachers grading the papers did not know the audience conditions of each essay, and independent raters, blind to the purpose of the study, scored the essays. Finally, interrater reliability was established for each aspect of the ratings.)

Results

. . . [T]eachers . . . scored the papers written to communicate with peers ($M = 75.11$) higher than those written for their midterm exam ($M = 69.66$), with the difference being significant, $F(1, 42) = 75.13$, $p < .001$.

(The square root of F *equals* t *for correlated samples with 43 df. The 42 df reported in the article also should be 43, but this error does not affect the results.)*

The results indicated that the teachers had judged the papers written to communicate with peers on the network higher, by more than half a standard deviation, than those written for the teacher to determine their midterm grade.

The papers written to communicate with peers were scored higher regardless of the order in which they were written in both classrooms. . . .

Table 1 presents the average score in each of the five composition criteria, as well as a total score for each set of papers scored by independent raters. These scores confirmed the effect found using teachers' wholistic scores. Students' writing is better when they are writing to communicate with an audience than when they are writing to demonstrate their skill in writing to the teacher. The strongest effects are in the organization, content, and language use of the compositions. . . .

A content analysis of the differences between the pairs of articles indicates that students did make decisions about their text based on audience considerations. . . .

The abbreviated account written by students to the teacher seems to assume that they share sufficient background knowledge . . . to understand the description without difficulty. When writing to communicate with peers in other countries, the students seem to realize their audience does not share their background knowledge; therefore they were far more explicit. . . .

. . . The students seemed to assume that explicitness and further elaboration was redundant when writing for the teacher. Their assumption of a shared background of experiences between themselves and their teacher resulted in more abbreviated writing. These compositions in turn received lower assessments by the teachers.

Audience awareness also led to a change in the use of colloquial expressions. When writing for their peers in other countries, the students were less likely to use slang or personal expressions. . . .

Though we lack the process information about the students' writing that is necessary to substantiate our claim, we have the impression that the students devoted more thought to the content and the organization of their compositions when writing for the network than when writing for the teacher. . . .

Discussion

The teachers' assumption that writing for a grade would result in higher quality writing was not supported. In this experiment, students wrote better compositions when they were trying to communicate information and ideas with their distant peers than when they were trying to write their best for an examination. The compositions written to communicate with peers were better organized and dealt with the content in a more informative and elaborate fashion. . . .

. . . [T]hese students tailored the content and the form of their writing to different audience conditions.

A property of school writing is the often unspoken expectation that directs students to write as if they were writing to a qualified audience. Teachers expect their students to understand the difference between writing *to* a specific teacher as a reader and writing *for* a teacher as evaluator. However, this may be a more difficult task than teachers imagine. Students are learning to write and therefore should practice writing as if they were planning to share their ideas with some readers. . . .

Conclusions

Learning does not have to be totally separated from the contexts in which it is applied. Writing is much more effectively learned when students direct their writing to specified audiences for purposes rather than practice writing in write-as-if settings, even when the imaginary audience and purpose is made explicit. By contextualizing the skill in communicative settings, students are more likely to utilize skills learned in classrooms outside of school. Studies on the transfer of a skill learned in one setting to another indicate that the best way to increase transfer is to make the contexts as similar as possible, thereby eliminating the problem of transfer. Thus, if we design an environment in which students write for specified audiences on topics about which they want to convey information, we will be developing the skill in a similar situation as will exist when they write outside of the classroom in the society at large. Computer networks make it possible to increase the range of goals and audiences for students' writing and in doing so may provide a first step in the reintegration of students into the larger society.

(Notice the conclusion that the audience does affect quality of writing. Students writing for peers in another country provide more information and richer content than when writing for their teachers. Presumably, when students are writing for the teacher they omit details because they assume that the teacher is familiar with the situation and experiences. Indeed, they found that quality of writing differs when it is for communication versus evaluation. And they found that students adjust their writing to suit their audience. The conclusion is justified. Students served as their own controls, and precautions were taken to guard against experimenter effects. However, these results and conclusions only generalize to seventh-grade students in Israel who write for their teachers and peers in Virginia on the topics introduced in this study.)

Supplementary Readings
on This Topic

- Cook, T. D., & Campbell, D. T. (1979). *Quasi-experimentation: Design and analysis issues for field settings.* Chicago: Rand McNally College Publishing.
- Kasdin, A. E. (1992). *Research design in clinical psychology* (2nd ed.). Boston: Allyn & Bacon.
- Neale, J. M., & Liebert, R. M. (1986). *Science and behavior: An introduction to methods of research* (3rd ed.). Englewood Cliffs, NJ: Prentice Hall.

2

CASE STUDIES

This chapter is concerned with a descriptive method of assessing behavior. The case study involves extensive observation of a single individual, several individuals, or a single group of individuals as a unit generally before, during, and after some intervention. Despite the fact that intervention is neither systematic nor methodical, there is sufficient justification for studying a single individual. The study may suggest factors that precipitate a disorder, concern a rarely occurring disorder, involve a treatment that is in limited supply, lead to the development of a new treatment, provide the opportunity to use a common technique in a novel way, and/or provide evidence against a generally held principle. Because of the nature of the study, only descriptive statistics are possible as indicators of changes in the targeted behavior. Likewise, because of the laxity of such studies (e.g., nonsystematic introduction of treatment) only tentative cause-effect conclusions are possible. Potentially, every threat to internal validity can plausibly account for the obtained results.

However, the extent to which these threats play a role depends on whether objective measures of behavior are made, when they are made, and whether more than one case is studied at a time.

Case studies range from those that are purely descriptive, with no measurements made, to those that include elementary descriptions of some behavior (e.g., frequencies, means, etc.). The latter extend from those that include pre- and posttreatment measures to those, better controlled, that include continuous monitoring. In this chapter, we examine two case studies. We evaluate the first together; the second is evaluated only by you. The former has no objective measures of the targeted behavior, whereas the latter includes a baseline measure of behavior as well as a description of the treated behavior in terms of frequencies and means.

STUDY EXAMPLE 2.1

This case study is of the treatment of a blind student by means of group therapy with sighted individuals. It includes no measures of behavior and no control conditions and therefore is potentially open to a host of threats to internal validity.

The Study

- Corazzini, J. G., Michaels, C., & Finer, W. Group therapy and the visually handicapped: A case study. *Professional Psychology, 13*(3), 444-452. Copyright © 1982 by the American Psychological Association. Adapted with permission.

Group therapy with the visually impaired is not a recent therapeutic strategy. . . . Regardless of the type of orientation, the membership in these groups has tended to be homogeneous. Except for the leaders, a typical therapy group is composed solely of visually handicapped members.

. . . [R]esults . . . as well as group therapy theory . . . suggest that heterogeneous group composition has distinct and important advantages over homogeneous group composition (e.g., more like the "real world," greater variety of coping styles available as models, etc.). Thus, both the law and group therapy theory and research argue for treating the mental health needs of a visually handicapped person in a group composed largely of sighted members.

Heterogeneity alone, however, does not guarantee therapeutic success. Deviance within a therapy group is a serious potential pitfall. Since the visually handicapped often have been seen as deviants within the majority population, it is consistent to expect them to be given that role in a therapy group of predominately sighted members. . . . There is no type of deviancy from "out there" that is too deviant for a group to accept once therapeutic norms are established and the member "joins." Research results suggest . . . that members are perceived as deviant if they use denial and communicate on a more superficial level than other group members. . . . Other . . . results . . . support the belief that if visually handicapped persons can be helped *not* to play deviant roles in the group, they and the other group members can experience the duration factors of universality by discovering that they have more in common than they have differences.

1. *What was the rationale for the study, that is, what led to it?*

Treatment for visually handicapped individuals has included group therapy, but the group has consisted of similarly afflicted individuals. This is not lifelike and does not allow the individual to overcome a feeling of being different. Research suggests that a heterogeneous group would be more beneficial by helping to teach such individuals that there are more similarities than differences between them and a sighted group.

This article will elaborate on the process of integrating a visually handicapped individual into an ongoing, process-oriented therapy group. . . .

2. What was the purpose of the study, that is, what did it intend to accomplish?

To expose a visually handicapped individual to a sighted group undergoing process-oriented group therapy, to teach him to accept the attitude that he is not a deviant because of his handicap.

Richard, the subject of the present case study, was a 25-year-old male student at a western university. He was congenitally blind, attended high school in a residential setting, and was a talented musician whose goal was to become a music therapist.

> (Note that the fact that Richard was congenitally blind is important. He never experienced being sighted and might not have resented what he was missing. Aside from not knowing why he was born blind, he may have been overprotected with little chance to develop self-confidence. This lack of self-confidence, rather than blindness, might be the source to anger that will be evident in this report.)

His wife of 1-1/2 years was visually handicapped, although not sightless. The instructor of a basic-helping-skills course referred him to the university counseling center for treatment, describing him as being so sarcastic and noncooperative . . . that he blocked his own and other class members' progress. . . . Richard had a history of poor interpersonal relationships and was perceived . . . as angry, demanding, and prone to violent outbursts. Many other students and university staff had expressed frustration in their attempts to relate to Richard and had chosen to avoid him. They considered him to be an articulate young man who was openly distrustful of them and resented anyone who treated him differently because he was handicapped.

Richard saw himself as dependent in his marriage relationship and frustrated in his attempts to establish independence and competence. He viewed his wife as constantly testing him or restricting his freedom. . . .

This issue of competence was pervasive; it was Richard's basic belief that others thought him incompetent because of his disability. Therefore, he either needed to work doubly hard to overcome this fundamental flaw and prove his worth or he needed to withdraw in order to protect himself from the negative judgments of others. For instance, he began playing the piano as a small boy and yet abandoned it completely when an instructor criticized his style. Richard consequently had become a loner with few friends and minimal emotional support.

(Note the many factors that could be contributing to his problems: blindness, unknown factors in his childhood, marriage, adjustment to college.)

?

3. What were the participant's major characteristics?

He was a 25-year-old congenitally blind college student, married for 1-1/2 years to a visually handicapped woman. He had some marital problems, which he attributed to his wife's attempts to make him feel dependent. He had a history of difficult interpersonal relations and was described as sarcastic and angry. He felt incompetent and was easily discouraged when his work was criticized. Because of his attitudes he was a loner, with few friends.

When Richard entered treatment once weekly in midfall of the academic year, individual therapy was deemed most appropriate. . . . The focus of therapy became the deeply held anger that lay beneath Richard's challenging and sarcastic style. However, working with his anger was difficult because he perceived its origin to be totally external to himself. . . . Therapy came to an impasse when Richard was unwilling to take any responsibility for the problems that he was facing.

. . . At this point it was considered necessary to make Richard's anger and its consequences more amenable to direct experience and evaluation by him. In order to do this, his wife was asked . . . to attend the . . . sessions. After two joint sessions it became apparent that Richard's wife played an instrumental part in maintaining his anger. . . . Her response to Richard's abuse was indirect and passive, which only reinforced Richard's anger.

The therapist . . . thought a therapy group for Richard might better help him experience and understand his anger while improving his interpersonal relationships. . . . In group therapy Richard would receive feedback from different group members, making it difficult for him to blame others for his unhappiness. . . .

?

4. What previous therapy experiences did he have?

Because of difficulties in a self-help course, he was recommended for therapy. He had weekly sessions for 3 months before the group therapy was recommended because of lack of progress in working through his anger.

5. Why did it fail?

He could not take responsibility for his anger or its origin and blamed his problems on external sources. Therapy could not lead to further progress.

6. *What role did the participant's wife play in his pathology?*

His wife was not sightless. He reported that she always tested him or attempted to restrict his freedom. When she had two joint therapy sessions with him, the therapist noted that she played a role in maintaining his anger.

7. *How long had the participant been in therapy prior to the current treatment plan?*

He was in therapy for 3 months prior to joining the group. (It is worth keeping in mind that prior therapy may not have had any obvious effect. Sometimes, effects accumulate, and one therapy works because of the previous experiences.)

. . . 3 months after he began treatment, Richard was referred to an ongoing, open (new members joined as old members terminated), process-oriented therapy group conducted in the same university counseling center. This group had formed approximately a month before Richard began individual counseling. It was led by two therapists, a male, who was Richard's individual therapist, and a female. The group met twice weekly for 50-minute sessions and, at the time of Richard's entrance, was composed of nine members (four men and five women), each of whom had been in the group for at least 2 months. . . . This particular group was chosen for Richard for two reasons: First, one of the leaders was his individual therapist with whom he already had a strong supportive alliance, and second, the group was mature enough to expect Richard to be responsible and strong enough to expect full membership rather than deviancy.

?

8. What was the nature of the group the participant joined?

There were 9 members, led by a female therapist and the male who had administered individual therapy. It was a cohesive group whose members shared their feelings and was expected to accept Richard as a member rather than as a deviant.

9. What else might have been happening in his life during this period of time?

He was getting older (i.e., maturing), interacting with his wife and colleagues at college, and receiving attention in, at least, therapy sessions.

A summary of Richard's involvement in the group follows. It is designed to highlight the more critical phases of his 4 months in the group: entrance, conflict/resolution, and outcome. . . .

Entrance

Richard's initial style of interacting in the group was to assume the same role he played . . . , the deviant. During the first few sessions no mention was made of Richard's disability, and group members made concerted efforts to include him in group interactions. . . . After four sessions, the pattern of Richard's interpersonal relationships had been reenacted in the group. His membership . . . was tenuous, and leaders and members alike questioned whether they could relate to him.

Conflict/Resolution

During the fifth session, Richard apparently decided to disclose more about himself. . . . He discussed in great detail his blindness and his marital problems. Eventually he was confronted by group members who asserted that Richard's talking about issues outside of the group was his way of avoiding making closer relationships with them. . . . As the sixth session opened, he sat sullenly with his arms crossed over his chest in apparent defiance of the group and refused to explain his feelings or behavior. Richard had become the deviant in the group. Group members had become increasingly angry with him. . . . Richard finally told the group that it had been difficult to attend the group, but he was there because he had a commitment to keep.

Instead of feeling sorry for him or apologizing for being so confrontive, the members and leaders of the group expressed anger at his rejection. They told him how he used his disability as an excuse for not relating to them. The group came to an impasse. . . .

The therapist informed him that she felt he was giving her one chance to care for him, and if she failed, she would not get another. This observation of the group's process had the effect of transforming the issue from one of competency in the group to the . . . issue of being cared for. At this point in the session, Richard visibly relaxed, dropped his defensive posture, and began to share his fears that the group was rejecting him. . . .

Richard had now become a full participating member. . . . He commented that it had been the caring, albeit unspoken, of the group that brought him back, and it was that perceived caring that he had not been able to experience from other people. . . . He no longer was a deviant in the group but was expressing feelings that everyone had felt.

10. What were the major steps involved in therapy?

This consisted of entry into the group as a deviant, resolution of conflict and disclosure of feelings of incompetence and fear of not being accepted, and final acceptance as a member of the group.

Outcome

Richard continued to make progress in the group and to contribute to the growth of other members as well. . . .

Discussion

As the therapists had expected, Richard's initial struggles in the group mirrored and focused those he was experiencing with his wife, his peers, and authority figures.

(Note that the therapist expected Richard to behave in a certain way, and he did.)

At first he attempted to use his visual handicap as a means to become a deviant, parallel to the process he used outside the group. However, the group refused to allow him to hide his sense of incompetence and fear of closeness with his anger, sarcasm, and sullenness. . . . The group members and leaders did not get caught up in feeling guilty for being sighted and persisted in confronting him with his attempts to reject them while still communicating a genuine caring for him. . . . Richard and the black member shared their anger and pain about being rejected for who they were, and a bond was established that brought about a strong feeling of universality. . . . From that point on, Richard participated as a fully functioning group member, making great personal progress and fostering growth in the other members and the leaders as well.

. . . 4 months after the termination of the group: . . . He had begun to write music again and was playing the piano both at home and in public . . . , his communication with his wife was much improved . . . , his wife was pregnant, . . . [and] he had taken a summer job as a roofer and expressed real delight about feeling competent, making money, and overcoming fears of not being able to succeed. . . . He mentioned that the group had helped him to begin to acccept himself . . . and to better relate to other people. . . .

?

11. According to the authors, how successful was the treatment?

Treatment was considered highly successful in terms of all the accomplishments that Richard reported: His marriage was better, he was playing piano again, he had a job, and he felt accepted as a member of the group.

12. What factors, other than the treatment, could equally account for the change in the person's behavior?

Feelings of incompetence and deviancy may have been unrelated to the blindness; the previous treatment may have had a delayed effect; the wife's attitude may have changed, independently of treatment; he may have adjusted to the university (maturation); and/or historical factors, such as he may have made new friends outside of therapy, the passage of time per se may have led to healing, and he was receiving extra attention. The therapist may have treated him in accord with his expectancies, or perceived changes in accord with his expectancies. Finally, any type of group therapy or regular group meetings might have been just as beneficial.

STUDY EXAMPLE 2.2

Whereas case studies are never free from threats to internal validity, some are better than others. Single-subject designs can be effective in eliminating many, and in some cases all, threats to a valid conclusion. They include a baseline measure of the targeted behavior, careful introduction of treatment and precise measures of posttreatment (or treated) behavior. Between these two extremes are studies that include modification of a treatment plan because the intended procedure is not effective, along with several measures of the targeted behavior. Such a case study is the subject of the present critique. This involves a boy who was treated for a phobia of dogs by means of a modified version of desensitization. In the classic version, the adult constructs a hierarchy of images of situations involving the feared object. Then the client is taught progressive muscle relaxation while imagining each situation, from the least to the most fear-provoking. Usually, sessions are conducted in a laboratory, but the client takes home tapes to practice the relaxation techniques.

The Study

- Chudy, J. F., Jones, G. E., & Dickson, A. L. (1983). Modified desensitization approach for the treatment of phobic behavior in children: A quasi-experimental case study. *Journal of Clinical Child Psychology, 12*(2), 198-201. Used with permission.

Although quite a few experiments have explored the efficacy of desensitization paradigms in adult fear cases, comparatively few have explored such procedures used with childhood fears. . . . Practitioners often appear to assume that children's fears can be treated through the same techniques that are applied to adults. . . . However, . . . data . . . suggest that childhood fears differ both qualitatively and quantitatively. In addition, there is a growing awareness that the goals of desensitization may differ. . . . Treatments should not only reduce fear, but also promote the acquisition of appropriate coping behavior since children may not possess requisite skills for successful coping.

One aspect of the "adult desensitization" paradigm that has proven difficult for use with children is the creation and maintenance of a state of relaxation. . . . A number of alternative competing responses have been reported: feeding, . . . playing, . . . and emotive imagery. . . . The latter procedure involves the creation of a strong positive emotion by having a child imagine a series of events similar to everyday experiences but within which is woven a story concerning a favorite hero. After inducing such a state, an item from a previously established hierarchy is introduced as a natural part of the narrative. . . . The procedure appears to be potentially effective in reducing fear, and in promoting cognitive rehearsal of coping strategies.

This case study illustrates a novel version of the emotive imagery paradigm. A self-created hero image . . . , as role-played by the child, was directed through "active imagination" to model more appropriate means for dealing with the aversive stimuli. The imagery of what the hero should do was . . . developed spontaneously . . . in response to a graduated hierarchy of fearful scenes. The procedure appears particularly useful for children because it depends less upon . . . concentrated imagery and more on modeling . . . and play. . . . The procedure also allows for the child to use the hero as a model for learning new behavior while concurrently allowing himself to be exposed to increasingly fearful scenes.

Method

John . . . was a seven year old white male referred for the treatment of a dog phobia. Approximately one year earlier, John had been knocked down and scratched by a German Shepherd dog. . . .

> (He became phobic and left the house less often. His parents bought him a puppy, to reduce the phobia, but it scratched him and he became even more phobic, and would not leave the house by himself.)

Baseline data were collected by the mother over a period of 21 consecutive days . . . during the summer school vacation. . . . Two behaviors were quantified. The first represented a frequency count of the number of times John left the fenced back yard or house unaccompanied by an adult (over a 24 hour day). Since this behavior was easily identified, interrater reliability was not calculated. The second behavior was a count (made by the mother) of the number of times he interacted with peers . . . in his house, yard or neighborhood. A behavioral avoidance test was also conducted in the clinic using a leashed dog of average size. . . . John's fearful reactions were felt to preclude the use of active-participation (in-vivo) desensitization procedures.

Clinical intervention began with the construction of a graduated hierarchy developed at home by the father and John. As a subjective unit of distress scale, John was asked to draw a line with the length representing his amount of fear. Ten scenes were developed. . . .

Muscle relaxation was initially used. . . . John practiced with his parents at home and during the weekly sessions, however, he was unable to relax for a sufficient period of time. . . . Emotive imagery was then chosen . . . using a fantasy hero called "Super Johnny." . . . Two sessions were spent in trying to interweave "Super Johnny" with the graduated scenes, however, John became bored after only several minutes. . . . It was decided that his natural playing ability would be used as a competing response. John was told that if he would imagine the graduated scenes he could then play by showing the examiner how "Super Johnny" would handle the scene. He was presented the graduated scenes and when he felt any anxiety or fear, as signaled by raising his hands, the scene was terminated and John was transformed into "Super Johnny." The transformation was elaborate and included having John put on a cape and drinking a "power-inducing potion." Following the transformation, the previous scene was reintroduced and "Super Johnny" was given instructions to use his arsenal of magic weapons against the dog only if absolutely necessary. . . . After "Super Johnny" successfully modeled appropriate behavior, "Super Johnny" was transformed back into John and instructed to image the same scene again, employing the more adaptive behaviors as modeled by "Super Johnny." . . .

Results

John successfully completed the hierarchy in eight sessions. For three weeks following the eighth session, the mother again recorded the number of times per day that John left his yard unaccompanied by an adult and the number of contacts he had with other children in the neighborhood. As compared to the baseline, there were dramatic improvements in these behaviors. . . . John left his house and fenced yard on only *two* occasions during the three-week baseline. This was an average of only .1 excursions per day overall. The number of daily contacts with neighborhood children ranged from no children to three children, with a mean of .85 contacts per day. After treatment, Johnny was leaving the yard unaccompanied an average of 1.76 times per day, and the modal frequency was twice a day. . . . The follow-up evaluation was conducted during school days and his chances for outside play were fairly restricted. The number of contacts with peers also increased markedly to 3.1 contacts per day. . . . In a post-treatment avoidance test with the same dog . . . Johnny was able to approach and pet the dog without either the parents or the therapist in the room. Observations indicated that he was slightly apprehensive.

A follow-up evaluation was conducted over a three-day period 15 months after termination of contact . . . [and] the improvements were still evident at follow-up. Johnny was leaving the yard unaccompanied an average of three times per day (range 2-4). . . . The child's parents reported that Johnny was still cautious around strange dogs, but that he was no longer phobic of dogs. . . .

Discussion

This case study describes a modification of desensitization procedure using emotive imagery, free play, and covert modeling in the treatment of dog phobic behavior in a seven year old male. The procedure reduced phobic isolation and fear and increased social contact. The integration of covert modeling and free play into the desensitization paradigm appears promising for use with young children. Although there are clear limits to the conclusions of the efficacy of a treatment analyzed in a case study design (unknown generality, inability to isolate most effective treatment components, comparison against treatment control procedures, etc.), the combination of treatment modalities (desensitization, fantasy, covert modeling, and behavior rehearsal) used in this procedure would appear to have solid theoretical support. . . .

. . . Pre- to post-treatment improvements were also evident on the behavioral avoidance test with a live dog. Although the phobic behavior had persisted at a stable level for over a year before baseline data were collected, a 15 month follow-up shows that all improvements at end of treatment were still apparent.

CRITIQUE OF STUDY EXAMPLE 2.2

1. What was the rationale (i.e., background thinking) for the study?

2. What was the purpose of the study?

3. What are the major characteristics of the participant?

4. What was the basic procedure for collecting baseline data?

5. What procedures were used before the final one?

6. What was the novelty introduced as a final course of action?

7. How much time elapsed since baseline data were taken and the end of treatment? (Keep in mind that the treatment began during summer vacation.)

8. What were the main results?

9. What are some possible reasons for the elimination of the phobia other than the specific therapy?

10. In view of your answer to #9, is the authors' conclusion justified?

ANSWERS

1. Although many studies have shown positive effects of desensitization for adult phobias, few have explored its efficacy with children. Child phobias differ quantitatively and qualitatively from adult phobias. It is hard to create and maintain relaxation in children. Emotive imagery involves imagining an everyday positive experience with a favorite hero interwoven in the tale. Then, an item from the fear hierarchy is introduced. This might be an effective way of reducing fear and was selected to treat a referred case of a phobia.

2. The original intent was to use emotive imagery to eliminate a dog phobia in a child. A novel variation was used instead.

3. A 7-year-old white male. One year earlier, he had been knocked down and scratched by a German Shepherd. He became fearful and was given a puppy, but it scratched him. He became phobic and would not leave his house without an adult.

4. The mother collected baseline data for 21 days: The number of times he left the house or yard without an adult and the number of times he interacted with peers were noted. An avoidance test also was administered using a dog on a leash.

5. Initially, the boy and his father constructed a hierarchy of 10 stimulus situations involving dogs. For each one, the boy drew a line to indicate the amount of fear each aroused. Muscle relaxation was not successful. Emotive imagery was tried next with "Super Johnny" as the hero. The therapist attempted to introduce him in a story involving a dog and required that the youngster imagine the hero's reaction, but he became bored.

6. Instead of imagining the hero in the scene, the boy role-played him and showed the therapist how the hero would deal with the dog in the scene. When the boy became too anxious, the scene was ended. The boy was transformed to

the hero and then reenacted that scene or one that was less anxiety provoking.

7. Three weeks were devoted to baseline data, and treatment occurred over 8 weekly sessions. This is the passage of 11 weeks and would bring the end of treatment to about the time that the child would be returning to school.

8. Prior to treatment, the mean number of times he left the house alone was .1 per day, with a mean of .85 peer contacts. After 8 weeks of treatment, he left the house a mean of 1.76 times per day (mode = 2) and had an average of 3.1 contacts with peers per day. On the avoidance test he was able to approach and pet the dog. Behaviors were maintained on follow-up tests.

9. Other events occurring during the 8 weeks that could have led to reduction of the phobia are the following:

    - *History.* Increased attention from the parents and therapist; TV shows and/or movies he might have seen with friendly, gentle dogs (no mention is made about giving away the puppy); return to school
    - *Maturation.* The boy was almost 3 months older
    - *Bias* in the mother's recording of data
    - *Cumulative effects* of earlier treatments

10. Tentatively, yes. Although some of the above explanations are plausible in accounting for improvement, measures of behavior over a period of months did show a reduction in fear.

Supplementary Readings
on This Topic

- Kasdin, A. E. (1992). Drawing valid inferences from case studies. In A. E. Kasdin (Ed.), *Methodological issues and strategies in clinical research* (pp. 475-490). Washington, DC: American Psychological Association.
- Kasdin, A. E. (1992). *Research design in clinical psychology* (2nd ed.). Boston: Allyn & Bacon.

3

NARRATIVE ANALYSIS

Many qualitative methods exist besides the case study. Participant observation, used by psychologists, sociologists, and other social scientists, involves observing group interactions by "joining" the group. Ethnographic analysis involves examination of cultural events or experiences. Originally, this entailed objective measures. The new ethnography also includes interviews with respondents. A more prominent "newcomer" stems from methodology that originated in Europe: narrative analysis. This entails analysis of a life story—a segment of one's life that is of interest to the researcher—including experiences of the narrator as perceived to be relevant to the life segment in terms of their impact, chronological sequence in the narration, and potential effect on the future course of actions by the narrator. The analyst is interested in why certain experiences were reported when they were and why some are emphasized. Explanations may be offered throughout as hypotheses, each tested by subsequent text. What is significant is the interaction between past, social, and present events in shaping the narrator's perception of these now and in the future. These narratives are assumed to provide more information on our perceptions about the effects of social variables than can be provided by traditional paper-and-pencil scales.

What is recognized, at the core of the analysis, is that the narration depends on the interaction between interviewer and narrator. Although researchers believe that this cannot be controlled, keep in mind that questions stem from a particular researcher, as do "all possible" hypotheses about why a report of event A led to a report of event B. In other words, tendered hypotheses may be a function of the experiences and/or beliefs of the interviewer. Moreover, the data obtained in an interview are structured by the question. The intent is to structure questions so that they encourage a narrative on the meaning of the life experience to the respondent rather than a mere report.

STUDY EXAMPLE 3.1

We will evaluate this study together. The example is from the field of social work. The investigator has conducted numerous interviews with homosexuals and their parents in order to understand the impact of "coming out."

The Study

- Ben-Ari, A. (1995). It's the telling that makes the difference. In R. Josselson & A. Lieblich (Eds.), *Interpreting experience: The narrative study of lives* (Vol. 3, pp. 153-172). Thousand Oaks, CA: Sage.

Mark was 27 when we met at one of the small cafes in Berkeley, California. His intense blue eyes stared at an invisible spot as he began to put together the pieces that made up his story:

It was during the holiday season. We had taken a
friend of ours to the doctor and were waiting for her
in the car. My mother raised the subject of the
dance planned for the following night. She asked
me why I had decided not to go. She waited a few
seconds, sighed, and said, "Well, I keep hoping that
sometime you are going to have a girlfriend that you
will bring along," and I said, "That's never going to
happen." She asked, "What?" and I said, "I am gay."
She was silent for a few minutes, then whispered,
"You must be kidding," and I quietly shook my
head, "No, I am not." That is how I told my mother.

Mary, a soft-spoken woman in her late 50s, began her story:

It was around Thanksgiving weekend. We were all
staying at our friend's house. There was a big dance
coming up the following night. I had bought tickets
for everyone. The whole family planned on going,
including my 87-year-old mother. A week before the
party, Mark asked me to take his ticket back. . . .
    We had taken our hostess to her doctor's appoint-
ment and were waiting in the car. We were very
quiet and didn't even look at each other. I have a
very clear memory of that moment. I remember
asking myself what was going through his mind and
if this silence was significant. Then, breaking the
silence, he asked, "Did you take back that ticket?"
"Yes," I said, disappointed, "I'd really like you to go
but there will be other times." But he shook his
head and said, "Oh no, there won't." And I asked,
"Why not?" and it was then he told me that he was
gay. This is how I learned that I have a gay son.

Two personal and distinctly different accounts of the very
same incident: a son's and a mother's attempts to arrange
their lives within a meaningful context. At present, both
Mark and Mary think of that weekend as a turning point in
their lives.
    The aim of this chapter is two-fold: It documents the
attempts of two individuals to personally organize their life

experiences around a particular turning point, using the narratives of Mary and Mark to illustrate what gay men, lesbians, and their parents may go through prior to, during, and following the discovery of a child's homosexuality. Researchers have argued that predictive and longitudinal research focuses mainly on demonstrating stability over time, which may result in neglect of a more interesting question, that of conditions accounting for change. . . . This chapter . . . examines a change in people's lives—a turning point— employing a narrative or interpretive approach.

. . . Little research has been devoted to understanding the reactions in the family to the discovery of a child's sexual orientation . . . and generally, the impact . . . on their parents' well-being has been overlooked. . . . I will confront these issues and look at coming out . . . by applying the concepts of privacy and intimacy and the dynamics between them to the process in which parents learn about their children's homosexuality. . . . I will also examine the . . . process and its implications for the well-being of the parents.

?

1. What is the rationale for the study?

Longitudinal studies have ignored factors accounting for changes in people's lives. Moreover, little research has looked at the family's reaction to learning of a child's sexual orientation and the impact on parents' well-being of a child's homosexuality.

2. What were the purposes of the study?

One was to examine how people attempt to organize their life experiences around a turning point in their lives, using the experiences of a gay man and his mother to illustrate what homosexuals and their parents go through before, during, and after the child's sexual orientation is disclosed. The second was to look at a change in a person's life using a narrative approach.

One of the main arguments of the narrative approach is that constructing a "subjective truth" is at least as important as revealing "objective truth." . . . Eliciting the significance of the experience and its meaning to the individuals involved in it is the principal concern. To elicit first impressions and minimize the potential influence of a theoretical framework, open-ended and almost identical questions were presented to Mary and her son. When interviewing Mary, I asked her to describe her experiences as well as her perceptions of her son's experience throughout the process of coming out. . . . Mark was asked to decribe his as well as his mother's experiences throughout the very same process.

> *(Note that there is no report of where and when interviews took place and whether there were just two interviews—one for each of them—or whether there were more than two interviews over a period of time.)*

Thus, two first-person accounts and two descriptions of the other person's perceived experiences were available on completion of the interviews. The following is a presentation of these four perspectives of a single incident: a son revealing his sexual orientation to his mother. Obviously, there are differences between the versions. Nonetheless, the purpose of discussing these differences is not to detect discrepancies among the stories but to interpret and understand in terms of their respective contexts.

In their stories, Mary and Mark differentiate between predisclosure, disclosure, and postdisclosure thoughts, feelings, and experiences. A similar sequence underlies the organization of this chapter. It is important to point out, however, that the distinction between predisclosure, disclosure, and postdisclosure is predicated on adapting a retrospective outlook.

?

3. Who were the narrators?

A 27-year-old gay man and his mother in her late 50s.

4. What was the procedure? What is lacking?

Both were interviewed, individually, using identically phrased open-ended questions that were designed to elicit first impressions, significance, and meaning of the experiences. However, we don't know anything about the circumstances of the interviews, except that at least one, Mark's, took place in a cafe.

Predisclosure

All that can be said with any certainty about predisclosure is that it ends at disclosure. Yet significantly, both Mary and Mark felt the need to somehow define this period and seemed to want to consider how long this stage lasted, when it started, what it referred to, and what characterized it.

Mark talked about wanting to come out as well as his reservations about it.

> I feel close to my mother. Her not knowing was an incredible barrier. I was hiding probably the most major facet of my life from her. I felt that I was living a lie by not telling her that I am gay.

(Note that he may be expressing a feeling of guilt.)

Reflecting on his fears, he added,

> I did not have any real ones, my mother is pretty liberal, I knew that there wouldn't be any major problems. And yet I knew that once I said it, I would never be able to take it back. The words would be out there and there would be no way to return. . . .

Mark characterizes predisclosure as a period of tension and conflict. He describes constant struggle: wanting to share and wanting to hide, on the one hand, longing to be open and honest about his homosexuality with his mother, and on the other hand wishing to remain secretive about the very same issue.

. . . Prior to disclosure, gay men and lesbians experience tension between the need to exercise control over the access to particular information (privacy) and the need to share that very same information (intimacy). . . . [D]isclosure occurs when the need to keep information private subsides and the wish to be open and share this information becomes more important.

I asked Mary what she had thought were Mark's motives in coming out to her. She replied,

> I used to constantly ask myself the same question. At different times I came up with different answers. At first, still in the grip of pain, I asked myself why he did it, whether he was trying to hurt me, or to get back at me. I found myself constantly thinking about what it was that I had done. Later, I learned that he had been tired of hiding and pretending to be someone he was not. It took me several years to realize that Mark came out to me primarily because he valued our relationship. He felt that hiding that aspect of his life from me would cause our relationship to stagnate or even deteriorate. I really think he wanted to be honest and to share with me what he was going through back then.

. . . Mary gives us a clear example of the developmental nature of interpretation. Her attempt to "make sense" of her son's behavior evolved through three major stages. Initially she focused mainly on herself, as if she or her behavior could possibly explain his behavior. She then moved to concentrating on him as the main locus of interpretation: He didn't want to live a lie, or he was tired of pretending to be someone he was not. Finally, she began to talk in terms of their relationship. It has been my observation that when parents . . . move away from seeking understanding in either themselves or their children, to thinking about the relationship between them, then they start adjusting to the discovery of their child's homosexuality.

Reflecting on Mark's then-anticipated fears, she said,

> Now, I can hardly think of Mark being afraid of telling me anything about his life. I don't think he was afraid that I would do something. But knowing that he did keep this information from me for a significant period of time is in and of itself indicative. Even now it is hard for me to admit that he did not tell me because he was afraid to and yet, between the time he himself discovered his sexual orientation and until he told me, well it has been a fair number of years. . . .

Studies . . . have suggested specific explanations for homosexuals' disclosure . . . to parents. . . . Hopes that disclosure will reduce the price exacted for "passing" (i.e., as heterosexual), permit greater honesty, open up channels of communication, strengthen family bonds, deepen love, and provide opportunities for mutual support and caring feature as reasons for disclosures.

However, self-disclosure is not always perceived as a positive experience. . . . Gay and lesbian children . . . avoid disclosures to their parents . . . because of fear of rejection, worry about parents' sense of guilt, guilt about parents' physical and mental pain, apprehension about being forced to seek treatment, desire to protect the family from crises, and uncertainty about their sexual identity. . . . Underlying all . . . is the realization that disclosure is irreversible. Mary describes being suspicious during the predisclosure stage. Suspecting that Mark was gay long before he told her, she recalls asking herself if it was normal that he didn't do the same things as his older brother . . . , that he never had a girlfriend, never expressed any interest in going out with girls? She also remembers, however, that as a teenager, he went through a period when he didn't want to be around anyone; days in which he stayed at home without leaving his room. She recalls that she often asked herself what the meaning of all this was and where it would all lead. Now she believes that it was during this period that he came to terms with his homosexuality. . . . [N]ote, however, that Mark did not discuss this period of time in his story.

Mark admitted that he knew his mother suspected he might be gay before he actually came out. Both the mother and her son, in fact, were withholding information. Mark was secretive about his sexual orientation; Mary kept her suspicions to herself. Yet Mark knew about his mother's secret, much as Mary knew about her son's. Thus a complex of secrets and concealed awareness of the other party's secrets evolved throughout the predisclosure stage.

The first family member with whom Mark shared his secret was his sister. Mark knew that she had many friends in the gay community and that she would not have a problem accepting him as a gay brother. Our data . . . suggest that the majority of gay men and lesbians would first disclose their homosexuality to a family member other than a parent: a sibling or a member of the extended family. They think of the first disclosure to a family member as a trial, a "rehearsal" before the real performance. . . .

Mary and Mark think of predisclosure as a period of time during which they felt distant from one another, and their relationship deteriorated. "Not telling" enabled both of them to keep their secrets and protect their privacy. By the same token, withdrawing to the safety of their secrets left little space for exchange, sharing, and closeness.

?

5. How was the period of predisclosure described?

For the son, as a period of conflict between wanting to come out and not wanting to relinquish his privacy. He also guessed that his mother knew. The motive was the need to be closer to her. For the mother, there were doubts about why he was different from his older brother and the suspicion that he might be gay.

6. Is any other interpretation of the motive plausible?

Yes. Mark may have felt guilty about his nondisclosure and/or his homosexuality and may have wanted to relieve the guilt.

Disclosure

Mary and Mark have different perceptions of what transpired during actual disclosure. . . . Mary is sure that Mark carefully planned the disclosure down to the very last detail. On the other hand, Mark casually implies that he intended to come out "sometime" during that weekend. Mary thought that Mark deliberately chose a time when she would be unable to make much fuss.

> Not only were we not at home; we were house guests. He made his disclosure when our friend was in the doctor's office, allowing only a very brief exchange beween us. When the friend returned, we both tried to act as if it had never happened, hadn't been said. But I think he was very stiff at that point, and felt a little self-conscious. Later that day, I asked him when he first knew, and he told me that was too private and personal a question.

Mark's narrative focuses on a different aspect . . . :

I was watching her through the rear mirror. She was in the back seat. I could see her. She could watch my eyes. We were both looking at each other through the mirror. . . . At some point I think we both avoided looking at the mirror. Later that evening, I was sitting in front of these people's house and my mother came to talk to me. She asked me if I was sure that I was gay, if I wasn't just going through a phase. She also said that if it was true, she wouldn't know what to do about it. That was all we talked about.

Mark and Mary's perceptions of the disclosure reflect the differences in the meanings they attribute to it. . . . Generally, the initiating person is more likely to recognize the planning involved. . . . It is interesting to note, however, that in our case Mary is sensitive to the planning aspect of disclosure.

Neither Mary nor Mark includes details that might imply doubts pertaining to issues about which they currently feel certain. Yet the other person does. . . . Mark emphasizes his mother's questioning of his homosexuality, and Mary doesn't mention it in her account. These differences can be explained in light of how they currently perceive themselves. Mary views herself as a very accepting person. . . .

(This contradicts Mark's account. Look at the end of above quote. Or, Mary's perception of herself may have changed.)

Mark, on the other hand, presents himself as never having doubted his homosexuality. . . .

On the basis of interviews with 27 parents and 32 gay men and lesbians, Ben-Ari . . . has developed the view that in most cases, gay and lesbian young adults disclose their homosexuality to their parents because they want to get closer to them. Indeed, telling parents about their homosexuality generally does improve the relationships between these children and their parents. Most of the interviews reflect a consensus during the time of the interviews, and in retrospect, the main motive for disclosure is "to be honest with parents; not to hide; not to live a lie."

Like their gay and lesbian children, an overwhelming majority of parents also prefer that their gay children disclose their sexual orientation to them. . . . They also prefer to receive "private" disclosure and that it be done in person. . . . [M]any parents expressed their regrets at not being told sooner. They feel that they missed an important part of their children's lives. Mary says,

> I really feel bad that I missed those years of his life, that I could not share with him when he was in high school, whatever he was going through. I think all mothers who have learned to accept this, feel this way. We miss. In my case, I missed 10 years of his life which he couldn't share with me, the questions and fears he had. Now, I wish I could replay those moments, hug him, and tell him how much I love him anyway.

?

7. How was the disclosure period interpreted?

The mother reported being convinced that Mark had carefully planned to tell her on a weekend when they were visiting friends and she could not make a fuss. Mark did not mention specific planning but said that he had intended to tell her sometime that weekend. Each omitted details about issues of which they were certain at present but which would imply doubt at the time.

8. How does the author interpret this discrepancy in reports?

In terms of how each perceives himself/herself today. For example, Mary perceives herself as accepting but may have had doubts about her acceptance then and omitted this from her account.

9. Are other interpretations plausible?

Yes. The omitted issue of past doubt might reflect denial. Psychoanalysts might attribute the omission to repression.

Postdisclosure

I met Mark and Mary more than 5 years after the initial disclosure. Mark remembers his mother right after disclosure:

> A little bit of surprise, quite a bit of disbelief, and unwillingness to deal with it. The hours and the days that followed, I think she kind of put it in the back of her mind and did not think about it because she had this social engagement she was going through, and she couldn't stop to process this knowledge. After that she talked a lot to my sister who has a lot of gay friends.

Mary remembers,

> I was pretty shocked, I think that when you are shocked like that you kind of have a dead feeling, you don't really know what to say next. I didn't cry, I was just shocked and thought what am I going to do now. I don't think I even reassured him that that's OK with me. . . . [Very quietly she added,] I don't think I even did that.

Parental reactions to learning about their child's homosexuality are often seen in terms of typical grief responses, including shock, denial, guilt, anger, and acceptance. . . .

Mary's experience, however, does not reflect a typical process of grief following disclosure. Although describing herself as being shocked initially, she could not recall going through denial, anger, self-blame, or guilt. . .

(Note that initially she reported thinking "what it was that I had done.")

Our data did not confirm the traditional view and did not reveal significant differences between specified grief reactions

. . . which may imply that parents do not necessarily go through a grief sequence after learning about their child's homosexuality. . .

(Note that a mother's reactions may differ from a father's reaction.)

Like many other parents, Mary thinks about her post-discovery stage in terms of a chronological sequence. She differentiates, for example, between her thoughts and feelings right after she was disclosed to, during the first year, and at the time of the interview:

> Later on, maybe 6 months later, I think that I came to gradually accept more and more that this was really true. I felt very protective towards him and extremely concerned. I was more worried about him than I was about how I was feeling. After realizing that he could not change, I didn't even think about it anymore, I started to accept reality.

The search for an underlying theme that would characterize a period of time or a certain experience is indicative of the effort to organize and create meaning out of a particular experience. . . .

> When I think about it now, the emotion I found that I had within the first 6 months, or the first year, and still have to some extent is loneliness. I tend not to share this with anybody who I think will think less of him. Everybody in our family thinks very highly of him. I guess, I don't want anybody to think: Ha, he is not what we thought he was. Among my closest friends, there is no one with whom I could share the experience of having a gay son.

Mark's recollection of his mother's postdisclosure experience is somewhat different. He remembers, for instance, that during the first 6 months, or even the first year, his mother didn't want to ask him about his personal life.

(Note that she reported earlier that when she asked him when he became aware of his homosexuality he answered "that was too private and personal a question.")

She was embarrassed to talk about it, or she thought it wasn't any of her business. I think she really didn't want to know what could be going on. She didn't want to know if I had a lover. She didn't know how to communicate about gayness with a gay child.

On completion of the interviews, I asked Mark and Mary, "What could the other person have done so it would be easier for you?"

Mark thought that if his mother had been able to communicate with him about his homosexuality earlier, it would have made the whole experience easier. He felt that his initiative to get closer to her was not reciprocated. Mary said that it would have helped if Mark were closer, physically and emotionally, so she would not have to be so alone.

. . . One of this chapter's main concepts is that gay men and lesbians come out to their parents mainly because they want to get closer and be able to share their lives with them. Parents can ease their experiences following the discovery of their children's homosexuality by perceiving it as a quest for intimacy. By the same token, gay and lesbian individuals are not the only ones to keep information about their homosexuality private before disclosure. In most cases, the parents of these individuals also keep related thoughts and suspicions secret.

10. What were the accounts regarding the postdisclosure reactions?

Mark described his mother's reaction as surprise (shock), disbelief, and putting her coping at bay. Mary also described being shocked and wondering how she would cope. Both describe a period of loneliness.

11. How were Mary's reactions interpreted?

The author claims that there was no evidence of a typical grief reaction, which fit in with other data she obtained.

12. Is there question about the interpretation?

Yes. First, Mary earlier had questioned what it was she had done. On the one hand, this may refer to "why is he trying to get back at me?" On the other hand, it may refer to "how did I contribute to his being gay?" The latter suggests guilt. Second, the conclusion that parents do not experience a typical grief reaction is based on a mother's account. The author does not report fathers' reaction to their sons' or daughters' homosexuality, nor mothers' reactions to their daughters' lesbianism, and we are led to believe that all reactions are alike.

13. Does the narrative analysis fulfill its purpose?

Yes and no. It describes recollections of the impact of an event that was the turning point in the lives of a gay man and his parent. It shows that certain issues are emphasized and others casually mentioned or omitted—perhaps the major future effect of the event. If the intent is to describe the actual (not perceived) impact, the method did not fully succeed. It relied on retrospection, when other factors can color objective reactions. Again, the author states that subjective truth is more important. Most important, interpretations of this narrative report are influenced by the theoretical leanings of the interpreter.

Supplementary Readings
on This Topic

- Josselson, R., & Lieblich, A. (1993). *The narrative study of lives, Vol. 1.* Newbury Park, CA: Sage.
- Josselson, R., & Lieblich, A. (1995). *Interpreting experience: The narrative study of lives, Vol. 3.* Thousand Oaks, CA: Sage.
- Riessman, C. K. (1993). *Narrative analysis.* Newbury Park, CA: Sage.

4

SURVEYS

The case study is the crudest of the descriptive methods for studying behavior; surveys can be better controlled. They obtain information that is otherwise inaccessible. Attitude surveys measure likes, dislikes, and so on. Research surveys test hypotheses. With both, responses are related to demographic information.

Two crucial aspects of surveys are the development of a valid and reliable questionnaire and selection of the sample. Because the intent is to generalize the results to the population, the sample has to be representative. Probability samples are representative: there is a certain probability that every member can be included in the sample. This may be a random or stratified sample. With the latter, the population is segmented on some basis (e.g., age, college level), and samples of each segment are in the same ratio as exists in the population. Nonprobability samples are not representative because they exclude members of the population. For example, telephone directories exclude people without telephones or with unlisted numbers. Quota sampling obtains samples with certain characteristics in the same ratio that exists in the population but only from a particular location.

The biggest potential drawback of surveys is that people are not always willing or able to respond to the questionnnaire. Therefore, what begins as a representative sample does not always end that way. There may be a difference between respondents and nonrespondents; that is, those responding may be a select group, and this can place serious limitations on the extent to which results can be generalized. For this reason, it is very important that, when reading results of a survey, you learn the initial size of the sample and the final percentage responding. This is true regardless of whether the survey was conducted by means of a written questionnaire, a telephone, or a face-to-face interview. It is equally important to know who gathered the data, how, and where.

Results of surveys are reported in terms of percentages. Tests of significance often involve chi-square. However, other analyses can be used (e.g., differences between proportions). Chi-square tests determine whether frequencies in certain categories differ from what would be expected on the basis of chance. When categories differ along a single dimension, the test is called goodness of fit. For example, all faces of an unbiased die should occur equally often when it is tossed many times. If you toss it 120 times, you would expect each face to appear 20 times (120/6 = 20). Suppose you obtain frequencies of 18, 20, 22, 30, 16, and 14 for faces 1 through 6, respectively. Is there evidence to suggest a biased die? The $\chi^2 = 8.00$ and you enter the chi-square table with $6 - 1 = 5$ *df.* A chi-square of at least 11.07 can occur by chance 5 times out of 100 ($p = .05$). A value of 8.00 can be expected more often, and you conclude that the obtained frequencies do not differ reasonably from the expected frequencies of 20. There is not sufficient evidence to consider the die biased.

Contingency tests determine whether frequencies in one category depend on membership in another. For example, does preference for rare, medium, or well-done steak depend on sex? Males and females are surveyed about their preference. You end up with a 3 (Steak Preference) × 2 (Sex) table of frequencies.

Expected frequencies are based on marginal totals across rows and columns for each cell ([row total × column total]N). Then, chi-square is calculated and compared with a tabled value for df = (rows – 1)(columns – 1). Here df = (3 – 1) (2 – 1) = 2. If the obtained value is lower than the tabled χ^2, you conclude that steak preference does not depend on sex. If the obtained value is significant, then steak preference depends on sex.

We begin our critical review by evaluating a survey together.

STUDY EXAMPLE 4.1

This survey, a follow-up study, determined whether former clients of a mental health center were satisfied with the services.

The Study

- Kirshner, J. H., & Hogan, R. A. Patient feedback at a community mental health center: Year three. *Professional Psychology, 13*(3), 431-438. Copyright © 1982 by the American Psychological Association. Adapted with permission.

Since most previous research in psychotherapy has not been conducted in community facilities and private practices, Parloff . . . questioned its value to practitioners and policymakers. Morrison . . . has advocated patient feedback in his community-oriented approach to psychotherapy. . . . [I]n this age of accountability, . . . patient's views require investigation.

In 1964 Schofield asserted that therapy is most effective with young, attractive, verbal, intelligent, and successful (YAVIS) patients. Research from community mental health centers . . . indicates that the poor receive the same therapeutic benefits as other groups. Studies from mental health centers may be a step towards a psychotherapy for the poor. . . . [T]he poor use mental health centers in greater proportion than . . . [others] in the population.

The present study represents the 3rd year of follow-up evaluation of former patients . . . in Muscatine, Iowa.

?

1. What was the rationale for conducting the survey?

Most research on psychotherapy is not conducted in community facilities; there is a question about its value for practitioners and policymakers. Moreover, whereas evidence suggests that young, attractive, successful, intelligent individuals gain the most from therapy, community mental health research suggests that the poor also benefit. Similar studies could benefit the poor, the greatest population of patients served by mental health centers.

2. What was the specific purpose of this survey?

To conduct a third-year follow-up on former patients at a rural community mental health facility.

Method

Questionnaire

As in previous surveys . . . a questionnaire was mailed to every former patient over 13 years of age who had not been seen in 3 to 11 months.

(Nothing is reported about reliability and validity.)

The sample was drawn from those serviced between July 1, 1977 and June 30, 1978.

A cover letter assuring former patients of our genuine desire to learn both the positive and negative aspects of service delivery and of the confidentiality of their response was included with the questionnaire. Of the 190 instruments delivered, 99 (52%) were returned after a maximum of two follow-up contacts.

(Although such a return rate is not uncommon, you must, at this time, wonder about the characteristics of the nonrespondents.)

Variables previously studied . . . included age; sex; marital status; number of therapy sessions; income categorized as below $5,000 a year, $5,000-$6,999, $7,000-$11,999, $12,000 and up, and unknown; and education, coded as 8th grade or less, 9-12th, 13th or more, and unknown. Other former variables were patients' perceived degree of help received through counseling and therapy, divided into extremely helpful, moderately helpful, of little help, and not helpful; patients' perceived seriousness of the problem that brought them to the center, categorized as very serious, moderately serious, or slightly serious in their lives; patients perceived interest of the therapist in them, rated as very interested, not as interested as they would have liked, or disinterested; and the self-reported behavior after termination, checked as not seeking further help, being seen by another professional, or not seeking further help but feeling that it was needed. . . .

(There are no guidelines for making these judgments, and they refer to perceptions of events that occurred up to a year ago.)

New variables . . . completed before the follow-up study included disposition, checked as ended by mutual consent; further care indicated but patient not ready; withdrew without notice or transferred; and staff's perception of the client's condition at termination, rated as improved, unimproved, deteriorated, or not changed.

?

3. What population was sampled?

Questionnaires were mailed to all former patients older than 13 years of age who had been seen from 3 to 11 months earlier.

4. What was the general nature of the questionnaire?

Demographics (age, income, education level), evaluations (of the seriousness of their problem, the extent to which the therapist was interested in the patient, the extent to which the patient felt helped by therapy and their behavior after therapy ended). Staff also rated patient's disposition at the end of therapy.

5. Can reliability and validity of the questionnaire be questioned?

Yes. Neither measure is reported here, although they may have been in an earlier publication. Moreover, some who were surveyed had to make judgments about feelings they had almost a year earlier. Third, there were no guidelines for judging seriousness of a problem, degree of improvement, and so on, and these could have been colored by patient expectations.

Results

Demographic Variables

Former patients ($N = 99$) fell within these age ranges: 13-17 (11%), 18-29 (37%), 30-54 (43%), and 55+ (8%). Of the 99 patients, there were more women (61%) than men (39%), and the marital status was divided into 32% single, 48% married, 13% divorced, 3% widowed, and 3% separated.

The majority (54%) were seen three times or less ($N = 98$), with 18% having 4-6 sessions, 15% having 7-10 sessions, 5% having 11-15 sessions, and 7% having 16 or more sessions.

Income data ($N = 98$) was available on most former patients. Twenty-four percent reported income below $5,000, 3% had income between $5,000 and $7,000, 19% declared income of $7,000-$11,999, and 34% reported income of $12,000 and up. Census data for 1970 revealed 9.2% of the Muscatine county population was at poverty level. With at least 24% of the study's sample having incomes below $5,000, the poor were well represented.

Educationally (*N* = 97), most (59%) had 9-12th grades of school, 26% had 13 years or more, 13% had 8 or less years; educational level for 2% of the sample was unknown.

?

6. What was the return rate of questionnaires?

After two follow-ups, 99 out of 190, or 52%, responded.

7. What were the major characteristics of the respondents?

They were 30-54 years old, women, married, seen three times or less, incomes of $12,000 or more, and 9th- to 12th-grade education level.

Client Perception Variables

Most former patients felt that they had been helped to some extent by counseling or therapy (*N* = 97). Thirty-six percent found the therapy extremely helpful, 31% moderately helpful, and 24% of little help. . . .

Patients (*N* = 97) considered the problem that brought them to the center as very serious. . . (64%). . . . Twenty-seven percent found the problems moderately serious. Nine percent had slightly serious problems.

Former clients (*N* = 99) perceived their therapist as very interested in them (61%). . . . Only 2% had therapists whom they considered disinterested. . . . Therapists were seen as moderately interested in 28%. . . . Nine percent felt that their therapist's interest in them was not as much as they would have liked.

After terminating (*N* = 97), 59% sought no further professional help. . . .Twenty-one percent were since seen by another professional. Twenty percent sought no further help but felt they needed it.

Closing Summary Variables

At time of termination, center staff rated the disposition of 93 patients as follows: 33%—further care indicated but patient not ready, 31% ended by mutual consent, 31% withdrew without notice, and 3% transferred. Condition at termination ($N = 91$) was evaluated as 48% unimproved, 47% improved, 3% no change, and 1% deteriorated.

> *(The N's keep changing because of missing data for particular items. Also note the discrepancy between the percentage of former patients who felt that they had been helped at least moderately—36% + 31% = 67%—and the ratings of therapists that only 47% had shown any improvement. Moreover, only 24% of the former patients said that therapy was of little help, but 48% were rated as unimproved.)*

?

8. What were the major findings of the survey?

Most felt that therapy had helped, very serious problems brought them to therapy, they sought no further help, and the therapist was interested in them. Forty-eight percent were rated unimproved.

Statistically Significant
Variable Interactions

The most consistent result of these follow-up studies has been the relationship between perceived therapist interest and perceived help received ($N = 97$), $\chi^2(9) = 53.15$, $p < .0001$. . . .33 of 35 persons who felt extremely helped, considered their therapists very interested in them. . . .

(Now check df to see if they are accurate.)

Perceived therapist interest was related to termination behavior ($N = 97$), $\chi^2(6) = 13.52$, $p < .05$. Forty of 58 persons who found the therapist very interested in them sought no further help; 10 sought no further help but felt they needed it; and 8 went to see another professional. . . .

?

9. *You read a list of levels for the categories of perceived interest and perceived help. Check these. Based on them, what should be the degrees of freedom for χ^2 that tested the contingency of these two variables? Does this change the conclusion reached?*

Based on four levels of perceived help and three levels of perceived interest, the $df = (4 - 1)(3 - 1) = 6$. The tabled value for 6 df at $p = .001$ is 22.46, so the conclusion is the same.

10. *What is the meaning of the χ^2?*

The extent to which the patient felt helped by therapy depended on the extent to which the therapist was perceived to be interested in the patient: those whose therapist appeared most interested felt they were helped.

11. *Now consider the relationship between perceived interest by the therapist and termination behavior. Are the degrees of freedom correct? Does the conclusion change?*

With 3 levels of perceived interest and 3 levels of termination, $df = (3 - 1)(3 - 1) = 4$. According to a chi-square table, a value of at least 9.49 will occur 5 times out of 100 when two categories have a total of 4 df. The obtained 13.52 will occur much less often and still is significant.

12. What is the meaning of this χ²?

What the patient did after therapy ended depended on how interested the therapist was perceived to be: those patients whose therapists seemed interested were less apt to seek additional help.

In the current sample a number of variables were related to termination behavior: marital status ($N = 97$), $\chi^2(8) = 19.28$, $p < .01; \ldots$ income ($N = 96$), $\chi^2(8) = 17.93$, $p < .05$; education ($N = 95$), $\chi^2(6) = 12.46$, $p < .05$; and disposition ($N = 92$), $\chi^2(6) = 12.77$, $p < .05$. The marital status-termination behavior is unique to the 1977-1978 sample. In other samples married persons did constitute the largest category, and most did not seek further professional help. . . .

Income was related to termination behavior largely because 33% (11 of 33) of persons with incomes of $12,000 or more did go to another professional after termination. It does not mean that poorer clients did not seek further help because they could not afford it, since 73% (17 of 23) of the clients with incomes below $5,000 neither sought nor felt they needed further professional help. . . .

Education and termination behavior were significantly related for the first time. Clients with 13 or more years of school were more likely (72%, 18 of 25) not to seek further professional help nor feel a need for it.

Disposition, a new variable, was significantly related to termination behavior largely because 72% of (21 of 29) clients who ended by mutual consent neither sought further help nor felt they needed it. However, 50% (9 of 18) of clients who did not seek further help but felt they needed it were judged by their therapist as needing further care at the time of termination, although they were not ready for it.

Disposition was significantly related to another new variable —staff's perception of the client's condition at termination ($N = 89$), $\chi^2(9) = 27.61$, $p < .001$. Of 28 patients who ended therapy by mutual consent, 82% were judged improved. . . .

Of 28 patients who withdrew without notice, 71% were considered unimproved. Of 29 patients for whom staff felt that further care was indicated but the patient was not ready, 62% were . . . unimproved, and 38% were . . . improved.

?

13. Check the df *associated with relationships between termination behavior and the listed variables. Are they correct?*

All four sets of *dfs* are correct: With five levels of marital status and three levels of termination behavior, $df = (5 - 1)(3 - 1) = 8$, and this is also true of the income variable; education had 4 levels and so did disposition, so *df* for each is $(4 - 1)(3 - 1) = 6$.

14. How do you interpret the significant chi-squares?

Married individuals, those with higher income and higher level of education, and those who ended therapy by mutual consent were least likely to seek further help.

Discussion

Therapists . . . have contended that the therapeutic relationship is crucial to patient change. . . . In the four samples, there has been a highly significant interaction between perceived degree of help . . . and perceived therapist interest. Therapist interest can be construed as part of a relationship variable. Interpreted in this manner, data from the four samples support the importance of that relationship; . . . our data are correlational. Correlations are not necessarily causations. Other explanations are possible.

. . . [C]lients rate therapeutic outcome more favorably than therapists do. Only 9% of clients rated therapy "not helpful." By contrast, staff rated 48% of clients unimproved, 3% no change, and 1% deteriorated. If it can be inferred that being helped results in improvement, it appears that professional staff is the stricter rater. . . .

Staff ratings appear to be influenced by disposition, since 82% of those who ended therapy by mutual consent were judged improved, and 71% who withdrew without notice were considered unimproved. Only 38% of patients whom staff felt needed further care but were not ready were considered improved. Yet there was no significant interaction between the amount patients felt they were helped and the disposition.

Neither income nor education, the YAVIS components, were significantly related to number of therapy sessions, patient evaluation of perceived helpfulness of counseling or therapy, or perceived interest of the counselor in the former patient. This . . . is consistent over two previous samples . . . and the present one. . . . Overall, data from the current sample lend additional support to the contention that the poor receive the same quality treatment and therapeutic benefits as other socioeconomic groups. . . .

(This is a sweeping conclusion based on self-reports of respondents' perceptions of how they felt up to one year earlier.)

Since 24% of . . . this sample had incomes below $5,000 . . . in a county in which 9.2% of the population was in poverty, the data also tend to support . . . that in proportion to their number in the population, the poor tend to be overserved by community mental health centers.

?

15. *Is the conclusion justified that the poor receive the same quality treatment and therapeutic benefits as other groups?*

No. Nonrespondents were almost half of the patients sampled. They may have been unable to read and thus unable to answer the questionnaire. Or, they may have been least satisified with the services and unwilling to answer. For respondents, expectancy for help would be greatest because money was scarce and they paid for therapy. Therefore, they would be more apt to rate the services favorably. Further, most respondents were young, with incomes above $12,000 a year and at least a high school education. Finally, *perception* of quality of treatment and benefits were surveyed. Actual quality and benefits require objective assessment.

Supplementary Readings on This Topic

- Selltiz, C., Wrightsman, L. S., & Cook, S. W. (1976). *Research methods in social relations.* New York: Holt, Rinehart & Winston.
- Weisberg, H. F., Krosnick, J. A., & Bowen, B. D. (1989). *An introduction to survey research and data analysis* (2nd ed.). Glenview, IL: Scott, Foresman.

5

CORRELATION STUDIES

Correlation studies attempt to establish relationships between two or more variables. Participants with the characteristics of interest are selected and measured. Because individuals have other characteristics as well, cause and effect conclusions about a relationship that might be established are not possible; the relationship may be due to an unmeasured variable or to chance. If only two variables are involved, we can end up with a correlation coefficient. This describes the strength and direction of the relationship, positive or negative. Positive relationships indicate that both characteristics co-vary in the same direction. Negative relationships indicate that both characteristics co-vary in opposite directions; an increase in one is accompanied by a decrease in the other. The correlation coefficient also describes the strength of the relationship. This is a value ranging from 0 to ± 1.00. The closer the value is to 1.00, the stronger the relationship or degree of covariation. However, a value *may be* obtained and still effectively be equal to zero. Thus, once the value is calculated it is then tested statistically to determine whether it is significantly greater than zero. The degrees of freedom associated with the test are $N - 2$, where N = number of pairs of scores. If the obtained value can occur by chance 5 or fewer times in 100, it is considered to represent a real correlation.

Whenever a correlation coefficient is declared significantly greater than zero, we run a risk that we've made an error in the decision we've reached: the coefficient may, in fact, be a chance occurrence. Such a value, on rare occasions, may occur even when two events are not correlated. When working at the .05 level of significance, we risk making this (Type I) error 5 times out of 100. If two coefficients are computed, each tested at the .05 level of significance, the risk of a Type I error with either decision is greater than .05. And the more coefficients we compute, the greater the risk of a Type I error when reaching a decision (i.e., declaring any coefficient significant when it is not) about a coefficient in the entire set. Behavioral and social scientists prefer to keep that overall risk of a Type I error at about .05. This can be accomplished in several ways. One way is to adopt a significance level for testing each coefficient that equals .05/C, with C = number of coefficients computed. If five coefficients are computed, each would be tested for significance at .05/5 = .01. Therefore, any coefficient that can occur by chance (when variables really are not related), more than 1 time in 100 (e.g., .02 or even .05) would be declared "not significantly greater than zero." Because such a procedure may be too conservative, an alternate remedy is to arrange coefficients in order of magnitude. The highest coefficient is tested at .05/C (e.g., .05/5 = .01). The next one is tested at .05/C – 1 (e.g., .05/4 = .0125). The next is tested at .05/C – 2 (e.g., .05/3 = .0167) and so on, with the lowest coefficient tested at .05/1 = .05. This is extremely important because many authors have not made the adjustment.

Therefore, some of the coefficients they declare significant, especially at the .05 level, may not be significantly greater than zero. In many cases, in the absence of the exact p value actually associated with each coefficient, that value can be approximated. If N is sufficiently large (at least 50), then we can determine the Z score for each r and read off the associated p value from the normal curve table. Here $Z = r/[1/\sqrt{N}]$. If the actual p value (depending upon Z) is equal to or lower than the critical p, then the r is significant.

The most common type of covariation is linear. And the most common linear correlation coefficient is the Pearson r. Thus, the relationship being established is assumed to be linear; Pearson r measures the degree to which the two variables are linearly related. If a relationship exists between two variables but is not linear, the calculated r may very well be close to zero.

A more precise description of degree of linear relation is r^2, the coefficient of determination. This describes the percentage of shared variance, or percentage of variability in one characteristic that is accounted for by the other variable. Thus, if r between IQ and grade point average (GPA) equals .45, then $r^2 = (.45)^2 = 20.25\%$ of variability in GPA is associated with IQ. Those with higher GPAs are likely to have the higher IQs. The remaining variability is due to time spent studying, other activities, and so forth.

Although cause and effect relationships are not likely to result from correlation studies, the effects of some obvious "third variables" can be removed statistically by means of a partial correlation. This removes the effect of a variable from the ones of interest and answers the question: If participants are equal on variable X, what is the true correlation between A and B?

The study to be reviewed is concerned with establishing relationships between two variables at a time. We will look at this study together. As in other studies, design issues are important. If tests are used to measure the characteristics, they should be reliable and valid, measurements should be made under uniform conditions, in counterbalanced order, and by a naive experimenter.

STUDY EXAMPLE 5.1

In this study, the focus was on relating ratings of school children by teachers and by other school children. A term with which you may not be familiar is "sociometric procedures" commonly used to assess popularity. Children are shown pictures or names of class members and asked to pick those they would want to play with, for example. Those picked most often are presumably most popular.

The Study

- Landau, S., Millich, R., & Whitten, P. (1984). A comparison of teacher and peer assessment of social status. *Journal of Clinical Child Psychology, 13*(1), 44-49. Used with permission.

Ever since the dramatic follow-up study of third grade children . . . it has been acknowledged that social status or peer reputation maintains a powerful relationship with adult outcome measures. . . . [C]lassroom nominations for negative roles (ostensibly peer rejection) was the most potent predictor of adult psychiatric problems 13 years hence, even when compared with teacher and clinician ratings of those same children. There has been a growing clinical interest in the implications of negative social status among children. . . .

Previous research has functioned primarily with the presumption that peer sociometric procedures are the most valid means of assessing the social status or social competence of children. . . . Even though the ratings by other informants (e.g., classroom teachers) show reasonable agreement with social status nominations, . . . it could be argued that it is the children . . . who provide the true "state-of-affairs" . . . via sociometric procedures. . . . [I]f teachers are asked to assess a child's social competence, this would be pursued as the more time-efficient . . . way of determining social status.

Recent research . . . provided evidence that seems to contradict this premise. When using various observed preschool social behaviors as criterion measures, . . . a simple teacher ranking of popularity, and not peer-generated sociometric popularity . . . made significant contribution to the predictions of the dependent variables. . . . [T]eacher ranking procedure . . . appeared to be the more valid way of determining a child's social skills with peers. In light of the immense credibility that researchers have invested in sociometric procedures, these are disquieting findings. Sociometric research generally reflects difficult and time consuming data collection procedures, especially with preliterate subjects. If more . . . or even equally valid, information regarding social status could be derived by a simple teacher ranking, investigatory effort would be . . . reduced.

The findings . . . need to be evaluated in light of the fact that popularity was used as the variable representing a child's status. . . . Surprisingly, there are no known longitudinal studies demonstrating the significant predictive validity of positive reputation or popularity. There is, in fact, research to suggest that popularity and rejection measures are separate dimensions. . . .

Apparently, being rated as unpopular suggests different implications than being rejected. . . . [T]he first purpose of this study was to gain a better understanding of the relationship of teacher-generated versus peer-generated social status data in order to assess the relative utility of the teacher ranking procedure. . . . Secondly, the actual relationship between the variables of popularity and rejection was investigated. . . .

?

1. What was the rationale for the study?
Previous research indicated that peer negative ratings are the best predictors of children's future psychiatric status

and that sociometric procedures are the most valid for these predictions, but other data suggested that teacher ratings of popularity might be a better (or equal) predictor of a child's social skills with peers. If so, it would be a time-saver over sociometric ratings. Moreover, while negative ratings by children are good predictors of later psychopathology, there appears to be a difference between being unpopular and being rejected. Similar studies have not been conducted for popularity ratings.

2. What were the specific purposes of the study?

To determine the relationship between teacher and peer ratings of popularity, including a measure of peer rejection, and to study the relationship between peer popularity and peer rejection as they related to social behavior in the classroom.

Method

Subjects

Subjects were 49 boys attending five kindergarten class-rooms in a small . . . Midwestern community. The boys ranged in age from 68 to 84 months, with a mean age of 74.6 months.

(Girls were excluded because of a larger study being conducted with male subjects.)

At the time of the investigation, each subject had been enrolled in his respective classroom for approximately eight months. . . . The number of boys per class ranged from 8 to 13.

?

3. Who were the participants?

Forty-nine boys in five kindergarten classrooms, 68-84 months old, with a mean age of 74.6 months. Each child had been enrolled in the class (with 8-13 boys) for at least 8 months.

Procedures

Three sources of information were collected for these boys;
teacher rankings and ratings, peer nominations of social
status, and observed social behavior during free-play activity. . . . [E]ach teacher was requested to rank, from an alpha-
betized list of their male students, each boy in terms of the
degree to which other children most like to play with him.
. . . They were instructed to apply a ranking of one to the boy
seen as most popular and continue until all boys were
ranked. These popularity rankings were then divided by the
number of boys in each class and transformed. . . . Teacher
ratings of aggression were also available for each boy. These
involved an empirically derived aggression factor. . . .

Peer nominations: In order to assess social status, peer
nominations of "like the most" and "don't like" were collected
from kindergarten classmates. This involved a sociometric procedure that had previously shown adequate retest-reliability
plus good concurrent and predictive validity in the preschool setting. . . .

Prior to the administration of this sociometric, each boy
was photographed from a distance of one meter. . . . Peer
nominations were then obtained from all boys and girls in
each classroom on whom parental permission had been obtained. The 49 subjects were rated by 46 boys and 50 girls.
Three kindergarten parents consented to have their son
rated but not to participate as rater. . . .

The 96 raters were individually interviewed by a male
doctoral student in school psychology. Each was initially
asked to name every boy from the array of photographs of
boys from his/her class. This naming procedure established
that the boys to be rated were known to their classmate
raters. . . . Each child was asked to nominate first one and
then a second boy (i.e., "who else . . .") who best fit the item
described. Scores for the popularity ("like the most") and
rejection ("don't like") variables consisted of the total number
of nominations received, divided by the total number of
raters in the class. . . .

Observed social behavior: Using a point-time sampling procedure, the social interaction of each subject was observed over a six-week period during free-play activities. . . . [T]he following social behaviors of each boy were coded using 10 second intervals: solitary/uninvolved activity (e.g., staring into space), solitary/parallel play (e.g., playing alone), positive interaction (e.g., playing together), negative interaction (e.g., snatching a toy from another child), and adult-only interaction (e.g., verbal exchange with teacher). . . . All subjects were observed for a minimum of 80 intervals except one boy who was observed, due to illness, for 52 intervals. . . . A subject's score for a given behavioral category was the number of intervals that behavior occurred divided by the total number of intervals observed. All . . . variables were transformed. . . .

Five observers, who were kept blind to all questions under investigation, comprised the observer corps.

(This is a good feature of the design.)

Assignment to kindergarten classrooms was rotated so that each had an opportunity to collect data in all settings.

(This is another good feature of the design.)

Observers targeted on each subject for a 10-second interval, progressing through all subjects before returning again to the first boy observed. The sequence . . . was randomized daily and each observation session lasted approximately 20 minutes. Training in . . . use of the behavioral categories involved repeated exposure to training tapes of social behaviors of kindergarten children not included for study. . . .

During the actual data collection phase, 25 percent of all observations were simultaneously observed by both an observer and the trainer for the purpose of establishing an estimate of the reliability of the coding procedure. . . . Effective percentage agreement . . . was computed. These were calculated by dividing the occurrence of agreements by the occurrence of agreements plus disagreements without the contribution of agreements of nonoccurrence. Effective agreement for the five categories of socal behavior ranged from 81.0% to 96.0% with a mean of 88.9%.

(Another good feature.)

?

4. What was the general procedure used in this study?

Teachers ranked each boy in the class for degree to which other children preferred to play with him and rated each for aggression. Boys and girls in each class looked at photos of the boys and chose the one they liked the most (popularity) and did not like (rejection). Nominations were obtained from a total of 46 boys and 50 girls. These were made via an interview by a male doctoral student. Finally, social behavior was observed by five rotated blind observers over at least 80 10-second intervals during free play for solitary/uninvolved activity, solitary/parallel play, positive interaction, negative interaction, and adult-only interaction.

5. Was observer/experimenter bias likely to play a role?

No. The graduate student had no expectancy about who would be nominated as being popular or rejected. And observers were "blind" with respect to the purpose of the study.

6. Could observations of social interactions be considered reliable? Why?

Yes. Observers first were trained with unrelated tapes. Interobserver reliability was established between an observer and trainer for 25% of all observations. Agreement was over 95%.

7. Could teacher rankings or ratings be considered free from bias?

If they were purely objective and based only on observation, then yes. However, teachers characteristically have their favorites or ones that they "take under their wings," and if either is the case, then bias may play a role here.

Results

. . . For the two social status items, correlations between the boy and girl nominations were computed. Both correlations were significant at $p < .001$ or better ($r = .67$ and $r = .74$ for popularity and rejection, respectively). These results . . . indicate that when boys and girls are requested to nominate only boys for social status information, they show significant correspondence in their selection. In the analyses that follow, results are reported using the boy nominations only.

Table 1 presents the correlations among the teacher and peer sociometric data. . . . There was a significant but modest negative correlation between peer nominations of popularity and rejection ($r = -.37$). . . . Further, there was significant agreement between teacher rankings of popularity and peer nominations of both popularity ($r = .50$) and rejection ($r = -.59$). . . .

Table 1 also presents the results of the correlations between the sociometric and the observational data. . . . In terms of the observational variables of Solitary Activity and Positive Interactions, all three sociometric measures provide significant and basically comparable information, the magnitude of the correlations are quite similar.

(Locate Solitary Activity and read across to see its correlation with Peer Popularity [−.30], Peer Rejection [.27] and Teacher Popularity [−.33]. Now do the same for Positive Interaction.)

Table 1   *Correlations Between the Sociometric and Observation Data*

	Peer popularity	Peer rejection	Teacher popularity
Peer popularity	—	−.37**	.50**
Peer rejection	—	—	−.59**
Solitary activity	−.30**	.27*	−.33**
Solitary play	−.25*	.07	−.12
Positive interaction	.34**	−.35**	.36**
Negative interaction	.17	.46**	−.25*
Adult-only interaction	−.13	.03	−.02

*p < .05; **p < .01.

However, in terms of Solitary Play and Negative Interaction, the peer measures appear to be supplying information beyond that offered by the teacher. . . .

> *(Do the same for these two variables and note that Solitary Play is correlated only with Peer Popularity, whereas Negative Interactions is correlated with both Peer Rejection and Teacher Popularity.)*

It is interesting to note that the more moderate relationship between Teacher Popularity and Negative Interaction ($r = -.25$) does not necessarily mean that teachers are insensitive to aversive classroom behaviors since ratings of aggression collected from these teachers correlated significantly ($r = .36$, $p < .01$) with Negative Interaction. It does tend to suggest, however, that peers apparently place more emphasis on negative interactions as determinants of friendship choices.

. . . [T]his study found that the behaviors associated with a boy's popularity are not necessarily identical to those related to his rejection. Even though both Peer Popularity and Peer Rejection were significantly related to Solitary Activity and Positive Interaction, only the former social status variable correlated significantly with Solitary Play and only the latter correlated significantly with Negative Interaction. These findings seem to offer further evidence that the social status variables of popularity and rejection are neither interchangable nor redundant. . . .

One other finding of interest reflected in Table 1 concerns the relationship between social status and the observation variables of Solitary Play and Solitary Activity. Although high rates of both are associated with decreased popularity, only Solitary Activity is related to increased rejection. . . .

?

8. *What is the meaning (verbal and by r^2) of the negative correlation found between peer popularity and peer rejection?*

The more the child is liked by peers, the less he was rejected or nominated as "don't like." In terms of r^2, approximately 14% of variability in the extent to which a child is rejected is associated with the extent to which he is not popular.

9. *As in #8, interpret the correlation between teacher's popularity rankings and peer nominations of the following:*

(a) *Popularity*

The higher the teacher's ranking of popularity of a child, the more the other children liked the boy or ranked him high in popularity. Approximately 25% of the variability in the teachers' ranking is associated with peer rankings.

(b) *Rejection*

The higher the teacher's ranking of popularity, the less the peers tended to reject the child or to select him as "don't like." Approximately 35% of the variability in teacher's ranking of popularity could be associated with the extent to which others rejected him.

10. Describe the relationships between the three socio-metric ratings (peer popularity, peer rejection, teacher popularity) and the child's

(a) Solitary Activity?

The more popular the child, as rated by peers or teacher, the less the child engaged in solitary activity. The more he engaged in solitary activity, the more he was rejected by peers.

(b) Positive Interaction?

The more the child played with other children, the more he was liked by peers and ranked high in popularity by the teacher, and the less he was rejected by peers.

(c) Solitary Play?

The more the child played alone, the less popular he was with peers.

(d) Negative Interaction?

The more negative the child was with other children, the more he was rejected by peers and the less popular the ranking by the teacher.

11. Regarding Solitary Play and Negative Interactions, which were better correlates of these social behaviors?

Peer nominations of popularity correlated with Solitary Play $r = -.25$), and peer rejection and teacher popularity correlated with Negative Interaction ($r = .46$ and $-.25$, respectively).

12. What evidence suggests that the factors associated with popularity of a boy is not related to the factors associated with rejection?

Solitary Play was associated with less popularity but not with Peer Rejection, and Negative Interaction was associated with Peer Rejection and reduced teacher popularity but not with less popularity among peers.

13. What are similarities and differences in predicting Solitary Activity and Solitary Play by the boys?

Both are related to Peer Popularity, whereas Solitary Activity also is related to Peer Rejection and teacher popularity rankings.

14. If you focus on the larger matrix of correlation coefficients, there are 15 of them, several of which were declared significant at p < .01, and several declared significant at p < .05. Are all of those declared significant at the .01 likely to be significantly greater than zero?

No. If we apply the correction to obtain critical p values, as discussed earlier, the highest $r = .46$ and the apppropriate (critical) p value is $.05/15 = .003$. According to what we said earlier, $Z = .46/[1/\sqrt{49}] = 3.22$ and the actual p of obtaining .46 is about .0007, so it is significant. The next higher $r = .36$ and the critical $p = .05/14 = .0036$. Here $Z = .36/[1/7] = 2.52$, and the actual p of obtaining .36 is .0059. This is higher than .0036, and therefore the r of .36 probably is not significant. The next higher $r = .35$, and the critical $p = .05/13 = .0038$. The $Z = .35/[1/7] = 2.45$, and the actual p is .007, so this r, too, probably is not significant. The same is true of the remaining rs declared significant at the .01 level and is also true of the coefficients declared significant at the .05 level.

15. In terms of this analysis, what was the major correlation between sociometric measures and the target boys' behaviors?

There was a correlation between Peer Rejection and Negative Interaction by these boys. The remaining correlations have to be considered suggestive.

Discussion

The primary purpose of the present study was to examine the utility of a teacher popularity ranking procedure as a viable alternative to sociometric nominations. Results were consistent in demonstrating that, even though teachers and peers show reasonable concordance in their respective perceptions of social status, the two sources were not providing entirely redundant information. . . . [P]eer nominations did as well as, if not better than, teachers in the prediction of observed social behavior. . . . [T]his study found that, at least relative to kindergarten sociometric popularity, the teacher ranking procedure was less comprehensive in explaining social behavior variance.

Several explanations for this inability to replicate . . . findings of the preschool study . . . are worthy of consideration. The fact that the current study was performed in a kindergarten setting may limit those transsituational generalizations that might otherwise be inferred. . . . [V]ariations in classroom structure can account for competing results in various sociometric studies.

A second and more critical explanation for the apparent discrepancy between studies relates to the nature of the social status variable investigated. . . . By looking at popularity as the exclusive measure of social status, the discovery of much information may have been precluded. Evidence is accumulating that being "not liked" is quite different than being "disliked." . . . Results indicate that, especially in terms of observed negative interaction, kindergarten nominations of rejection provide significantly more information than teacher perceptions of popularity. This differential relationship does not exist, however, when employing peer nominations of popularity, as teacher and peer popularity variables offered essentially redundant information.

. . . The longitudinal implications of popularity . . . are yet to be established. If researchers are interested in demonstrating the utility of a teacher ranking procedure, the present results would suggest that teacher-perceived rejection may be the construct of choice. To rely upon teacher rankings of popularity may mask that information regarding the presence of peer problems and inappropriate classroom behaviors.

. . . The correlations presented in Table 1 suggest that, especially with Solitary Play and Negative Interaction, low popularity and high rejection scores involve different observable correlates. Consistent with previous research . . . this study provides further evidence that argues for the distinction between unpopular and rejected children in order to enhance an understanding of the distribution of peer reputation.

. . . For both economical and ethical reasons it may be necessary to use teachers as informants of social status, but as this study and others . . . indicate, important information may be lost if peer rejection is not evaluated.

?

16. *What conclusions were drawn regarding peer nominations, teacher rankings of popularity, and social behavior correlates?*

Peer nominations are as good as, if not better than, teacher rankings in predicting social behaviors. Although peers and teachers equally predicted positive behaviors, peers were better at predicting negative interactions—or at least in rejecting those boys who demonstrated the most negative interactions. The study also concluded that unpopularity is not the same as rejection.

17. *On the basis of results, should investigators rely on teacher ratings to predict social behaviors of children? Why?*

No. Although teacher ratings correlated with peer rejection, they were not correlated with negative activity, whereas peer rejection was correlated with negative activity and this is one of the predictors of later difficulties in social adjustment.

Supplementary Reading
on This Topic

- Howell, D. D. (1992). *Statistical methods for psychology* (3rd ed.). Boston: PWS-Kent.

6

REGRESSION ANALYSIS STUDIES

Regression analysis deals with predicting certain variables on the basis of knowledge about other, independent variables. Or it deals with the role played by certain independent variables in a particular dependent variable. Thus, it may deal with how well GRE scores predict performance in graduate school, or it may deal with the average amount of change in blood glucose for each unit change in stress. When we are concerned with more than one independent (or predictor) variable, then the problem is called multiple regression analysis. In this instance, the regression equation is

$$\hat{Y} = b_0 + b_1 X_1 + b_2 X_2 + \ldots + b_p X_p.$$

Assuming a straightline relationship between Y and Xs, b_0 is the Y intercept, and the remaining bs are regression coefficients.

Each reflects the average amount of change predicted in Y for each unit change in the corresponding X *when all other variables are held constant.* Therefore, if several predictors are correlated with each other (called multicollinearity), all but one provide redundant information, and each uniquely contributes little to the prediction (i.e., one or more of the bs will be relatively low).

Because we often want to know the relative importance of a variable in predicting Y, βs (beta weights) or standardized regression coefficients, based on Z scores, are computed instead of bs, based on raw scores. Here, each β reflects the average amount of change predicted in Y in terms of standard deviation units for each unit change in X. Each of the βs is tested for significance. If one is not significant, then it does not significantly contribute to the predicted $\hat{Y}$ once the other variables are included, even though it may correlate highly with these other variables. If βs are tested for significance, df for an F test (analysis of variance test, covered in Chapter 11) are 1 and N (number of sets of scores) $- p$ (number of predictor variables) $- 1$.

Another bit of information that emerges from multiple regression analysis is multiple R: the correlation between the dependent variable and the predictor variables. Its square is interpreted as any r^2 as percentage variance in the dependent variable that is associated with the predictor variables. It is calculated by $R = \sqrt{\beta_1 \, r_{1y} + \beta_2 \, r_{2y} + \ldots + \beta_p \, r_{py}}$ and its significance is tested by an F test with p (number of predictor variables) and $N - p - 1$ df.

If the intent of the analysis is to determine whether certain predictor variables *are related to* an outcome measure, all variables are entered into the equation simultaneously. However, if the intent is *to predict* the outcome (criterion) variable, alternate multiple regression procedures are available. The best known is stepwise multiple regression. After the significance of all predictor variables has been determined, the most significant predictor, in terms of having the highest correlation with the dependent variable, is entered into the equation and R^2 determined. Then, the second most significant predictor, the one with next highest partial correlation with the dependent variable, is added and R^2 is redetermined. If the change in R^2 is significant, the effect of the first variable is reexamined. If it is still significant (i.e., still accounts for a reasonable amount of variance, the next variable is entered and the process is repeated until the change in R^2 no longer is significant. That last variable is removed. If significant variables are added successively, the procedure is called forward selection or variable-added-last regression analysis. If the procedure involves the successive elimination of the least significant variables, the procedure is called backward elimination regression analysis.

Use of multiple regression analysis is not without cautions. Sloppy data yield misleading results of the analyses. In addition, if extreme scores (outliers) are included, these can distort results. If no mention is made about tests for outliers, an examination of means and standard deviations can give you some idea about the shape of the distribution of scores.

Other problems can occur with stepwise regression analysis. Some variables declared to be significant predictors may be significant by chance because so many tests are conducted (especially with a large number of predictors). Variables that are significant when one sample is measured may not be so for another sample and vice versa. For these and other reasons, the results of stepwise regression analyses should be interpreted cautiously.

Regarding design issues, multiple regression studies should be as rigorously conducted as an experiment. Given that some of the predictors are scores on psychological tests, the tests should be reliable and valid and be administered in counterbalanced order; that is, each test should appear in each position an equal number of times. Moreover, the individuals administering the tests should be naive with respect to crucial bits of information so as not to influence the testees. Finally, testing conditions should be uniform to reduce variability, and volunteer participants should not differ radically from those who refused to take part in the study; that is, there should be no selective loss of participants.

Two studies are presented, the first of which we will evaluate together. You will evaluate the second one alone.

The first study analyzes its data by variable-added-last regression analysis. It is an attempt to learn why patients with probable Alzheimer's disease deny that they have a memory deficit.

The Study

- Sevush, S., & Leve, N. Denial of memory deficit in Alzheimer's disease. *American Journal of Psychiatry, 150*(5), 748-751. Copyright © 1993, the American Psychiatric Association. Reprinted with permission.

Patients with clinically diagnosed Alzheimer's disease often deny either the presence or severity of their deficits in memory and activites of daily living. . . . The reasons for this . . . have not been established, but two studies have provided . . . data on the relationship between this variable and demographic, cognitive, and psychiatric factors in . . . groups of patients with Alzheimer's disease.

In one study . . . clinical interviews were used to assess denial of deficit in 25 subjects with possible Alzheimer's disease who had cognitive impairment of varying severity as well as in five subjects with "senescent forgetfulness." Subjects with possible Alzheimer's disease were found to be more likely to deny their deficits than were individuals with senescent forgetfulness, and subjects with marked cognitive impairment suffered from greater denial than did those with mild cognitive impairment. Another study . . . provided additional data by comparing "awareness of illness" with severity of disease and severity of depression in 38 patients with probable Alzheimer's disease. Awareness of illness was measured by administering a memory self-assessment questionnaire to the patients and comparing the results to parallel assessments made by the patients' caregivers. . . . [A] negative trend was found in the relationship between awareness of illness and severity of dementia: awareness decreased as dementia severity increased. The negative correlation was strongest between awareness of deficit and performance on verbal and visual secondary memory tests. A trend was also found relating awareness of illness to severity of depression: awareness was greatest in those patients with the most marked depression.

These studies, although suggestive, are limited by small numbers of subjects and by restriction of cognitive testing to assessment of memory function and overall disease severity. In the present study, we used a larger group of subjects and compared denial of memory deficit with demographic indexes, overall cognitive decline, presence of sad affect and depressed mood, and impairment in a variety of specific cognitive abilities.

?

1. What was the rationale for the study?

Patients who are clinically diagnosed with Alzheimer's disease deny the severity or presence of memory deficits. The reason for this denial is not clear. Two studies suggested cognitive deficits and/or depression as possible causes. However, they involved small numbers of cases and did not use comprehensive measures of cognitive performance.

2. What was the purpose of the study?

To establish the relationship between denial and demographic, cognitive, and emotional variables with many patients.

Method

Patient Selection

Out of 179 consecutively evaluated patients seen at our clinic for a complaint of progressive intellectual decline, 128 patients satisfying the criteria . . . for probable Alzheimer's disease were identified. Excluded subjects were eliminated because their scores on the cognitive examination were not low enough to satisfy standard cutoff criteria or because another cause of dementia was suggested by clinical or laboratory findings. . . . Informed consent to participation . . . was provided by all patients or their legal representatives.

Cognitive ability was measured with the Assessment of Cognitive Abilities in Dementia, . . . a cognitive examination with 16 subtests requiring 30 minutes to administer. . . . [S]cores on the Assessment of Cognitive Abilities in Dementia (range = 0-80) correlated with scores on the Mini-Mental State Examination . . . (range = 0-30) for a patient group with comparable dementia ($r = 0.86$, $df = 23$, $p < 0.0001$). . . . [P]atients were included only if their Assessment of Cognitive Abilities in Dementia scores fell below 62 (corresponding to Mini-Mental State scores below 25). Reliability and validity measures for Assessment of Cognitive Abilities in Dementia subtest scores and a detailed description of the battery have been presented elsewhere. . . . For analyses in the present study involving individual subtests, subscores were converted to T scores . . . with a mean of 50 ($SD = 10$).

Age at onset of Alzheimer's disease was estimated by structured interview of the patient's primary caregiver. The caregiver was asked to identify the first symptom that was noticed and then to determine when the first symptom was initially observed.

(That is a huge task, open to error, because initial symptoms are so subtle, as to go unnoticed.)

Specific anecdotes pertaining to the time of disease onset were elicited when possible.

The clinical characteristics of the patient group are given in Table 1. The ratio of men to women was 59:69. Seventeen patients have died and been autopsied since the start of the study; 16 (94%) of these patients were diagnosed as having definite Alzheimer's disease . . . but no abnormalities were observed in the remaining subject.

Table 1   *Clinical Characteristics of 128 Patients With Probable Alzheimer's Disease*

Characteristic	Mean	SD
Age at disease onset (years)	69.23	8.49
Education (years)	12.41	3.22
Duration of illness (years)	3.82	2.33
Denial score (0-2)[a]	1.07	0.68
Assessment of Cognitive Abilities in Dementia score (range = 0-80)[b]	35.24	15.39
Mini-Mental State equivalent (0-30)[b]	17.07	4.62
Depression score (0-6)[c]	1.18	1.29

[a]A higher score indicates more denial.
[b]A lower score indicates greater impairment.
[c]A higher score indicates greater depression.

3. Who were the participants?

128 patients seen at a clinic who met accepted criteria for a diagnosis of probable Alzheimer's disease. There were 59 men and 69 women, with a mean age of onset at about 69 years and mean duration of illness at about 4 years. Of 17 patients who died later, autopsy verified that all but one had the disease.

Measurement of Denial

Denial of memory deficit was evaluated by a structured clinical interview. . . . In the structured clinical interview, patients were asked whether they had a problem with memory, whether it was a serious problem, and whether it interfered with their function. They were asked if they thought their memory was worse than that of other individuals their age and whether they thought they were suffering from an illness affecting their memory.

(This, too, is a tall order for someone with a memory deficit and loss of other cognitive functions. Moreover, the likelihood is that the interviewer is one of the authors.)

Patients were rated as having no denial of memory deficit (score = 0) if they acknowledged the presence of a memory deficit and expressed awareness of its severity. They were rated as having mild denial of memory deficit (score = 1) if they acknowledged their memory deficit but underestimated its severity. They were rated as having marked denial of memory deficit (score = 2) if they denied an impairment in their memory. An interrater reliability estimate of kappa = 0.837 (N = 20) was obtained with two raters, indicating excellent reproducibility for the denial measure.

Measurement of Sad Affect and Depressed Mood

Depression is difficult to measure in patients with Alzheimer's disease because the disease itself may cause . . . symptoms used in depression scales that have been validated on samples of patients without dementia. . . . In the present study, presence and severity of sad affect and depressed mood were assessed by using a simple three-item scale (total score = 0-6) that included the patient's self-report (not depressed = 0, mildly depressed = 1, markedly depressed = 2), the caregiver's assessment (not depressed = 0, mildly depressed = 1, markedly depressed = 2), and the examiner's assessment of the patient's affect (0 = absence of sad affect, 1 = mildly sad affect, 2 = markedly sad affect). An interrater reliability of kappa = 0.714 (N = 20) was obtained with two raters, indicating good reproducibility for the depression measure.

?

4. What independent variables were included? How were they measured?

Age of onset was determined by extensive interview of the primary caregiver. Cognitive abilities were measured by the Assessment of Cognitive Abilities in Dementia, a valid and reliable battery containing 16 subtests and requiring 30 minutes to administer. Performance on this test was one of the criteria for inclusion in the study. Sad affect and depression were measured by a 3-item depression scale completed by the patient and caregiver and presence or absence of sadness scale completed by the examiner. Two independent raters of depression ($N = 20$) yielded interrater reliability of .714.

5. Who was the examiner likely to be?

One of the authors.

6. What was the dependent variable and how was it measured?

Denial was determined by a structured interview and rated as 0, no denial and awareness of severity of memory deficit; 1, mild denial involving an underestimation of severity of deficit; or 2, marked denial of deficit. Interrater reliability was .837.

7. Who was the rater likely to be?

One of the authors.

8. Examine Table 1. Based on the supposition that approximately 68% of a large group of scores should range between M±SD, and 95% should range between M±2SD, are any entries suspect of a skewed distribution?

Yes. Denial scores can range from 0 to 2, yet 68% of the scores should range between .39 and 1.75, whereas 95%

range between −.29 and 2.43, both impossible. Likewise, abilities scores could range from 0 to 80. Whereas 68% of the scores should range from 19.85 to 50.63, 95% of the scores should range from 4.46 to 66.02. But patients scoring above 62 were excluded.

Analysis

SAS statistical software was used to derive Pearson correlation coefficients relating denial **to the remaining independent variables.** . . . To control for covariance among variables, a variables-added-last strategy . . . was adopted in which the addition of a variable is assessed . . . after all other variables have already been entered. . . .

To further examine the correlation between denial and cognitive function, a stepwise multiple regression analysis was performed with the 16 cognitive subtests serving as independent variables. . . . [T]he best single predictor was selected first and other variables were added only after the effects of previous variables were fixed. . . . [A] variables-added-last analysis was done to control for the covariance between cognitive variables.

To further examine the correlation between denial and depression, Pearson correlation coefficients were used to relate denial to individual depression-component items (patient report, caregiver report, and examiner observation).

Results

Of the 128 patients with probable Alzheimer's disease, 25 (19.5%) displayed no denial of their memory deficit, 69 (53.9%) displayed mild denial . . . and 34 (26.6%) displayed marked denial. . . . Denial scores were not significantly correlated with age at onset of Alzheimer's disease . . . , years of education . . . , or duration of illness. . . . Significant correlations were found, however, between denial and gender

Table 2 *Results of Variables-Added-Last Regression Analysis*
of the Correlation Between Denial of Memory Deficit and
of Demographic, Cognitive, and Depression Variables
in 128 Patients With Probable Alzheimer's Disease

| Variable | Variables-added-last analysis | |
	Partial F $(df = 1,121)$[a]	p
Age at disease onset	0.27	0.61
Duration of illness	0.13	0.72
Years of education	0.02	0.89
Gender	5.19	0.02
Total assessment of Cognitive Abilities in Dementia score	4.47	0.04
Depression score	17.15	0.0001

[a]The partial *F* tests the statistical significance of the contribution of each variable to a model that already includes all the other variables. Specifically, it tests whether the coefficient for each variable in the overall model is significantly different from zero.

(women exhibited greater denial than men . . .), between denial and Assessment of Cognitive Abilities in Dementia score (more impaired subjects exhibited greater denial than less impaired subjects [$r = -0.392$, $df = 126$, $p = 0.0005$]), and between denial and depression score (nondepressed subjects exhibited more denial than depressed subjects [$r = -0.377$, $df = 126$, $p = 0.0001$]). These correlations remained significant even with a variables-added-last analysis that controlled for the covariance among variables (Table 2).

9. *Which variables correlated with denial scores? Interpret each r in terms of r^2.*

Denial correlated with gender, cognitive abillities (–.392), and depression (–.377). Greater impairment was associated with more denial: $.392^2 = 15.37\%$ of variance in denial was associated with cognitive impairment. Greater depression was associated with less denial: $.377^2 = 14.21\%$ of variance in denial was associated with depression.

A significant regression model related denial of memory deficit to scores on the 16 subtests of the Assessment of Cognitive Abilities in Dementia. . . . Stepwise multiple regression identified object naming as the only subtest that alone correlated significantly with denial ($F = 22.87$, $df = 1,126$, $p = 0.0001$); no other subtest added significantly to the model. The contribution of object naming remained significant with the variables-added-last analysis as well. The relationship between object naming and denial of memory deficit followed a negative slope ($b = -0.032$, $t = -3.74$, $df = 126$, $p = 0.0001$).

?

10. Interpret the last F ratios in Table 2.

The first shows that depression alone contributes significantly to denial. The next shows that cognitive abilities produces a significant increase in R_2 (percentage variance in denial associated with depression and with abilities), above that due to depression. The third shows that gender also significantly increases R_2.

11. Describe the relationship between denial and cognitive abilities.

Only object naming correlated with denial. The lower the ability, the greater the denial.

Analysis of the relationship between denial and depression revealed significant correlations between denial and patient self-report of depressed mood ($r = -0.338$, $df = 126$, $p = 0.0001$) and between denial and examiner assessment of patient's affect ($r = -0.333$, $df = 126$, $p = 0.0001$), but only a trend was found between denial and caregiver report of patient's mood. . . .

?

12. *What were the findings regarding the separate measures of depression and denial?*
Denial was negatively correlated with depression rating by the patient and examiner, but not the caregiver.

Discussion

A significant effect of gender on denial was found: Women exhibited greater denial than men. . . . Unfortunately, the present study was not designed to assess the relative influence of premorbid personality, social learning, examiner bias, or differences in the disease process itself on the relationship between gender and denial.

A significant correlation was found between denial of memory deficit and degree of cognitive impairment. . . . In contrast to previous reports . . . examination of individual cognitive subtests revealed a significant negative correlation between denial and object naming but did not identify other independent correlations.

Denial of memory deficit correlated significantly with the measures of sad affect and depressed mood used in our study. . . . Examination of individual measures of depression indicated significant correlations between denial of memory deficit and patient self-report and examiner assessment but not caregiver assessment, raising questions regarding the validity of assessment of mood by untrained caregivers. The negative direction of the correction between denial and depression may indicate that depression in patients with Alzheimer's disease is, in part, a reaction to perceived loss of ability and therefore functional in nature. . . .

?

13. What were the major conclusions reached by the authors?

The correlation between denial and object naming suggests that impaired cognitive ability underlies denial of memory deficits in the patients. And the correlation between denial and depression suggests that depression is a reaction to symptoms of Alzheimer's disease.

14. Are these conclusions justified? Why?

They are questionable. The major measures of denial and depression probably were made by one of the authors and may have been subject to expectancy bias. Moreover, distributions of denial, depression, and abilities scores appear to be skewed and outliers may have distorted results. Finally, only object naming correlated with denial and this may be just a chance correlation. Assuming that it is not, none of the remaining subtests may correlate with denial, or 128 patients may not have provided enough power to detect other cognitive variables related to denial.

STUDY EXAMPLE 6.2

This study is in the area of education and makes use of a kind of stepwise regression analysis known as hierarchical regression analysis. In contrast to the former, in which predictors are added to the regression model in terms of their significance, the latter uses a preselected set of predictors to determine whether each changes R^2 as it is added to the model. The focus of the present study is to demonstrate that academic and nonacademic variables contribute to variability in test performance of college students.

The Study

- Woehr, D. J., & Cavell, T. A. (1993). Self-report measures of ability, effort, and nonacademic activity as predictors of introductory psychology test scores. *Teaching of Psychology, 20*(3), 156-160. Used with permission.

At many colleges and universities, the majority of students enrolled in introductory psychology classes are freshmen. For some, the leap into college is a difficult one. . . .

Difficulty making the transition from high school is evidenced by students who begin their college careers with disappointing course grades, despite academic credentials indicating they can do the work. Identifying the factors that contribute to a student's poor test performance is often a complicated matter for the student and the instructor. . . .

In trying to understand why these students do poorly on their exams, we have recognized three areas worthy of inquiry. The first area pertains to students' academic ability to do college work—the blend of aptitude and educational skills that enables them to compete with their classmates. Students in introductory courses may do poorly on their tests because they overestimate the extent to which sheer academic ability will enable them to score well. Students whose grades and SAT or ACT scores easily surpassed those of their high school peers must learn to compete with college classmates who are equally capable. Leveling of the competition sets the stage for other, nonability variables to play a determining role in students' grades. A second area of inquiry is the amount of effort that students put into preparing for exams. Students who could easily earn top grades in high school may underestimate the effort needed to prepare for college-level examinations. The third area of inquiry concerns students' involvement in nonacademic aspects of college life. . . . [M]any freshmen probably misjudge the degree to which extracurricular pursuits can interfere with academic tasks.

Previous researchers have examined some of these variables in attempting to predict students' overall college performance.

. . . The variable that has received the most attention from researchers is academic ability, typically indexed by SAT scores. . . . Students with varying SAT scores earned significantly different psychology test scores. . . . Beck et al. . . . reported a correlation of .42 between total SAT score and mean test performance in a sample of students from a general psychology class (76% freshmen). . . .

The total amount of variance in test scores that can be explained by academic ability, academic effort, and nonacademic activity has not been addressed empirically. Our study is an attempt to determine how these variables are related to students' psychology test performance. We hypothesized that measures of ability, effort, and activity will explain significant amounts of variance in introductory psychology test scores. We also hypothesized that information regarding academic effort and nonacademic interference will provide explanatory power over and above that attributable to academic ability alone.

Method

Subjects

Subjects were 325 students from two large introductory psychology classes (64% freshmen, 26% sophomores, and 10% juniors or seniors). Fifty-four percent of the participants were men, and 46% women; these percentages roughly correspond to the percentages of men (56.6%) and women (43.4%) at the university in general.

Measures

Criterion variable. The criterion variable was students' scores on their first exam in the course. This criterion minimizes the influence of factors that arise as a consequence of one's test score (e.g., a drop in motivation) and that further cloud the question of why a student did poorly. The exams in each class, although not identical, overlapped substantially. Both exams used a 50-item, multiple-choice format covering the same four chapters from the same introductory psychology text. . . . Approximately 80% of the items on both exams were drawn directly from the test bank . . . that accompanied the text. . . . For one exam, 70% of the questions were factual, 15% were conceptual, and 15% were applied. The other exam consisted of 65% factual questions, 5% conceptual questions, and 30% applied questions. Items not drawn from the test bank . . . were used primarily to test material presented only in lectures. The two exams were also similar with respect to the percentage of items that covered material presented only in the text (approximately 20%).

Predictor variables. Information on several predictor variables were obtained with a brief, self-report questionnaire. All items were open-ended questions in which students simply filled in the blank with the appropriate response. The questionnaire contained items reflecting each of our three target constructs: academic ability, academic effort, and nonacademic activity.

Ability was assessed with three indicators: high school grade point average (HSGPA) indexed on a 4-point scale, SAT-V, and SAT-M. . . .

Three indicators were also used to assess effort: number of hours per week the student spent studying for the exam, number of times the student had read the chapters covered by the exam, and number of lectures the student had missed before the first exam. . . . [W]ith the first indicator subjects were instructed to estimate the average number of hours per week that they devoted to the course outside of class. This included time spent reading the text as well as engaging in any other study activity related to the course. . . . Although the amount of study time and number of chapter readings are not completely independent, we expected these indicators to tap different aspects of study effort.

Items measuring nonacademic activity asked students to indicate the number of hours per week they spent in each of three types of activities: school-based extracurricular activities, work, and television viewing. . . . [R]eported hours engaged in each type of activity were summed to form a single nonacademic activity score.

Procedure

Participants completed the self-report questionnaire just before the start of their first exam. Data were collected in the context of a demonstration conducted over a series of classes and designed to illustrate several issues related to psychological research (e.g., the rights of subjects, measurement of variables, prediction, and correlation). As part of this demonstration, students were informed about the nature of the study and given the opportunity to participate. Although participation was entirely voluntary, nearly all students (94%) elected to participate.

Results

Preliminary analyses supported both the reliability and the comparability of the two exams. Coefficient alpha estimates of internal consistency for the two exams were .80 and .82 respectively. Also, the difference between the mean scores for each exam was not significant ($M = 73.8$; $M = 72.2$, $t = .73$, ns). Because of these findings, as well as the significant overlap in test content, all subsequent analyses were performed on the combined data set from both classes.

Table 1 lists means and standard deviations for each of the variables. Mean scores for self-reported HSGPA and SAT scores in our sample paralleled figures obtained from the university for students campus-wide, thus supporting their use as a proxy for students' actual HSGPA and SAT scores. . . . Not shown in Table 1 is the number of hours spent in each of the three activities assessed. Students reported spending most of their nonacademic hours on extracurricular activities ($M = 9.30$) or viewing television ($M = 9.02$) and relatively little time working ($M = 2.86$).

Correlations among the variables measured are presented in Table 2. Significant zero-order correlations were found between psychology test scores and each of the predictor variables except time spent studying introductory psychology. Hours of studying was significantly related, however, to the other indicators of academic effort (i.e., number of times students read the assigned chapters and number of classes missed).

Table 1   *Means and Standard Deviations for Test Score and Indicators of Ability, Effort, and Interference*

Variable	M	SD
Test score	73.18	12.57
Academic ability		
HSGPA	3.56	0.36
SAT-V	512.91	84.18
SAT-M	573.69	86.52
Academic effort		
Time studying[a]	4.31	3.40
Chapter readings	1.38	0.60
Classes missed	0.45	1.00
Nonacademic activity		
Total time[a]	21.19	15.35

[a]Average number of hours per week.

Table 2   *Intercorrelations Among Predictor and Criterion Variables*

Variable	2	3	4	5	6	7	8
1. HSGPA	.06	.09	.02	.06	−.07	−.14*	.31*
2. SAT-V	—	.05	−.07	.00	.19*	−.07	.20*
3. SAT-M		—	−.15*	−.04	.11	.04	.14*
4. Time studying[a]			—	.25*	−.12*	−.06	.01
5. Chapter readings				—	−.06	−.07	.22*
6. Classes missed					—	.20*	−.22*
7. Nonacademics						—	−.12*
8. Test score							—

[a]Average number of hours per week.
*$p < .05$.

To examine how well our three target constructs predicted students' test performance, a hierarchical multiple regression analysis was conducted in which specific indicators for each

Table 3   *Hierarchical Regression Predicting Psychology*

	Test scores		
	R^2	ΔR^2	ΔF
Academic ability	.13	.13	12.45*
Academic effort	.23	.10	10.28*
Nonacademic activity	.25	.02	7.74*

*$p < .01$.

construct were entered as a set. Academic ability indicators were entered first, followed in turn by indicators for academic effort and nonacademic activity. Results of this analysis are summarized in Table 3. The value of R^2 indicates the total amount of variance in test performance accounted for by the variables entered, and the change in R^2 (ΔR^2) indicates the amount of variance accounted for by each set of variables over and above previously entered sets. For the full model, R^2 was significant, $F(7, 241) = 11.74$, $p < .0001$, and indicated that 25% of the variance in test scores was explained when all three sets of predictors were included. Academic ability variables accounted for approximately one half (13%) of all the variance accounted for in test scores. Measures of academic effort, however, contributed significantly for an additional 10% of the variance. Involvement in nonacademic activities, although reflecting only a 2% increase in explained variance over that attributable to academic ability and academic effort, was also significant. When the order of entry for academic effort and nonacademic activity was reversed, the amount of variance explained at each step was still significant but slightly different: Nonacademic activity predicted an additional 8% in psychology test scores, whereas academic effort yielded only 4% increment in explained variance.

To explore further the link between test scores and individual predictor variables, standardized regression coefficients that comprised the full prediction model were examined. Standardized beta weights allow for a comparison of the magnitude of effects of the different indicators on a common metric. . . . Only coefficients for time spent studying . . . and for SAT failed to reach significance.

Finally, analyses were conducted to examine the extent to which the inclusion of students beyond their first year (36% of the sample) influenced our results. Previous analyses were repeated using a reduced sample of participants that included only first-year students. Results of this analysis revealed that none of the coefficients obtained with the full sample was significantly different from those obtained with the reduced sample.

Discussion

We hypothesized that measures of students' academic ability, academic effort, and nonacademic activity would predict test scores in an introductory psychology class. Our results support this hypothesis in that a regression model containing these predictor variables accounted for a significant amount of the variance in students' first exam scores. Academic ability alone accounted for approximately 13% of the variance in test scores. . . . In our study, the prediction of introductory psychology test scores was improved significantly by the use of self-report measures of academic effort and nonacademic activity. These variables accounted for 12% of the variance in test scores beyond that attributable to students' academic ability. . . . Students should also be advised that academic ability explains only about 13% of the variance and that other, nonability factors are also important. One factor is the effort students devote to the course, both the amount of time and the type of effort. For example, our findings indicate that regular class attendance and multiple readings of assigned chapters are associated with higher test scores. . . .

Our findings do not support the strategy of simply telling students to study more; the bivariate correlation between hours spent studying psychology and psychology test scores was .01! This finding is also in line with previous results. . . .

. . . We often encounter students who attend class regularly and who claim to devote considerable time and energy to our class but do poorly on their tests. Further inquiry often reveals that these students spend much time on potentially nonproductive study activities. . . . Many of these activities are very time-consuming, and most invite shallow processing of information that is incomplete and possibly inaccurate. We routinely caution our students that such activities are no substitute for careful and comprehensive reading of the text and regular class attendance. . . .

Several factors limit the conclusions we can draw from our study. Our set of predictor variables is not exhaustive; other variables may also influence students' test scores. Moreover, variables that are correlated with exam scores may not be causally linked to these scores. For example, the number of classes students missed was inversely related to test scores, but attending all future classes may not raise students' grades. Missing class may simply be more common among students who lack adequate study skills or who are indifferent about their grades. Our findings are also limited by the self-report nature of our predictor variables. . . .

Finally, our results did not change when we excluded from the analysis students who had advanced beyond their first year of college. However, given that first-year students made up a very large proportion of our sample, the similarity in findings is not surprising. Because the small number of upper level students in our sample argued against a separate set of analyses, the issue of whether these findings generalize to more experienced students enrolled in introductory psychology is still unresolved. Also unresolved is the degree to which our three target constructs predict test scores in more advanced psychology courses. Because upper level courses rarely involve first-year students or the use of multiple-choice tests, our findings may not generalize to students' performance in those courses.

CRITIQUE OF STUDY EXAMPLE 6.2

1. What was the rationale for the study?

2. What was the purpose of the study?

3. Who were the participants?

4. Could the two classes have differed in the distribution by level of students?

5. What was the criterion variable? How did it differ between classes? What does this suggest about level of students and/or instructors of each class?

6. What were the predictor variables?

7. What was the procedure? What questions have you regarding it?

8. Examine Table 1. Are any entries questionable?

9. Table 2 lists 28 intercorrelations, some of which are declared significant at $p < .05$. Using the rule of $.05/C = p$ required for significance of the highest r, $.05/C - 1 = p$ required for significance of the next highest r, and so on and determining the actual p associated with each r by $Z = r/[1/\sqrt{N}]$, which rs actually are significant?

10. What is the nature of hierarchical regression analysis that distinguishes it from stepwise regression analysis?

11. The full model R^2 (which includes all predictor variables) is reported to be significant with 7 and 241 *df*. Are these *df*s accurate? What does it suggest about total number of entries?

12. What was the most potent predictor of test score?

13. Did inclusion of upper-level students make any difference in the analysis?

14. What were the major conclusions reached by the authors?

15. Were these conclusions justified on statistical grounds?

16. Were conclusions justified on the basis of the design?

17. Do these results have practical application?

ANSWERS

1. Freshmen, many of whom take Introductory Psychology, often have difficulties in adjusting to college courses. Although three variables may contribute to poor exam performance (academic ability, time spent studying, time spent in nonacademic activities), the relative contribution of each has not been determined empirically.

2. To determine the contributions of each variable in explaining variance in academic performance and to show that variables unrelated to academic ability also contribute to the variance.

3. Of the 325 students in two Introductory Psychology classes, 64% were freshmen, 26% sophomores, and 10% juniors and seniors.

4. Yes. One class could have consisted mainly of upper-level and the other of lower-level students, depending on when they were offered, and no mention is made of who taught the courses.

5. The test score on the first exam was the criterion. It was based on a test that measured factual, conceptual, and application of knowledge gained from the text and lectures. For one class, 15% of the questions were applied and for the other 30% of the questions were applied. This suggests that levels of students differed between classes and/or that different instructors taught the classes.

6. Academic ability was measured by self-reported GPA in high school, SAT-V(erbal) and SAT-M(ath) scores. Effort expended was measured by self-reported time spent studying for the exam, number of times required chapters had been read and number of classes missed. Time spent in nonacademic activities was measured by self-report of time spent in extracurricular activities, watching television and working.

7. Students gave self-reports prior to the first class exam in the context of design issues in research. The nature of the study was explained and students were asked to volunteer. Because this was obtained just before the start of the exam, the students had to give self-reports when they were anxious.

8. Yes. High school grade point mean is 3.56 and $SD = 0.36$. With such a large group, 68% have averages between 3.56 ±0.36 = 3.2 and 3.92, and 95% have averages between 2.84 and 4.28 (impossible). This suggests a skewed distribution with large variability and possible outliers.

9. All rs of at least .19. Thus, the test score correlated with HSGPA, SAT-V, number of chapter readings, and number of classes missed. Moreover, SAT-V and classes missed also were correlated; however, r is positive and makes no sense. Finally, number of classes missed correlated with time spent in nonacademic activities.

10. In hierarchical analysis, order of entering each variable into the model equation is specifically determined before the analysis is conducted. In stepwise analysis, the most powerful predictor is entered first, then the second most powerful, and so on until R^2 fails to change significantly and all predictors have been tested.

11. The $df = 7$ is correct because seven predictors were used. However, if $N = 325$, then error df should be $325 - 7 - 1 = 317$. If 241 is correct, then there were $241 + 7 + 1 = 249$ entries, not 325.

12. Academic ability accounted for 13% variance in test scores: Those students who achieved the highest scores were likely to have reported the highest HSGPA and SAT scores, and vice versa for low scores.

13. No. When data were reanalyzed with freshmen and sophomores scores only, results were essentially the same.

14. First, exam performance is predicted by academic ability and also by academic effort (fewer missed classes, more readings of the chapters) and nonacademic activities. But self-reported time spent studying is unrelated to the test score.

15. They appear to be. Analyses were conducted three different ways (with original order of variables entered, with order of effort and nonacademic time reversed, and by simultaneous entry to determine beta weights) and results were essentially the same. Although there may have been some outliers for HSGPAs, the obtained correlation between ability and test score is reasonable and in line with other findings. The only question is with respect to the size of sample used in the analyses.

16. Probably. Although two different classes and, apparently, two different teachers were used, no differences were found between them. Moreover, the participation of upper-level students did not change the results. However, it might have been wiser to obtain the information after the exam when students probably were calmer. And because there was no acknowledgment about calculations, it is likely that these were conducted by the authors; it would have been preferable to have a naive individual do so.

17. Yes. Students with lower academic ability (as measured by the same variables) can be encouraged to put more quality time into studying (e.g., reading and testing themselves) and less time into nonacademic activities to boost grades. However, motivated students probably know this.

Supplementary Readings
on This Topic

- Cohen, J., & Cohen, P. (1983). *Applied multiple regression/ correlation analysis for the behavioral sciences* (2nd ed.). Hillsdale, NJ: Lawrence Erlbaum.
- Hays, W. L. (1988). *Statistics* (4th ed.). New York: Holt, Rinehart & Winston.
- Howell, D. C. (1992). *Statistical methods for psychology* (3rd ed.). Boston: PWS-Kent.

7

FACTOR-ANALYTIC STUDIES

Factor analysis attempts to reduce a large set of correlated variables to a smaller set of hypothetical characteristics, traits, or factors that underly the correlations. Sometimes, the purpose of factor analysis is to determine the minimum number of factors accounting for the correlations. Sometimes, it is to determine the underlying factor structure of the original variables (i.e., their underlying traits). And at other times, the intent is to test a hypothesis that certain factors account for the observed variables.

Of the various methods, the most popular is principal components: an attempt to determine the main factors (components) accounting for the largest proportion of variability in all the scores. An important assumption, here, is that all the factors are orthogonal, uncorrelated, or independent. The advantage is parsimony, or the simplest explanation of the observed data. The disadvantage is that the factors, in reality, may be correlated.

A brief review of the various steps involved in the principal component analysis should clarify terms you are likely to encounter when reading a factor-analytic report. Consider that five variables, in the form of five different tests, are routinely administered to new admissions to an institution. Because some of the tests may be measuring the same basic underlying factor, a factor analysis is conducted. The net result of the analysis is that all the tests may not have to be administered.

A correlation matrix will, by eyeballing, reveal how many factors are likely to account for the data. If, for example, A and E are correlated with each other and B, C, and D are correlated with each other, one factor may account for the former and a second for the latter. To extract the first factor, a mathematical procedure is used to arrive at a weight (w) for each of the five variables such that the factor will account for the largest proportion of variance for all of the data. Imagine a table consisting of the standardized (Z) scores of all participants on all of the variables (tests). This yields five columns of Z scores, with each participant providing 5 scores. A factor score can be determined for each participant. This is the sum of the Z scores weighted by the appropriate weights for each variable, or

$$F_i = w_A Z_A + w_B Z_B + \ldots + w_E Z_E.$$

This yields an additional (sixth) column of scores for each participant, namely, factor scores. Now we proceed to determine the correlation between Z scores of variable A and the factor scores, Z scores of variable B and the factor scores, Z scores of variable C and the factor scores, and so forth. Each of the five correlations between the variable and the factor is known as factor loading. The higher the correlation (i.e., factor loading), the more that Factor 1 underlies that variable.

We have five factor loadings, or correlation coefficients. If each is squared and the sum obtained, that sum is called the eigenvalue; that is, Σ(factor loadings)^2 = eigenvalue. When the eigenvalue is divided by the number of variables, we have the proportion of variance accounted for by Factor 1. Generally, when factors have eigenvalues of at least 1.00, the factors are considered stable and replicable. Those with eigenvalues less than 1.00 are not considered stable. (Eigenvalues are also properties of correlation matrices that indicate the number of factors that can be extracted.) For example, given .8A, .2B, .7C, .65D, and .9E, eigenvalue = 2.4025 and 2.4025/5 = .48. Thus, Factor 1 accounts for 48% of total variability of all the scores.

The second factor is extracted in exactly the same way, with new weights applied to the Z scores of each of the five variables and with the stipulation that these weights are orthogonal to the first set. The factor loadings will, of course, differ from those for the first factor; the eigenvalue will be smaller as will the proportion of variance accounted for by Factor 2. Now we can also obtain an additional bit of information. If the Factor 1 and Factor 2 loadings on variable A are squared and summed, we have a measure of the proportion of variability in variable A accounted for by Factors 1 and 2. This can be done for each of the variables, and each sum is called a communality.

The final step of this first phase involves setting up a table of the Factor 1 loadings and Factor 2 loadings (or more if additional useful factors are extracted) for each variable. Such a table is a factor structure matrix, and it would be considered to have a simple structure if each variable loads heavily on one factor and very lightly on the remaining factors. This seldom occurs and leads to the second phase, rotation. Imagine a plus sign with Factor 1 loadings on the vertical axis and Factor 2 loadings on the horizontal axis. Now plot each variable to correspond with its Factor 1 and Factor 2 loadings. Correlated variables will tend to cluster together in one quadrant. The aim of rotation (performed mathematically) is to bring one of the axes (e.g., Factor 1 loadings) closer to the variables so that they are simultaneously farther from the other axis (e.g., Factor 2 loadings). Because the plotted variables remain in the same original physical location in the quadrant, their factor loadings will change so that they load heavily on one factor and lightly on the others. If both axes are rotated together as a unit, we have orthogonal rotation and the factors are considered to be uncorrelated. If each axis is rotated separately, we have oblique rotation and the factors are considered to be correlated. Investigators often do both to see which results in a factor structure matrix that has simple structure. As a final note, because factor analysis is basically complex, the analysis is likely to be performed by a well-versed statistician.

From a design point of view, threats to internal validity are the same as those for any correlation study. The administration of several tests requires that they be reliable and valid and that the orders be counterbalanced to rule out the chance that performance on one test is a function of what came before. The sample is expected to be representative, and participants should be tested under uniform conditions. Finally, the administrator should be naive regarding the purpose of the study.

Two factor-analytic studies are presented. We will evaluate the first one together, and you will evaluate the second.

STUDY EXAMPLE 7.1

The following study relates to diabetes and deals with the important issue of adherence or compliance to the diabetic regimen as a means of achieving diabetic control. In this instance, based on responses to interviews regarding 13 areas of compliance, factor analysis was performed to determine the factors underlying adherence to various aspects of the regimen. Along with the orthogonal varimax rotation, an oblique promax rotation was performed. This involves two stages: Following a varimax rotation, an oblique rotation is performed so that simple structure is achieved in the factor structure matrix. Remember, this involves high loading on one factor and low loading on the remaining factors for a given variable.

The Study

- Johnson, S. B., Silverstein, J., Rosenbloom, A., Carter, R., & Cunningham, W. (1986). Assessing daily management in childhood diabetes. *Health Psychology, 5*(6), 545-564. Used with permission.

Inadequate adherence to treatment regimens is considered a major problem in the management of chronic disease. It is estimated that half of these patients do not adhere to their medical regimens. . . . Watkins and his colleagues published some of the first empirical documentation of the extent of this problem in adults with diabetes. . . . In their sample, over half of the patients were making insulin dosage errors, two thirds were incorrectly testing their urine for glucose, and only 25% were judged to have acceptable dietary habits. . . .

The clinical literature suggests that adolescence is a particularly difficult time; desires for peer conformity and independence may interfere with daily diabetes management routines. . . . However, few empirical studies have addressed this issue. . . .

Measuring adherence behaviors relevant to diabetes is difficult for several reasons. Disease management is complex, requiring numerous daily behaviors in the areas of insulin injection, glucose testing, diet, and exercise. Although there is a tendency to treat "adherence" or "compliance" as a unitary construct, findings . . . suggest that adherence to one aspect of the treatment regimen may be unrelated to adherence to a different regimen component. . . . [P]atients may . . . exhibit variable behavior across the different aspects of the treatment program. . . .

1. What was the rationale for the study?

Adherence to the diabetic regimen is a major problem in management of the disease. Although errors have been made by over half of a tested sample of adults, data suggest that the problem is greater among adolescents. However, this has not been empirically established. Moreover, adherence is not a unitary concept. Patients can comply well with one aspect of the regimen and make mistakes in complying with another aspect.

In our study, we tested the viability of the 24-hr recall interview as a method of assessing adherence behaviors in a population of youngsters with childhood diabetes. This procedure is a standard dietary assessment technique, considered . . . best of the available self-report methods. . . . We modified the 24-hr recall interview procedure to collect information on all diabetes management behaviors. Unlike the usual dietary assessment procedure in which one interview is conducted with a single informant, we utilized three interviews with patient and parent independently to obtain a more representative and comprehensive sample of daily diabetes management behavior. We also attempted to test the unitary versus multivariate nature of adherence as a construct in childhood diabetes and the relationship of patient age, sex, and disease duration to daily disease management.

2. What were the purposes of the study?

To assess diabetic management behaviors of children and adolescents by means of three separate interviews of parent and child and to determine the relationship between compliance and age, sex, and duration of diabetes.

Method

Subjects

Youngsters attending clinics of the North Florida Regional Diabetes Program or the 1982 Florida Camp for Children and Youth served as subjects.

(Note that the study was conducted during summer months.)

Both patient and parent were contacted by telephone to solicit participation; informed consent was obtained. One hundred sixty-eight patient-parent pairs volunteered.

(The total number of possible participants approached is not reported.)

Subjects ranged in age from 6 to 19 years, with diabetes duration of 1 to 17 years. Most patients were white (88%) and were evenly distributed between the sexes (53% male, 47% female). Annual family income varied from less than $10,000 to over $40,000, with most families earning between $10,000 and $29,000. . . .

?

3. Who served as participants?

168 patient-parent volunteers from a clinic or diabetes camp.

Patients were mainly white, from low to middle income families, about half were males, with ages ranging from 6-19 years and duration of diabetes ranging from 1-17 years.

Procedure

Participants were told that the investigators were interested in what patients and families "usually do" to manage diabetes. . . . To encourage unbiased reporting, all interviews were conducted by trained nonmedical personnel who were not associated with the clinic staff.

> *(This is a good feature of the design. Interviewers were trained but were naive with respect to the purpose of the study.)*

Each subject and one parent (usually the mother) were interviewed on three occasions over a 2-week period. The first . . . was conducted during the patient's clinic visit or by telephone. All subsequent interviews were conducted by telephone. . . . Subject and parent were always interviewed separately. The same parent was interviewed on all three occasions. Information was obtained about the activities of 2 weekdays and 1 weekend day.

Respondents recalled the previous day's events in temporal sequence, beginning with the time of wakening in the morning and ending with retiring to bed. The interviewer recorded all diabetes relevant activities. If the respondent did not spontaneously offer the necessary information, the interviewer prompted with questions. . . .

Each interview took approximately 20 min.

4. What was the general procedure?

Over a 2-week period parent and patient were separately interviewed about daily activities, including those related to diabetes management. The first occurred at the clinic or by telephone and the last two were by telephone. Interviews were about activities 24 hours earlier on 2 weekdays and 1 weekend day.

5. What precautions were taken to guard against expectancy effects and reactive measures?

Interviewers were nonmedical personel who were not associated with the clinic and were trained to interview. Reactive measures were controlled for by telephone interviews because participants did not know when they would be called and were only told that the study was concerned with what people usually do to control their diabetes.

Measures

Thirteen measures of compliance or adherence were developed. All were constructed so that a range of scores was possible, with higher scores indicating relative noncompliance and scores close to zero indicating relative compliance.

Injection regularity . . . was calculated by measuring the standard deviation of injection times reported across the three interviews. If the youngsters took both an a.m. and p.m. injection, the standard deviations of the a.m. and p.m. injections were calculated separately and then averaged.

Injection interval. The absolute difference between a patient's average interval between injections and an ideal injection interval was calculated for each patient. For youngsters who took only one shot per day, the ideal interval was defined as 24 hr. For youngsters who took an a.m. and a p.m. injection each day, an ideal injection interval was arbitrarily defined as 10 hr between a.m. and p.m. injections on the same day, and 14 hr between the p.m. injection and the following a.m. injection.

Injection-meal timing . . . was calculated by subtracting meal times from injection times and calculating the average of all these difference scores. Then, we added 60 min to this average, and the resulting sum was divided by 60 so that youngsters who, on the average, took their injections 60 min to 1 min before meals would receive scores from 0 to .99. Youngsters who usually took their injections at the time of their meals or after eating would receive scores of 1.0 or greater.

Regularity of injection-meal timing. We also considered the regularity of intervals between injections and eating. This was measured by calculating the standard deviation of the intervals between injections and eating across the three interviews.

Calories consumed. For each youngster, an ideal number of total daily calories was estimated based on age, sex, and ideal weight for height. . . . Each patient's ideal total number of daily calories was then subtracted from the patient's reported average daily calorie consumption. . . . A positive score . . . indicated that the subject ate more than his or her ideal total number of daily calories. A zero score indicated that the youngster's actual calorie consumption equaled that of his or her ideal calorie consumption. A negative score indicated that the youngster ate less than the ideal.

Percentage of calories from fat. . . . [T]he percentage of total calories consumed as fat was calculated. . . . Ideal fat consumption (25%) was subtracted from actual fat consumption. Scores above zero indicated that the patient consumed more than 25% of his or her calories in fats. Scores below zero indicated fat consumption less than 25% of total calories.

Percentage of calories from carbohydrates. . . . [A]ctual carbohydrate consumption was subtracted from the ideal (60%) so that scores above zero indicated insufficient carbohydrate ingestion. A score of zero indicated the patient's diet consisted of 60% carbohydrates. Scores below zero indicated that more than 60% of the calories consumed consisted of carbohydrates.

Concentrated sweets. . . . [A] separate exchange unit category was developed for concentrated sweets. Forty calories of any concentrated sweet was equivalent to one concentrated sweet exchange unit. The average number of these exchange units consumed per day was calculated.

Eating frequency. Based on an ideal of six meals or snacks per day, the percentage of snacks or meals not eaten across the three interviews was calculated and multiplied by 100. A high score indicated that the patient ate infrequently. A low score indicated frequent eating. A score of zero indicated the patient averaged six meals or snacks per day.

Exercise frequency. Exercise on six possible occasions per day was noted for each of the three interviews. The percentage of these 18 periods without exercise was used as an estimate of exercise frequency. A score of zero indicated the patient reported exercise on all 18 occasions. A score of 100 indicated no reported exercise on any occasion.

Exercise duration. The average amount of time spent exercising across the 18 possible exercise occasions was calculated, and a constant (1) was added to each value to avoid subsequent division by zero. The reciprocal of this score was used, so that low scores indicated lengthy exercise and high scores indicated little or no exercise.

Exercise type. Each . . . activity was given an energy expenditure rating, . . . with higher ratings indicating more strenuous exercise. The patient's average expenditure rating across the 18 possible exercise periods was calculated and, again, a constant (1) was added to avoid subsequent division by zero. The reciprocal of this score served as the measure of exercise type. Low scores indicated more strenuous exercise whereras high scores indicated less strenuous exercise.

Glucose testing frequency. The frequency of glucose testing across the three interviews was calculated. Using an ideal testing frequency of 4 times per day, the number of glucose tests was divided by this ideal (12) and multiplied by 100. The total was subtracted from 100 so that high scores indicated few glucose tests and low scores indicated frequent tests. A score of zero meant that the youngster tested 12 times over the 3 days. A score of 100 meant no reported glucose tests over the 3 interviews.

?

6. *What was the general nature of the 13 measures derived from the three interviews?*

They measured aspects of insulin injections, diet, exercise, and glucose testing.

7. *Are there any concerns about these measures?*

No. The measures are part of a standardized procedure. Moreover, they were not taken in any order but based on reports given during each interview.

Results

Parent-Child Agreement

Because parent and child were interviewed separately, comparisons between their reports provide some information on their reliability and validity. Complete concordance between respondents was not expected because few parents . . . observe all of their child's activities.

. . . All of the correlations for the total sample were statistically significant ($p < .0001$), ranging from $r = .42$ . . . to $r = .78$. . . . For a number of the measures, however, parent-child agreement appeared to differ depending on the age of the child. A statistical test for differences between correlations across the four age groups was conducted for each adherence measure. . . . Statistically significant differences were found for 6 of the 13 measures. The youngest children (6 to 9 years) showed poorest parent-child agreement for measures involving time (i.e., the injection measures and exercise duration); moderate agreement for type of diet (percentage of calories from fat, percentage of calories from carbohydrates, and concentrated sweets); and strongest agreement for calories consumed, exercise type, and frequency measures (eating frequency, exercise frequency, and glucose testing frequency). The 10- to 12- and 13- to 15-year-old groups showed the most consistent parent-child agreement across all measures, whereas the oldest age group (16 to 19 years) had highly variable parent-child correlations.

?

8. *What was the purpose of correlating parent-child measures? What were the general findings?*

Correlations established reliability and validity of the measures. For the total sample, correlations were significant for all 13 measures. The most stringent $\alpha = .05/13 = .003$ and in all cases $p < .0001$. However, when correlations were compared across age groups, differences were found for six measures. Least agreement occurred for the youngest group for injection time measures and duration of exercise. Best agreement between parent and child occurred for children between 10 and 15 years of age, whereas agreement was variable for the oldest age group.

Relationships Among
Adherence Measures

To assess the relationship among the 13 adherence measures, data from the parent and child interviews were combined. If data from one respondent was missing, data from the other respondent was retained. . . . The 13 adherence measures were then subjected to a principal-component factor analysis. . . . Using a criterion of eigenvalues greater than one, a five-factor solution resulted, accounting for 70.6% of the variance. The five factors were rotated to simple structure using the varimax procedure. The factor loadings are presented in Table 4. Oblique promax rotations were also carried out. The pattern of simple structure was virtually identical to the orthogonal varimax solution. Factor intercor-

Table 4   *Factor Analysis of Adherence Measures: Factor Loadings*

Adherence Measure	Factor 1 Exercise	Factor 2 Injection	Factor 3 Diet Type	Factor 4 Frequency	Factor 5 Diet Amount
Injection reg.	−.071	.736	.054	.018	−.077
Injection int.	.095	.852	.176	.005	.102
Inj.-meal timing	.041	.724	.038	−.068	.003
Reg. of inj.-ml tim.	.007	.522	−.022	.361	.190
Calories consumed	−.090	.079	.262	−.408	.696
% cals. from fat	.006	.124	.965	.090	.070
% cals. from carb.	.010	.108	.971	.028	−.008
Concentrated sweets	−.011	.024	−.088	.216	.845
Eating frequency	−.048	−.075	.250	.740	−.116
Exercise duration	.959	.007	−.017	−.005	−.042
Exercise type	.941	−.086	.040	.028	−.007
Exercise frequency	.667	.109	−.010	.151	−.022
Glucose test. frequ.	.239	.116	−.082	.656	.121
% var. acct. for	18.0	16.4	15.8	10.5	9.9

Note. High factor loadings are underscored, indicating the adherence measures belonging to each factor.

(Names of measures are in abbreviated form and fully reported in the article.)

relations were nonsignificant and varied from $r = .17$ to $r = .03$. Because differences in solution were so slight, the orthogonal factors solution depicted in Table 4 was retained in view of its statistical advantages.

Factor 1 consisted of high loadings on the three exercise measures, whereas Factor 2 consisted of high loadings on all four injection measures. The dietary measures loaded on the three subsequent factors. Factor 3 consisted of measures of diet type (i.e., percentage of calories from carbohydrates and percentage of calories from fat). Factor 4 included measures of eating frequency and glucose testing frequency; patients who tested for glucose frequently also ate more often. Factor 5 included measures of total calories consumed and the amount of concentrated sweets ingested; youngsters who ate excessive calories also ate more sweets. . . .

?

9. *A principal-component factor analysis was performed on the 13 measures. What was the rationale for reporting results of the orthgonal varimax rotation?*

An oblique promax rotation arrived at essentially the same results and revealed little correlation among the extracted factors.

10. *Five factors were extracted with eigenvalues greater than 1.00. What were the eigenvalues?*

$\Sigma(-.071^2 + \ldots + .239^2) = 2.34$; $\Sigma(.736^2 + \ldots + .116^2) = 2.132$; alternatively, for Factor 3: $.158 \times 13 = 2.054$; $.105 \times 13 = 1.365$; and $.099 \times 13 = 1.287$.

11. *What were the bases for the names of the five factors?*

Although names are arbitrary, Factor 1 most highly correlated with the three measures related to exercise, Factor 2 had the highest factor loadings with the four measures related to insulin injections, Factor 3 was most highly correlated with the two measures related to composition of diet, Factor 4 had the highest factor loading for eating and exercise frequency and Factor 5 was most highly correlated with the two measures related to amount of foods consumed.

12. *Calculate the 13 communalities. Each reflects the extent to which variability in the measure is accounted for by the 5 factors. The variabilities of which measures are least associated with the 5 factors?*

Communalities are .5559, .7763, .5319, .4394, .7339, .9632, .9554, .7691, .6315, .9218, .8953, .4802, and .5223. The weakest associations were with regularity of injection-meal timing and with exercise frequency. Moderate associations were with injection-meal timing and with glucose testing frequency.

Patient Characteristics
and Adherence Behavior

Based on the results of the factor analysis, the 13 adherence measures were organized into five groups of measures: (a)Exercise, (b)Injection, (c)Diet Type, (d)Testing/Eating Frequency, and (e)Diet Amount. . . .

Exercise measures. . . . The 16- to 19-year-olds exercised less frequently than the 6- to 9- and 10- to 12-year-olds. The 13- to 15-year-olds also exercised less frequently than the 10- to 12-year-olds. . . .

Injection measures. . . . The oldest age group (16 to 19 years old) was . . . less adherent than all other age groups on all three measures. The 13- to 15-year-olds were also less adherent than the two younger age groups on injection interval and injection regularity.

. . . Oldest girls had the most irregular injection times. Patients with diabetes less than 5 years who were 16 to 19 years of age also had highly irregular injection times. . . . Oldest patients with shorter disease duration had the most inappropriate meal-injection intervals.

Diet type. . . . The two oldest age groups (16- to 19-year-olds and 13- to 15-year-olds) ate too much fat and too few carbohydrates compared with one or more of the younger age groups.

Testing/eating frequency. . . . The oldest age group ate less frequently and glucose-tested less frequently than all other age groups. The 13- to 15-year-olds ate and glucose-tested less often than the 10- to 12-year-olds. . . . Boys with shorter diabetes duration ate more frequently, whereas girls with longer diabetes duration glucose-tested most often.

?

13. *Which two age groups showed the least adherence to their exercise regimen?*

The oldest 16- to 19-year-olds and the 13- to 15-year-olds.

14. *Which age groups showed least adherence to aspects of the injection of insulin regimen?*

The oldest 16- to 19-year-olds, particularly females and those who had diabetes for the least amount of time, and the 13- to 15-year-olds.

15. *Which age groups least adhered to their diet regimen?*

The two older age groups: 16-19 and 13-15.

16. *Which two age groups ate less frequently and tested their glucose less frequently?*

The two older age groups: 16-19 and 13-15.

Discussion

When the 13 adherence measures were subjected to a principal-component factor analysis, five independent factors resulted, accounting for a substantial amount of the variance (70.6%). When the factors were rotated to simple structure an easily interpreted factor pattern emerged, with each measure loading strongly on only one factor. These results suggest that compliance or adherence with recommended treatment is not a unitary construct or a general characteristic of the patient. In fact, there are at least five aspects of diabetes management that are unrelated to one another. A patient's behavior in one area is not predictive of his or her behavior in another area. Describing a patient as "compliant" or "noncompliant" is insufficient, and probably inaccurate. Adherence with each of the regimen components must be assessed to have an accurate reflection of the patient's daily management behaviors.

In our sample, daily diabetes management behaviors were strongly influenced by the youngster's age. On 8 of the 13 measures, older subjects were significantly less adherent than their younger counterparts. Teenagers ate less frequently, monitored their glucose less often, exercised less often, had more variable injection times, deviated more from the ideal interval between injections, and often took their injections at the same time as, or even after, a meal. Most youngsters deviated from the American Diabetes Association's dietary recommendations, ingesting too much fat and too little carbohydrates. However, older adolescents deviated more than their younger counterparts. . . .

The fact that teenagers were less adherent in many areas of diabetes management is consistent with clinical experience, but has received little empirical documentation. Christensen et al. . . . studied dietary behaviors and reported teenagers to be less compliant than younger and older age groups. The results of the present investigation not only replicate the findings of Christensen et al., but suggest that adher- ence problems during adolescence are not limited to dietary management.

In comparison to the consistent association of age to adherence behaviors, few other patient characteristics were found to be significantly associated with one or more of the adherence measures. . . . Girls in the oldest age group spent the least time exercising and had the most variable injection times. . . . Youngsters in the oldest age group (16- to 19-year-olds) with diabetes less than 5 years had the most irregular injection times and the most inappropriate meal-injection intervals. Disease onset during the teenage years may be associated with less parental supervision and the consequent development of poor habits with regard to appropriate timing of injections on a daily basis and in relationship to meals. . . . **This was true** on only 2 of 13 measures, indicating that the effect of disease onset during adolescence is not pervasive.

. . . Documentation of greater adherence problems during the teenage years provides much needed empirical support for the widely held clinical impression of the "problem" adolescent with diabetes. The existence of similar adherence problems in other chronically ill childhood populations remains to be seen. Among teenagers with diabetes, however, intervention programs need to be developed and tested.

17. What were the general conclusions reached by the authors?

The major conclusion is that compliance is not a unitary concept but consists of 5 independent factors. The second conclusion is that teenagers have the biggest problems in adhering to aspects of the regimen, especially in terms of diet and exercising frequently enough.

18. Are the conclusions justified? Why?

Yes. No cause and effect was implied; the study was descriptive. The method used to obtain the measures is standardized and precautions were taken to guard against experimenter effects and reactive measures.

19. What are the limitations to generalizing these results?

The results were most likely obtained during the summer and may not generalize when school is in session. The sample was primarily white and may not generalize to other races. The sample was primarily low to moderate income and may not generalize to lower or higher socioeconomic levels. And the age range, from 6 to 19 was the targeted ages, so results do generalize to these age groups.

STUDY EXAMPLE 7.2

This factor-analytic study also relates to participants with diabetes but deals with strategies used by teenagers to cope with life stress—the focus of the factor analysis—and factors that predict the coping strategies.

The Study

- Hanson, C. L., Cigrang, J. A., Harris, M. A., Carle, D. L., Relyea, G., & Burghen, G. A. Coping styles in youths with insulin-dependent diabetes mellitus. *Journal of Consulting and Clinical Psychology, 57*(5), 644-651. Copyright © 1989 by the American Psychological Association. Adapted with permission.

Coping styles may be viewed as the cognitive and behavioral efforts used in response to stressful conditions. . . . Compast . . . emphasized the importance of understanding the contextual framework of coping behaviors in youths. The youths' individual characteristics and resources interact with environmental characteristics (e.g., family strengths, community resources, the nature of the stressor) to produce certain coping responses. . . . Although several areas of child research would suggest that this type of contextual model best explains coping styles, empirical investigations of these models are limited. . . . Moreover, Compas . . . suggests that an examination of the role of the family in predicting coping styles in children and adolescents is an empirical priority.

Coping adaptively with the demands and stressors of insulin-dependent diabetes mellitus (IDDM) can be a formidable task for adolescents. . . . The daily treatment demands of the illness require vigilance and perseverance with several onerous tasks. . . . Moreover, normal alterations in day-to-day activities . . .

require compensatory adjustments in dietary intake and/or insulin dosages in order for the youth to maintain good metabolic control. In addition to the daily treatment demands, the youth is faced with emotional stressors related to the illness. . . . Additional stressors that the youth faces include feeling different from peers during a developmental stage in which identification with the peer group is extremely important, and striving to emancipate from parents while simultaneously feeling dependent and vulnerable to the illness. Thus, the demands of IDDM and its treatment require continual adaptation to stressful events.

Little is known about the associations among coping strategies, psychosocial functioning, and health outcomes (e.g., adherence, metabolic control) in youths with IDDM. . . . To our knowledge, only two studies have evaluated the relations among coping styles and health outcomes. . . . In a sample of 39 adults with IDDM, Frenzel et al. . . . found that coping styles were not associated with adherence behaviors. . . . The researchers suggested that there is a greater use of coping strategies by individuals who are experiencing the stress of being in poor metabolic control. . . . [I]n a sample of 27 adolescents, Delamater and colleagues . . . found that adolescents in poor control used coping strategies more frequently than those in good metabolic control. . . .

The purposes of this study are twofold. First, we examine the relationships between coping styles and health outcomes (i.e., adherence and metabolic control) in a large sample of youths with IDDM. Second, we examine the family environment and its interaction with individual characteristics to predict coping styles in these youths. We evaluate how the age of the youth and the duration of IDDM are related to coping styles. . . . Because family relations and chronic stress are associated with health outcomes in youths with IDDM . . . these variables were chosen as important contextual factors. Thus, we assess whether individual characteristics (i.e., age, duration of illness), the environmental context (i.e., family relations, stress), and/or the interactions between the individual characteristics and the environment predict the youths' coping styles.

Method

Subjects

Subjects were 135 adolescents with IDDM and their parent or parents. Twenty-nine families were father-absent; the remainder were two-parent families. The adolescents' mean age was 14.5 years (*SD* = 2.4, range = 10.4 to 20.0), the average duration of IDDM was 66.3 months (*SD* = 46.2), the average age at diagnosis was 8.9 years (*SD* = 3.8), and 53% were female. Twenty percent of the families participating were Black (the remainder were White), and the sample was predominantly middle class. . . .

Procedure

The parents of all adolescents who were scheduled for a clinic appointment at a large children's hospital during a 7-month period were contacted and asked to participate in a study examining how adolescents and their families learn to live with diabetes. Only 8% of the families declined to participate. Families who lived in the immediate area were interviewed in their homes, and out-of-town families were interviewed at the hospital.

Written consent was obtained, and the confidentiality of all information was assured. The questionnaires were administered in a counterbalanced order, and interviews were conducted to accommodate the eating and glucose-testing schedule of the adolescent. . . .

The interviewers included three doctoral students and two advanced undergraduates who received extensive training (100 to 120 hr, with approximately 70% of the time spent in group training sessions and 30% in individual training) regarding the nature of IDDM, testing and observational instruments, and interviewing techniques. Interviewers were uninformed as to the subjects' level of metabolic control.

Measures

Adherence. The youths'adherence to the IDDM treatment regimen was assessed with an instrument originally developed by

Hart and colleagues. . . . Self-report and observational methods were used to measure adherence across five areas designated as important by the American Diabetes Association and researchers of adherence behaviors. . . . The 5 areas were diet, insulin adjustment, hypoglycemia, glucose testing, and foot care. Scores from each area were summed to provide an overall index of adherence. . . . Three-month test-retest reliability of the composite index is $r(17) = .70$, $p < .001$. . . .

(Validity measures also are reported.)

Metabolic control. The metabolic control of the adolescents was determined by averaging the hemoglobin A_{1c} (HbA_{1c}) levels taken at the time of the clinic visit and during the year prior to the interview. . . . In our laboratory, the range of HbA_{1c} values for children and adolescents without diabetes is 3.0% to 7.4%, with a mean of 5.2%. The HbA_{1c} values in the present sample ranged from 4.6% to 14.4%, with a mean of 9.4% ($SD = 2.02$). High HbA_{1c} values reflect poor metabolic control. Ideally, the HbA_{1c} values for children with diabetes should be as close as possible to the range of values for children without diabetes.

Coping. The coping styles of the adolescents were assessed using the 54-item Adolescent-Coping Orientation for Problem Experiences (A-COPE). . . . Youths rated how often they engaged in each coping behavior when faced with difficulties or when feeling tense from 1 (*never*) to 5 (*most of the time*). The A-COPE was originally factor-analyzed into 12 factors. . . . The 12 factors included Ventilating Feelings, . . . Seeking Diversions, . . . Developing Self-Reliance and Optimism, . . . Developing Social Support, . . . Solving Family Problems, . . . Avoiding Problems, . . . Seeking Spiritual Help, . . . Investing in Close Friends, . . . Seeking Professional Support, . . . Engaging in Demanding Activity, . . . Being Humorous, . . . and Relaxing. . . .

Family relations. The 30-item Family Adaptability and Cohesion Evaluation Scales (FACES-II . . .) was used to assess family cohesion and family adaptability. FACES-II has discriminated between functional and dysfunctional families in several samples . . . and is considered one of the best instruments to assess families on a system level. . . .

Table 2   *Factor Loadings From the Two-Factor Rotation of the A-COPE*

Coping scale	Factor 1	Factor 2
Ventilating feelings	−.075	.767
Seeking diversions	.648	−.007
Developing self-reliance	.813	.083
Developing social support	.794	.111
Solving family problems	.657	−.370
Avoiding problems	.093	.831
Seeking spiritual help	.666	−.215
Investing in close friends	.675	.215
Engaging in demanding activity	.694	−.288
Being humorous	.625	.001

. . . The scores of the adolescent and the parent or parents were summed to provide a global assessment of the family's perception of family cohesion and adaptability. . . .

Stress. Chronic life stress was determined by the adolescents' responses on the 50-item Adolescent-Family Inventory of Life Events and Change (A-FILE . . .) . . . [T]est-retest reliability is .80 over a 4- to 5-week period. . . . The A-FILE also possesses strong convergent validity. . . .

Results

Coping Scales

Correlational analyses of the 12 scales from the A-COPE indicate a high degree of intercorrelation among the scales. To obtain a smaller number of more unique coping indices, the 12 coping scales were subjected to a principal component factor analysis using the varimax method of factor rotation. The factor analysis derived a two-factor solution accounting for 51.6% of the variance in the scales. One of the scales, professional support, had relatively high loadings on both factors (i.e., .50 and .58). In order to obtain as much orthogonality between the factors as possible, this scale was dropped from further analyses. A second scale, relaxation, was also removed because it had a very low communality value (.23). The remaining 10 scales were subsequently reanalyzed, and a similar two-factor solution was

Table 3   *Correlations Between Coping Factors, Health Outcomes, and Individual Characteristics*

| | Coping | |
| | Utilizing personal and | Ventilation and |
Variable	interpersonal resources	avoidance
Adherence	−.055	−.367**
HbA$_{1c}$	−.025	−.045
Age	.042	.347**
Duration of IDDM	−.146*	.144*
Gender	.078	.021
SES	−.111	.083

Note. Because of the number of correlations, correlations that are significant at the .05 level should be considered only of marginal statistical significance.
*$p < .05$; **$p < .0001$.

obtained, accounting for 55.4% of the variance in the scales. Factor loadings for each of the scales are presented in Table 2.

Eight scales loaded on Factor 1. . . . This factor represents behaviors that involve the acquisition of emotional support and assistance from family members, participation in social relationships and activities, the diversion of attention from problems to positive interests, a reliance on personal skills to manage problems, attending church activities, and maintaining a sense of humor. Two of the 10 coping scales (i.e., ventilating feelings and avoiding problems) loaded strongly on the second factor. These coping responses involve getting angry and blaming others for problems, avoiding the problem by minimization, and engaging in negative activities such as drinking, smoking, and using drugs. Based on the grouping of the scales, Factor 1 is labeled Utilizing Personal and Interpersonal Resources and Factor 2 is labeled Ventilation and Avoidance.

Coping and Health Outcomes

Pearson product-moment correlations were conducted to assess the zero-order associations between the two coping factors, the health outcome variables, and the pertinent demographic characteristics (see Table 3).

Adherence to treatment and metabolic control. The ventilation and avoidance coping style was negatively related to adherence behaviors, whereas utilizing personal and interpersonal resources was not associated with adherence to the IDDM regimen. Neither coping factor significantly correlated with HbA_{1c}.

Individual characteristics. The ventilation and avoidance coping style positively related to the age of the adolescent and was marginally related ($p < .05$) to the duration of IDDM. In contrast, utilizing personal and interpersonal resources was negatively associated with duration of IDDM ($p < .05$). Neither coping style related significantly to gender or SES.

. . . [W]e tested whether ventilation and avoidance coping contributed a significant amount of the variance to adherence after the effects of disease duration and adolescent age had been taken into account. In the first step, disease duration and adolescent age were entered, and only adolescent age marginally predicted adherence, . . . $p < .059$. In the next step, ventilation and avoidance coping significantly accounted for an additional 10% of the variance, . . . $p < .0001$.

Predictors of Coping

Because the ventilation and avoidance coping style was associated with adherence, a simultaneous MRA

(multiple regression analysis)

was conducted only on this coping style. . . . Table 4 presents the standardized beta and the associated *F* values for the final regression equation. Beta indicates the strength and direction of the association between the predictor variable and the coping style and the *F* tests whether the predictor variable is statistically significant.

High ventilation and avoidance coping was predicted by high life stress, low family cohesion, and older adolescent age (i.e., youths in late adolescence). In addition, ventilation and avoidance coping was predicted by the interaction of Family Adaptability × Duration of IDDM. The R^2 for the five significant predictors was .32. . . .

Table 4   *Summary of Findings from Multiple Regression Analysis of
Predictors of Ventilation and Avoidance Coping*

Variable	β	F $(df = 1, 128)$	p
Main effects			
Age	.207	7.16	.008
Stress	.189	6.27	.014
Family cohesion	−.298	13.97	.000
Family Adaptability × Duration	−.196	6.95	.009

Note. Beta is the standardized regression coefficient. Percentage of variance in the coping factor accounted for by the regression equation (R^2) is .32.

. . . [L]ow family adaptability (i.e., rigidity) was strongly related to high levels of ventilation and avoidance coping in adolescents with long duration of IDDM. In contrast, when families demonstrated high adaptability (i.e., flexible relations), the adolescents with long disease duration used low levels of ventilation and avoidance coping.

Discussion

The first goal of this study was to examine the relationships between coping styles and health outcomes in youths with IDDM. Two factor-analytically derived coping styles were identified in these youths: utilizing personal and interpersonal resources and ventilation and avoidance. The frequent use of avoidance and ventilation coping related to nonadherence to IDDM treatment, whereas the use of personal and interpersonal resources was not related to health outcomes. . . . [T]he frequent use of avoidance and ventilation coping seems to reflect a poor fit between the child's style of coping and effective management of the diabetes. Although older adolescent age has been associated with poor adherence to treatment, . . . our results also indicate that it is ventilation and avoidance coping, not adolescent age, that predicts poor adherence.

Secondly, we examined whether individual characteristics (i.e., adolescent age, the duration of IDDM), the environmental context (i.e., family relations, life stress), and/or the interaction between individual and environmental factors predicted the use of ventilation and avoidance coping. Independent of family relations and life stress, older adolescent age was related to the more frequent use of ventilation and avoidance coping. . . .

Longitudinal research, however, is necessary to determine (a) what developmental changes occur in the type and use of emotion-focused coping strategies (e.g., avoidance and ventilation) and (b) whether these changes result in differential outcomes. . . . Perhaps ventilation behaviors (e.g., yelling, blaming others) do not change substantially over time, nor do the negative outcomes; but the alternatives chosen for avoiding stressful situations develop with age and become more adaptive. The sequence of using such strategies over the course of a stressor may also differ for adults compared with youths. . . .

Low family cohesion was also related to the frequent use of ventilation and avoidance coping, independent of other individual and environmental conditions. Low family cohesion has been associated with a variety of problems during adolescence. . . . The youths' coping style could as likely contribute to low cohesion among family members, as low family cohesion contributes to the more frequent use of ventilation and avoidance coping in the youths. The relatively strong contribution of family cohesion in predicting ventilation and avoidance coping seems consistent throughout the entire span of adolescence. . . . These results are similar to other recent research that indicates the influence of family relations on psychosocial functioning does not decrease in magnitude during later adolescence, as once thought. As Harter . . . speculates, it is the nature of family relationships that changes with development . . . not necessarily the relative importance of family relations.

One reason for the absence of relationships between the coping styles and metabolic control might be that the stressors were not diabetes specific, nor were the coping behaviors related to diabetes management. The relationships may have been stronger if, for example, the youth was asked how he or she copes with the fear of experiencing hypoglycemia when going to a social event, and if the coping responses were diabetes specific. . . .

CRITIQUE OF STUDY EXAMPLE 7.2

1. What was the rationale for the study?

2. What were the purposes of the study?

3. Who served as participants in the study?

4. What was the general procedure?

5. What were the good features of the design?

6. What general measures were made?

7. Are there any concerns about reliability and/or validity of any of the measures?

8. Scores on the coping scale were factor analyzed. How many factors accounted for variability in the scales? What are their eigenvalues?

9. Verify that, in the final solution, 55.4% of the variance is attributed to the two factors.

10. What two variables did not load heavily on Factor 1?

11. Which variable had the lowest communality? What does it mean?

12. Which variable had the highest communality? What does it mean?

13. When demographic variables were correlated with Factors 1 and 2, two of them highly correlated with Factor 2. Interpret the coefficients.

14. Does coping style have any relationship to metabolic control?

15. Examine Table 3 and determine the rationale for attempting to predict only ventilation and avoidance (Factor 2) coping styles.

16. What did the multiple regression analysis reveal?

17. Interpret the R^2 of .32.

18. What did the interaction indicate?

19. To what extent was the first purpose of the study fulfilled?

20. To what extent was the second purpose of the study fulfilled?

21. Are the conclusions justified?

22. To what extent do the results generalize?

ANSWERS

1. Whereas coping styles refer to cognitive and behavioral responses to stress, Compas believes that coping style is an interaction (i.e., joint function) between characteristics of the individual and his/her resources and environmental features. However, this model of understanding coping styles has not been tested. Adolescents with insulin-dependent diabetes constantly have to cope with stressors associated with their disease and peer pressure. Despite this, little is known about the interrelationship between their coping strategies, psychological functioning, and health outcome (adherence and metabolic control). The few studies reviewed found little association between coping strategies and psychological functioning and between coping strategies and health outcome, although one study found more coping strategies used by adolescents in poor metabolic control. However, all studies used small *N*s.

2. First, to evaluate the relationship between coping styles and health outcome in a large sample of teens with insulin-dependent diabetes. Second, to study the interaction be- tween family environment and characteristics of the teen in order to predict coping styles. This includes the characteristics of age of the teen and years with the disease.

3. One hundred and thirty-five teens and their parents. Twenty-nine of the families had no father present. Average age of the teens was 14.5; they had had diabetes for an average of 5.5 years and were first diagnosed at about 9 years of age. About half were females, 80% were White, and they were mainly middle class.

4. Families of teens attending a clinic were contacted and requested to take part. Only 8% refused. Those living near the clinic were interviewed at home; out-of-towners were interviewed at the clinic. All gave written consent, tests were

counterbalanced, and interviewers were intensively trained, although naive about the level of metabolic control of the teens.

5. Questionnaires were administered in counterbalanced order; independent interviewers were used; interviewers were naive with respect to health status of the teen.

6. Adherence by the teen to the diabetic regimen, metabolic control by glycosylated hemoglobin averaged over two measures made a year apart, coping styles when stressed, family functioning, and chronic life stress.

7. No, all are well-established tests.

8. Two factors with eigenvalues of 3.9287 and 1.6104.

9. $(3.9287 + 1.6104)/10 = .55391 = 55.4\%$.

10. Ventilating feelings and avoiding problems.

11. Being humorous (.391). This means that 39% of the variance of these scores that reflect a means of coping with stress is accounted for by Factors 1 and 2.

12. Avoiding problems (.699). This means that 69.9% of the variance of these scores that reflect a means of coping with stress is accounted for by Factors 1 and 2.

13. Adherence is one variable. The more the teen adhered to the regimen, the less he/she used ventilation and avoidance as ways of coping with stress. Age is the second variable. The older the teen, the more he/she used ventilation and avoidance as ways of coping with stress.

14. No. The correlations between HbA_{1c} and Factors 1 and 2 both were nonsignificant.

15. Adherence was the only behavioral variable associated with this factor. This variable was not related to Factor 1. And only duration of IDMM was (marginally) related to Factor 1.

16. The use of ventilation and avoidance is predicted by higher age of the teen, greater life stress, less cohesion in the family, and the interactive effects of the family's adaptability and length of time the teen had diabetes.

17. Approximately 32% of variability in (these) coping scores is associated with the predictor variables.

18. Teens from rigid (low adaptability) families tended to use more ventilation and avoidance to cope with stress, especially when they had had diabetes a long time. Teens from highly adaptable families tended to use less ventilation and avoidance to cope with stress, especially when they had had diabetes a long time.

19. The authors related coping style and health outcome, but only in terms of adherence. They concluded that ventilation and avoidance (both related to denial and projection) predicted adherence: High use of this style of coping is associated with poorer adherence to the diabetic regimen.

20. The second purpose was to determine predictors of coping style. They focused on ventilation and avoidance and found that it is predicted by age, stress, family cohesion, and family adaptability × duration of IDMM. However, the predictors only account for 32% of the variability in these coping behaviors.

21. Yes. This was a well-controlled study.

22. To similar teens with IDDM, who come from similar homes and who experience similar life stresses (specifically measured by the stress scale). As the authors note, if a different stress scale had been used—one directly related to diabetes management—results might have differed.

Supplementary Readings
on This Topic

- Diekhoff, G. (1992). *Statistics for the social and behavioral sciences: Univariate, bivariate, multivariate.* Dubuque, IA: Wm. C. Brown.
- Duntman, G. H. (1984). *Multivariate analysis.* Beverly Hills, CA: Sage.
- Kleinbaum, D. G., Kupper, L. L., & Muller, K. E. (1988). *Applied regression analysis and other multivariable methods* (2nd ed.). Boston: PWS-Kent.

8

DISCRIMINANT
ANALYSIS STUDIES

Discriminant analysis is a technique that bears some similarity to multiple regression, analysis of variance (discussed in Chapter 10), and factor analysis. Multiple regression attempts to establish a linear combination of independent variables that results in the most accurate prediction of some quantitative criterion (dependent) variable. Analysis of variance establishes whether group differences are evident in a dependent variable as the result of some manipulation of an independent variable. Factor analysis establishes which independent variables contribute to an underlying characteristic or trait (factor). And discriminant analysis attempts to arrive at a linear combination or combinations of quantitative discriminant variables that result in the largest separation of groups of individuals or objects. It also establishes patterns among the discriminant variables that discriminate or differentiate the groups. Whereas multiple regression yields a dependent variable score (e.g., grade point average) based on several predictors (e.g., SAT, GRE, high school average), discriminant analysis yields most likely group membership (e.g., barely succeeds, clearly succeeds, succeeds with honors). Whereas analysis of variance yields group differences based on a single independent variable (or combination of single levels) per case, discriminant analysis usually is based on several different discriminant variables per case. And whereas factor analysis determines correlations between factors and independent variables (loading), discriminant analysis determines correlations between discriminant function scores and original discriminant variable scores (also called loading) to see just which variables differentiate the groups.

Discriminant analyses are conducted for one of two reasons. First, groups may differ and the researcher wants to determine those characteristics that differentiate them. For example, which variables differentiate college majors in clinical, industrial, and physiological psychology? Second, given that established groups have been differentiated, to which group does an unknown data case belong? For example, is a given case to be classified as autistic, learning disabled, or mentally retarded?

The discriminant function is at the heart of each goal. This is the weighted sum of certain discriminant (independent) variables, sometimes referred to as predictors. These may be a number of different scores obtained from the members of each of the groups to be differentiated. If the intent is to discriminate among groups, a number of discriminant functions may be derived. Generally, the maximum number of functions depends on the number of criterion groups being measured. This number is one less than the number of groups or the number of discriminant variables, whichever is smaller. If there are three groups and four discriminant variables, there can be two discriminant functions. The first function will provide the best separation among groups and may discriminate one group from the others. The second may differentiate between the remaining two. These functions are derived simultaneously by determining the weights of the discriminant variables in such a way that they maximize group differences and minimize errors in classifying data cases.

The first function will have the greatest discriminating power. This means that if the mean discriminant function scores for each group is determined, the average difference among the group means will be largest for the first function and smaller for those mean differences for the remaining functions. These functions can be tested for significance by a multivariate statistic called Wilks's lambda, which is often converted to an F ratio: a ratio of between-group variability to within-group variability. The more the groups have been differentiated by a discriminant function, the greater the between-group variability and the larger the F ratio. If the ratio for the first overall test is significant, it is concluded that at least the first discriminant function differentiates among groups. The next step removes discrimination provided by the first function and repeats the test of significance to determine whether groups still can be separated by the remaining functions, each of which are orthogonal or independent of each other. If the first F ratio is not significant, none of the functions are significant, and it would be concluded that the discriminant variables do not differentiate the groups.

Values equivalent to R^2 can be determined to indicate percentage variability in the discriminant function scores for a particular function that is associated with the different groups. Therefore, these values indicate discriminating power of the function. The values may be reported as squared canonical correlations (correlations between discriminant scores and independent variables) or in terms of eigenvalues. In the latter, the ratio of an eigenvalue for a function to the sum of eigenvalues for all functions yields discriminating power of that function. And because the first function always indicates greatest differentiation, its value always will be largest, with remaining functions accounting for less of the variability.

Once significance of discriminant functions has been demonstrated, it is useful to determine the relative importance of each predictor variable in the discrimination. This can be achieved by converting scores on the predictor variables to standardized scores so that the function is expressed in terms of standardized scores weighted by beta weights. The squared value of each beta weight indicates the relative contribution of each variable. However, these relative contributions depend on which predictor variables are included in or excluded from the function and can very well change with deletions and/or additions of other variables—just as is true in multiple regression.

To get the flavor of discriminant analysis, imagine that we want to know what variables differentiate clinical psychologists, general practitioner physicians, and psychiatrists. We choose 10 of each professional and administer a battery of three tests. Say they measure empathy, locus of control (the extent to which one attributes experiences to one's own control as opposed to fate), and self-esteem. This yields a column of 30 group identification scores, 30 empathy scores, 30 locus of control scores, and 30 self-esteem scores. Because there are three groups and three discriminant variables, two discriminant functions are possible. Each function is derived mathematically so that the weights assigned to each predictor variable (the three tests) score for the first function will maximally separate the groups and the weights assigned to those variables for the second function will be such that the second function is orthogonal to the first. When the weights are applied to the scores of each participant, we have two additional columns: discrimiant function 1 scores and discriminant function 2 scores.

One of the first analyses on these discriminant function scores lets us know if they are significant. If so, all that this indicates is that the groups differ. We can determine how much of variability in each of the two sets of scores is associated with group membership, but these tests do not indicate which of the three variables separates the groups. One useful step would be to determine the intercorrelations between the scores on the three predictor variables. It might reveal that empathy is uncorrelated with the remaining two but that locus of control and self-esteem are correlated and might be measuring, say, self-confidence.

Now, correlations between discriminant function scores and scores on each of the three variables will indicate which variable (or variables) is the differentiator in the first and second function. For example, the highest correlation for the first function may be for locus of control and self-esteem. The second function may yield the highest correlation for empathy. These analyses plus a scattergram of each group member's first and second discriminant function scores might reveal that psychologists are relatively more empathic than the remaining two groups, whereas general practitioners and psychiatrists are relatively higher in self-confidence. Or the latter two groups might be differentiated in the degree to which each feels self-confident.

The bulk of published research focuses on group differentiation. Classification of unknown cases, the second purpose of the discriminant analysis, is achieved by setting certain discriminant scores as "cutoff scores." One now sets standards on the order of what follows: If the discriminant score of the unknown case is greater than the cutoff, that case is classified one way; otherwise, the case is classified another way. Concern here is with errors in classification and relative cost of the errors.

Two research articles that included discriminant analysis are evaluated, the first one together and the second study only by you. As is true of multiple regression and factor analysis, statistical analysis probably will be performed by a statistician who is knowledgeable about assumptions that have to be met. Our concern is with the bases for obtaining the data for the analysis. We want some assurance that testing conditions were about the same for all groups, that a naive data collector was employed, that the tests are reliable and valid, and that tests were not presented in the same order for all data cases.

STUDY EXAMPLE 8.1

This study is from the education field and deals with an attempt to determine whether handicapped and nonhandicapped students could be differentiated on the basis of test performance when tested under two different conditions. This study reports the results of the discriminant analysis in terms of Wilks's lambda. Moreover, another analysis is conducted: analysis of variance for a two-factor mixed design. This design is covered in

Chapter 11. Two terms that are discussed are main and interaction effects. Briefly, main effects are the average, overall, effects of each independent variable—here, the two groups and the two conditions under which they were tested. Interaction effects are differential effects on performance of each group under the two test conditions.

The Study

- Munger, G. F., & Loyd, B. H. (1991). Effect of speededness on test performance of handicapped and nonhandicapped examinees. *Journal of Educational Research, 85*(1), 53-57. Reprinted with permission of the Helen Dwight Reid Educational Foundation. Published by Heldref Publications, 1319 Eighteenth St, NW, Washington, DC 20036-1802. Copyright © 1991.

Standardized tests of academic achievement are designed to measure student growth and performance in fundamental skill and content areas. The skills measured are typically those necessary for further educational development. In addition, . . . standardized achievement tests are intended to provide all examinees with an equal opportunity to demonstrate their level of knowledge and skills. Standardized achievement tests are administered and scored under uniform conditions to increase the objectivity of the testing process. The procedure permits the comparison of the performance of a student or group with a norm or reference group that has taken the same or an equivalent test under similar conditions.

One aspect of test uniformity is timing. Most standardized tests are administered under timed conditions. . . . [A]ny items not completed within the prescribed time limit are considered to be incorrect or unattempted. Achievement tests are intended to be measures of skills and knowledge, therefore, time limits on those tests tend to be imposed primarily for administrative convenience, and they are designed to allow for 80 to 90% of all examinees to complete the test within the prescribed amount of time.

. . . [T]esting conditions such as timing may disadvantage examinees with disabilities. If, as a function of a disabling condition, an examinee's knowledge and skills cannot be fully demonstrated under standardized testing conditions, the obtained score will not accurately reflect the examinee's level of achievement but, rather, the extent of the disability.

To allow handicapped examinees to more easily participate in standardized testing programs, . . . the conditions of testing may be modified. In most cases in which the conditions of testing are modified for examinees with disabilities, the time limits are extended or waived. . . . [L]imited research has been conducted to examine the effect of testing time on the performance of handicapped examinees or to determine the amount of time actually needed by persons with various handicapping conditions.

. . . [H]andicapped examinees tested from 1979 to 1983 took considerably more time to complete the SAT than nonhandicapped examinees did. However, the relationship between amount of time and performance on the verbal portion of the test varied by type of disability. In contrast, . . . disabled examinees who spent more time on the mathematics sections tended to achieve higher mathematics scores.

Centra . . . also examined the effects of extra time on test performance by comparing the scores of handicapped examinees on timed and untimed administrations of the SAT. The results indicated that the performance of the handicapped students improved with extended time, the increase in scores being greater than that observed for nonhandicapped examinees who were allowed extra testing time. This suggests that the additional time allowed to handicapped students may be important in reducing the effects of the examinee's disability on test performance and in creating a comparable task.

1. What was the rationale for the study?

Standardized achievement tests measure proficiencies gained thus far. They are administered under uniform conditions so that comparisons can be made with performances by standardization groups. Timed testing is one component of uniform conditions, and items not completed within the time limit are counted as wrong. This may result in a poor measure of achievement by disabled students. The test might be measuring extent of the disability rather than level of achievement. To get a better measure of achievement by the handicapped, time limits can be waived. But the effect of this has not been studied much.

Comparable Time and
Test Speededness

When time limitations affect examinees' scores, a test is considered to be a partially speeded instrument, and scores are determined by the number of items attempted as well as the accuracy of responses. The greater the proportion of items unattempted is because of insufficient time, the greater is the speededness of the test. A pure speed test is a test with severe time constraints, but it is composed of items so easy that few errors are expected. In a pure power test, sufficient time is allowed for most students to attempt all items, but the items tend to be difficult. . . .

2. What was the operational definition of speededness of a test?

The number (or proportion) of test items not attempted because of time constraints.

Although most aptitude and achievement tests purport to be measures of power, . . . some tests may be more speeded for members of particular groups. If a test acts as a speeded measure for one group and a power measure for another group, timing may be a potential source of test bias.

. . . [I]ncreasing the time limits of standardized verbal and quantitative tests does not differentially affect the scores of groups defined by ethnic identity, sex, rural or urban residency, and years out of school.

. . . [T]he findings may not necessarily extend to other standardized tests or to members of other groups. . . . [F]or examinees who are younger, less experienced, or less successful academically, increasing the time limits of standardized tests may dramatically affect test performance.

One such group that clearly tends to be younger and less experienced in taking standardized tests that demonstrates varied academic performance is the handicapped population in elementary schools. That group may be particularly affected when time limits are imposed. Examinees with learning disabilities may require additional time to read and respond to test items. Similarly, physically handicapped examinees may require additional time to turn pages, record responses, and perform written computations or draw diagrams helpful in solving problems.

If handicapped examinees attempt fewer test items than nonhandicapped examinees do, then the test may be considered to be more speeded for examinees with disabilities. The purpose of this study was to investigate whether there is a difference in test speededness for handicapped and nonhandicapped examinees.

?

3. What was the purpose of the test?

To determine whether fewer test items would be attempted (speededness) by handicapped than nonhandicapped students.

Method

Test Materials

The standardized achievement test selected for this study was the Iowa Tests of Basic Skills (ITBS). . . . This comprehensive achievement battery for Grades kindergarten through 9 is designed to measure growth in fundamental skill areas. Together, the Primary Battery and the Multilevel edition consist of 10 test levels, numbered from 5 to 14, which correspond approximately to the median chronological age of students within each grade.

> *(At this point you might want to write those ages down to check that there are 10 levels. Also write the grades under age level, starting with kindergarten for age 5.)*

Each of the levels contains tests that measure achievement in the basic skills and content areas appropriate to the grade covered.

The two tests selected for this study were Language Usage and Expression and Mathematics Concepts, Level 11. The Language Usage and Expression test consists of 38 items with a range of difficulty appropriate for Grade 5. . . . The usual time allowed to complete the language usage test is 30 min.

The Level 11 Mathematics Concepts test consists of 35 items appropriate for fifth-grade students. . . . The usual time allowed to complete the Mathematics Concepts test is 25 min.

?

4. What standardized test was used?

Language Usage and Expression test and Mathematics Concepts test of the Iowa Tests of Basic Skills.

5. *Is there any concern about reliability or validity of the test?*

No. The test is standardized and known to be reliable and valid.

6. *The test consists of 10 levels, from kindergarten to 9th grade. They are labeled 5 to 14, corresponding to the median age of children at each level. Level 11 was selected as appropriate for 5th grade. In fact, to what grade is Level 11 (median age) appropriate?*

appropriate for Grade 6.

Age:	5	6	7	8	9	10	11
Grade:	K	1	2	3	4	5	6

Subjects

The Iowa Tests of Basic Skills was administered to 222 fifth-grade students selected from school systems in Virginia. Six of the students were physically handicapped, 94 were learning disabled, and 112 had no handicapping condition.

(Note that what is reported as 112 should be 122.)

The physically handicapped sample included students with neurological and orthopedic disabilities who were capable of taking the test independently under timed conditions. Students with visual or hearing impairments were not included. The learning-disabled sample included students identified as having specific perceptual, neurological, and cognitive deficits, and receiving special educational services in either self-contained classrooms or resource programs. All the students included in the study possessed normal-range intellectual function.

The students were selected from 18 elementary schools in six school districts. In 10 of the schools, physically handicapped, learning disabled, and an approximately equal number of randomly selected nonhandicapped fifth-grade students participated in the study. In 6 of the schools, only students with learning disabilities were tested. In one school, all fifth graders were tested, and, in another school, all learning-disabled fifth-gade students and an entire regular class were tested.

(Note the diverse source of students for each group. Keep in mind that students drawn from different schools may not be equivalent.)

7. Who served as participants?

A total of 222 fifth graders from 18 different schools in six school districts. Of those, 100 were handicapped (mainly learning disabled), and 122 were not handicapped.

8. Could the two groups be considered otherwise equivalent?

No. Aside from presence or absence of a handicap, all handicapped students were drawn from 17 out of the 18 schools (presumably from all school districts), but non-handicapped students were a random sample from 10 of the 18 schools (N unknown), all fifth graders from one school (potentially the largest proportion of this group) and one regular class of another school.

The Language Usage and Expression test of the ITBS was administered to 109 fifth-grade students. Of those students, 52 (48%) were handicapped, and 57 (52%) were nonhandicapped. Sixty-two (57%) were boys, and 47 (43%) were girls. The Mathematics Concepts test of the ITBS was administered to 113 fifth-grade students. Of those students, 48 (43%) were handicapped, and 65 (57%) were nonhandicapped. Sixty-three (56%) were boys, and 50 (44%) were girls.

(Note the difference between the total number and the break-down of those who received the Language and those who received the Mathematics test. Also note the grouping of disabled and handicapped.)

Test Administration

Parallel forms G and H of the Language Usage and Expression and Mathematics Concepts tests were administered to handicapped and nonhandicapped students in Grade 5. Each student took two forms of either the verbal (Language Usage and Expression) or mathematics (Mathematics Concepts) test. One form was timed; the parallel form was untimed. The order of the forms was varied to control for practice effects. Approximately half the students took the timed test first, and approximately half took the untimed test first.

(The procedures are called counterbalancing and control for the effects of practice and fatigue as accounting for a change in performance on the second test.)

The examinees were tested under one timing condition (timed or untimed), given a short break, and then tested under the other condition. The usual time limits were observed for the timed condition. For the untimed condition, the students were allowed as much time as necessary to complete the test. Large format answer sheets were provided to all the examinees.

(Note that there is no indication of who administered the tests, whether they were given to a group or administered individually, or both.)

?

9. What was the general procedure?

Roughly half of each group was administered the Language test and half of each group had the Mathematics test. Each student took parallel forms of one of the two tests. One form was timed and the parallel form untimed.

10. What were the good features of the design?

The orders of the parallel forms were counterbalanced, with half of the students receiving the timed condition first and the other half receiving the untimed condition first.

11. What were some questionable features of the design and/or report of the design?

It is not clear whether only one test was administered to all in a given school or to half the sample in that school. The two groups were not likely to be equivalent. Some students may have been individually tested and the rest tested as a group (e.g., an entire class was tested).

Analysis

To determine whether a difference in test speededness exists for handicapped and nonhandicapped examinees when tested under timed conditions, we conducted a two-group discriminant analysis. The two groups were handicapped examinees and nonhandicapped examinees. The independent variables were (a) completion or noncompletion of 90% of the test items . . . and (b) the number of items attempted by the examinee. The procedure was conducted for verbal test performance and mathematics test performance.

To determine whether reducing the amount of speededness has a differential effect on handicapped and nonhandicapped examinees, we used a two-factor mixed analysis of variance design. The first factor was timing condition. The second factor was group. The dependent variable was test scores. The procedure was conducted for verbal test performance and mathematics test performance.

?

12. What data served as the basis of the discriminant analysis for the Language test?

The percentage of items attempted, regardless of whether the items were answered correctly or not.

Results

A two-group discriminant analysis was conducted to examine whether a difference in test speededness exists for handicapped and nonhandicapped examinees. Predictor variables were completion or noncompletion of 90% of the test items and the number of items attempted. . . .

All of the nonhandicapped students who were administered the Language Usage and Expression test attempted all 38 items. Therefore, the mean number of items attempted by this group was 38.00; the standard deviation was 0. Two of the handicapped students attempted only 23 items, and one student attempted 29 items. The mean number of items attempted by the handicapped group was 37.25; the standard deviation was 3.14.

On the basis of the two predictor variables, a discriminant function was calculated. . . . The discriminant function was not significant, $r_c = .18$, Wilks's lambda = .97, . . . $p = .19$. This finding suggested that the handicapped group cannot be discriminated from the nonhandicapped group on the basis of completion or noncompletion of 90% of the test items nor the number of items attempted.

Table 1   *Grade-Equivalent Scores on Language Usage and Expression Test*

Examinee	M	SD
Handicapped		
Timed	4.3	1.6
Untimed	4.5	1.5
Nonhandicapped		
Timed	6.3	1.8
Untimed	6.4	1.4

(Note that the analysis was not the most appropriate because only one dependent variable was involved; t tests would have yielded the same results.)

?

13. What were the overall results of the discriminant analysis for the Language test?

The two groups were not differentiated in speededness when the test was timed. Approximately the same proportion of items was attempted by handicapped and nonhandicapped students.

A two-factor mixed analysis of variance procedure was conducted to determine whether reducing the amount of speededness has a differential effect on handicapped and non-handicapped examinees. The mean grade-equivalent scores on the Language Usage and Expression test under timed and untimed conditions are reported for the two groups in Table 1. When the test was administered under untimed conditions, the increase in mean scores was .2 grade level for the

handicapped group and .1 grade level for the nonhandicapped students. . . . Only the main effects for group were
significant, . . . $p < .01$.

> (This means that there was an overall difference in perform-
> ance of the two groups when the two test conditions are
> ignored, namely, the nonhandicapped students consistently
> outperformed the handicapped students.)

?

14. *What were the overall results of the analysis of mean
number of correct items achieved by both groups when
the Language test was timed versus untimed?*

Handicapped students, overall, achieved fewer items correct
regardless of whether the test was timed or untimed.

The discriminant analysis and analysis of variance procedures were repeated for performance on the Mathematics
Concepts test. Of the nonhandicapped students who were
administered the Mathematics Concepts test, 85% attempted
all 35 items, and 92% completed at least 90% of the test
items. The mean number of items attempted by the group
was 34.43; the standard deviation was 1.64. Seventy-five
percent of the handicapped students who were administered
the Mathematics Concepts test attempted all 35 items, and
83% completed at least 90% of the test. The mean number
of items attempted by this group was 33.52; the standard
deviation was 3.33.

On the basis of the two predictor variables, completion or
noncompletion of 90% of the test items on the Mathematics
Concepts test and number of items attempted, we computed
a discriminant function. The discriminant function was not
significant, $r_c = .18$, Wilks's lambda = .97, . . . $p = .15$, and it

Table 3   *Grade-Equivalent Scores on Mathematics Concepts Test*

Examinee	M	SD
Handicapped		
Timed	4.5	1.3
Untimed	4.6	1.4
Nonhandicapped		
Timed	6.4	1.5
Untimed	6.5	1.5

did not distinguish between the handicapped and nonhandi-capped groups.

?

15. What were the overall results of the discriminant analysis for the Mathematics test?

The groups were not differentiated by speededness of the test. Both attempted approximately the same proportion of items when the test was timed.

The two-factor mixed analysis of variance procedure was repeated using scores on the Mathematics Concepts test as the dependent variable. The mean grade-equivalent scores on the Mathematics Concepts test under timed and untimed conditions are reported for the two groups in Table 3. When the test was administered under untimed conditions, the increase in mean scores was .1 grade level for both the handicapped and nonhandicapped groups. . . . Main effects for group were significant, . . . $p < .01$.

?

16. *What were the overall results of the analysis of mean number of correct items achieved by both groups, when the Mathematics test was timed or untimed?*

Handicapped students, overall, achieved fewer correct responses, regardless of whether the test was timed or untimed.

Discussion

Our study was conducted to examine whether a difference in test speededness exists for handicapped and nonhandicapped examinees and whether the test performance of handicapped and nonhandicapped examinees is differentially affected under timed and untimed conditions. The results of the study provide no evidence of a difference in test speededness for the two groups nor evidence that the groups are differentially affected when the amount of speededness is reduced.

The results of the discriminant analysis procedures support the null hypothesis that . . . the two groups could not be distinguished on the basis of the number of test items attempted and completion or noncompletion of 90% of the test. This result . . . suggests that the handicapped group was not disadvantaged by timing.

The results of the analysis of variance procedures also fail to reject the null hypothesis of no interaction between group and timing condition. Although the difference in mean scores for the two groups was significant, timing condition was not, and the interaction between group and timing was close to zero . . . suggest[ing] that timing had little effect on the performance of either group. . . .

Our findings support and extend the work . . . which demonstrated that increasing the time limits of standardized verbal and quantitative tests did not differentially affect the scores of groups defined by ethnic identity, sex, rural or urban residency, and years out of school. Although the subjects in those studies were candidates for college and graduate or professional schools, the present findings, based on the performance of a much younger sample, are consistent with . . . previous studies, and reveal no differential effect of increasing test time limits on the performance of any group.

. . . The results of this study suggest that additional testing time may not affect student performance and that students with physical handicaps or learning disabilities may perform equally well under timed or untimed conditions. One . . . implication of our findings is that members of handicapped groups may reasonably be included in the standardized testing situation with the other members of their class. . . . This would provide handicapped students with the practice and experience of a group-administered test and the same opportunity to demonstrate their level of achievement as that given to nonhandicapped students.

?

17. What were the authors' major conclusions?

Handicapped and nonhandicapped students did not differ in number of items attempted when tests had a time limit (speededness). Moreover, removing the time limit did not benefit performances of either group.

18. In view of the report that all subjects were of normal intelligence, the questionable appropriateness of the level of the test, and the finding that handicapped children consistently performed at a lower grade level than did the nonhandicapped children, is the conclusion valid? That is, can any other factor(s) account for the results?

It is quite possible that the grade level chosen was too high for the handicapped group. As a result, if the test was too hard for them—as their performances suggest—removing a time limit would be of no help. Moreover, if the handicapped children were at the same grade level as the nonhandicapped children, they should have performed at the same level on, at least, the untimed conditions of the tests. Because they performed at a lower level, they were not equivalent to the nonhandicapped group. Finally, if handicapped children were not part of the standardization procedure, their performance cannot be compared with norms based on nonhandicapped children. These weaknesses mean that the hypothesis was not appropriately tested.

STUDY EXAMPLE 8.2

This study is from the field of education and deals with an attempt to accelerate the cognitive development of kindergarten children from impoverished environments. Piaget's theory of development guided the research. Accordingly, youngsters at first think very concretely, and their behavior is tied to specific stimuli. As more mature thinking emerges, they are capable of classifying objects such as tools, serializing, and applying principles of conservation (e.g., five pennies are still five pennies regardless of whether they are close to each other or spread over a surface). Whereas many studies determine characteristics that differentiate groups, this experimental study assigned individuals to two methods of training and then determined whether the training differentiated the groups on two standardized tests. Although the bulk of results are analyzed by determining discriminant functions, the authors also performed analyses of variance—univariate F tests.

The Study

- Pasnak, R., Holt, R., Campbell, J. W., & McCutcheon, L. (1991). Cognitive and achievement gains for kindergartners instructed in Piagetian operations. *Journal of Educational Research, 85*(1), 5-13. Reprinted with permission of the Helen Dwight Reid Educational Foundation. Published by Heldref Publications, 1319 Eighteenth St., NW, Washington, DC 20036-1802. Copyright © 1991.

Five-year-old children are highly variable in their cognitive functioning. Some 5-year-olds are still in the preoperational state of cognitive development. Their thinking remains closely tied to perceptual properties of the objects or events that they are considering. Consequently, the children frequently classify items inappropriately, even on simple properties such as form, size, orientation, function, or type. These failures result, at least in part, because the children cannot resist intrusions of irrelevant perceptual characteristics of the items to be classified. Such disorganization often occurs even when the physical objects to be classified can be inspected at length, and it is even more likely when purely mental representations form the basis for classification by similarities and differences.

Likewise, at 5 years the mental operation of seriation—arranging objects sequentially according to some gradation of size, space, number, time, etc.—is often deficient. Children whose thinking is still preoperational may be unable to seriate more than four or five tangible objects . . . and their finding the place for a new object within an already formed series is much more difficult. (It is much easier for a child to build a series by sequentially adding to the end of it. . . .) Mental seriation of items named is still more demanding. And, preoperational children typically do not understand or apply the operations of addition/subtraction, reversibility, reciprocity, and identity. . . .

Other children, at 5 years, evince more cognitive development. They have progressed to an early form of concrete operational thought and suffer less from perceptual intrusions into their thinking process. . . . Those 5-year-olds have the early concrete operations necessary to classify objects or events along one dimension by singling out the relevant characteristic, and they can easily seriate by one dimension and can conserve number, substance, and some other properties. The progressive development of concrete operational thought throughout the elementary school years involves many other abilities, but classification, seriation, and conservation are probably the key mental *operations* at the outset.

At the beginning of elementary school (kindergarten), performance on classification, seriation, and conservation problems predicts performance on a variety of standard and nonstandard achievement measures . . . and a variety of informal measures contrived by teachers and researchers. Significantly, kindergartners' abilities to classify, seriate, and conserve predict their achievement not only in kindergarten but also subsequently in Grades 1 through 4. . . . The relations of Piagetian operations to achievement suggest that trying to improve kindergartners' concrete operation functioning may be profitable.

Such an intervention seems especially appropriate because it would be intended to benefit children old enough to have need of the thought processes that are normal for their age peers. In many cases, the potential for better cognitive functioning exists, but the children need help in developing it, especially if the children are products of deprived or disadvantaged . . . environments.

Among the successful methods used to teach concrete operations are the learning set techniques favored by some psychologists and educators. A learning set consists of a large number of problems involving a broad variety of concrete objects. . . [T]hey can all be solved by the same abstract principle. . . . The variety of objects used to construct problems . . . solved via the same principle governs the extent to which the principle is learned and generalized. . . .

The Piacceleration instructional method was developed out of efforts to use learning sets to teach classification, seriation, and number conservation to blind and mildly mentally retarded students. Success with these . . . students . . . led to attempts to use this instructional method to help nonhandicapped children who were slow in developing these three concrete operations and who were not doing well in their kindergarten classrooms.

Preliminary tests of this program with small samples of 5-year-olds who had no identifiable handicaps but who had not been making normal progress indicated that Piacceleration instruction produced significant cognitive gains on a variety of non-Piagetian measures, and that the gains persisted for at least a year. There was no evidence for academic achievement gains in the preliminary studies. . . . However, achievement measures were taken . . . just 2 weeks after the intervention was concluded. . . .

Genuine progress in cognitive ability, as defined either by Piaget . . . or by standard psychometric instruments, should eventually be followed by improved academic performance and achievement gains. Hence, we decided to test Piacceleration with a larger sample and more extensive achievement measures taken after more time had elapsed. The target population was children, especially minority children, who were not doing well in their first encounter with a public school system. Because the children were engaged in making both the transition from home to school environment and the transition from preoperational to concrete operational thought, they might represent an especially vulnerable group with great potential to profit from intervention.

Our approach in this study was to offer half of the children instruction on the concrete operations of classification, seriation, and conservation instead of the conventional mathematics instruction that they would otherwise have received for part of the school year. The rationale was that the mastery of the three concrete operations gained from Piacceleration instruction might generalize to improved conceptual functioning and problem solving and . . . subsequently lead to improved achievement not only in mathematics but also in verbal comprehension. . . .

The other half of the children involved in the study served as a control or reference group. They were offered the conventional mathematics instruction from the program of studies used in the cooperating school system. . . . In essence, the comparison provided a test of whether a conventional mathematics curriculum or one that uses hundreds of manipulatives to ensure competence in the key concrete operations would produce the greatest gains in kindergarten mathematics, reasoning ability, and general comprehension for poorly performing kindergartners.

Method

Subjects

Selection. We asked the teachers of all 17 kindergarten classes in six neighboring Northern Virginia schools to select the 5 children in their classes who were lowest in ability, excepting those who had noticeable language difficulties or other special problems. . . . [T]he average ability of the children selected was low, as shown by the Otis-Lennon School Ability Index (SAI) for the untreated children (SAI = 33rd percentile). There were no data on the average ability or intelligence of kindergartners from those schools, but the 56th-percentile average of their fourth graders on the Stanford Achievement Test (SAT) provides a rough estimate. The schools . . . serve a high proportion of low-income and minority families.

Assignment. We assigned the groups of 5 students to experimental or control conditions according to a restricted randomization. The restrictions were to equalize the number of children from each teacher, school, and morning or afternoon kindergarten sessions in the experimental and control groups. This equalization was essentially achieved with one extra afternoon group assigned to the control condition.

Attrition. Two sets of experimental children were lost because of extended illness and eventual resignation of the classroom aides assigned to instruct them. The corresponding sets of control children were also deleted, leaving 30 experimental and 35 control children. Then 2 experimental and 6 more control children were lost because of moves or extended absences. The difference in attrition for the two groups did not approach statistical significance. . . .

Of the children remaining in the experimental group, 17 were White and 11 were minority (7 Black). For the control group, 15 were White and 14 were minority (10 Black). Differences in the ethnic composition of the groups did not approach structural significance. . . . [T]he average age was 6.01 years (*SD* = .42) for the experimental group, 5.99 years (*SD* = .42) for the control group. No representative socioeconomic measures were available.

Materials

Standardized tests. . . . We selected the Otis-Lennon School Ability Test (O-LSAT) and the Stanford Early School Achievement Test (SESAT) to measure the variables.

The O-LSAT was designed . . . to provide a measure of reasoning especially predictive of success in school. . . . [S]cores on the Primary I version used in this research correlated with end-of-year course grades in reading (.40) and mathematics (.48). Dyer's . . . review provides additional evidence of validity: correlations with first year Metropolitan Achievement Test scores are .61-.68.

At the 5- to 6-year-old level, this group test has a 15-item Classification scale, a 15-item Analogies scale, and a 30-item Omnibus scale. . . . All the scales consist of multiple-choice questions—one of four drawings to be marked in answer to a question read aloud. The School Ability Index (SAI) is derived from the scales, with all items having equal weights.

The O-LSAT manual indicates that minority students, primarily Blacks, were slightly overrepresented in the 130,000 O-LSAT standardization sample. . . .

. . . Primary I level . . . with a fall-spring test-retest reliability of .84. . . .

The SESAT (Level 2) was especially selected for this research because it measures knowledge of the physical and social environment. . . . Level 2 of the SESAT, for use in kindergarten, also provides measures of achievement in mathematics concepts and skills, verbal comprehension, vocabulary, letters, and phonetics, and has a total of 308 four-item multiple-choice questions. . . .

Median . . . reliabilities of .87 for Level 2 are given in the manual. The split-half reliability coefficient of the SESAT for the present sample [was] r = .84. . . . [T]he test has been favorably reviewed by experts, including a minority panel, for content validity. The manual reports median correlations of .62 with the O-LSAT.

Classification instruction. We used 20 problems for each of five types of classification. Texture classification. . . . Size, form, and orientation classification. . . . Nonverbal. . . . Verbal discovery of class. . . . In each problem, three objects or types of objects were the same and one was different, except for orientation problems. For the latter, all four objects were identical, but one was oriented differently. . . .

Seriation instruction. We used a set of 75 problems, each consisting of three to nine similar objects. The objects within each problem differed in height, length, width, or overall size, so that the children could order them from the largest to the smallest. . . .

Number conservation instruction. This set consisted of 120 problems using 24 types of objects. Each problem had identical items arranged in two rows. . . .

Conventional mathematics instruction. Uniflex cubes, geoboards, pattern blocks, number bingo boards, a large variety of household items kept in "junk" bags, and numerous teacher-prepared work sheets were used for the control instruction.

Procedure

The control children received the standard curriculum throughout the experiment in the normal classroom format. During December through February. . . .

The experimental children received the Piacceleration instruction from their classroom aide during the time ordinarily devoted to mathematics instruction. The aides pulled the group over to a corner of the classroom and worked through the Piacceleration program . . . 15 to 20 min per day, 3 to 4 days per week for 3 months, commencing November 30.

The aides were monitored twice a week by the first author, and they also were provided with lesson plans describing each phase of the instruction.

The children were taught to classify objects according to four primary dimensions: form, size, texture, and orientation. They were also taught to discover the class of an object, . . . to relate it to other objects of similar function, purpose, origin, or identity.

During a session on form classification, a set of four objects that constituted a classification problem was placed in front of each of the children. . . . The children, in turn, were asked which object was different from . . . the other three, and were praised enthusiastically for a correct choice. If the choice was incorrect, the child was coached and encouraged until a correct choice was made. The choices and feedback were seen and heard by all the children. . . . This process continued until the children had solved each problem. Effort and attention were always praised, and successful solutions were greeted enthusiastically. . . . The procedure continued until all the subjects could solve all of the problems and had been vigorously applauded for diligence and accuracy.

For orientation problems, all four items were identical, but three were presented upside down and the other right side up (or vice versa). . . . [T]he relevant dimension was orientation. We used the same procedure as that used for size or form. . . . Again, praise and attention were used to reward the children's continuing efforts.

> (Nonverbal and verbal discovery of classes is described in the following sections, along with seriation instruction.)

Children were always congratulated for their diligence, and correct solutions were applauded vigorously.

> (Number conservation training is described next.)

The endpoint of instruction varied somewhat depending on the group's rate of progress. Thus, in each group, those children who were the slowest to master the most difficult constructs . . . received more instruction than those who learned quickly. All Piacceleration instruction was finished by February 21.

When the children had mastered all three constructs, they joined their classmates, who were receiving the standard mathematics instruction . . . instead of Piacceleration.

The O-LSAT and the SESAT's Environment, Mathematics, Sounds and Letters, and Words and Stories scales were administered during the third and fourth weeks of May. . . .

Results

The main thrust of our study was to determine whether children who received the Piacceleration curriculum performed differently than did comparable children in the standard mathematics curriculum on the variables measures. Accordingly, the children's summary scores on the O-LSAT and on the SESAT Environment, Mathematics, Sounds and Letters, and Words and Stories scales were first used in a step-wise discriminate function analysis to assess how the variables contribute to group differences. . . .

. . . Because we expected that many of the predictor variables would be intercorrelated, we used a stepwise discriminant function analysis to avoid any potential problems with multicollinearity and to ensure that the predictors entered into each discriminant function reached the .05 alpha level.

Accordingly, the discriminant analysis was set to include only variables significant at the .05 level. The O-LSAT sum was included, and the discrimination was significant, . . . $p < .01$. Because the analysis was significant, we analyzed the components of each sum to obtain a more detailed picture of the differences caused by the Piacceleration curriculum. The analyses showed that the components for two O-LSAT scales and the SESAT Mathematics and Words and Stories measures were significantly affected by the difference between the two curricula, whereas the components of Environment and Sounds and Letters were not affected.

Discrimination with
O-LSAT Components

The O-LSAT components were more strongly affected by the curricula—the discriminant function was highly significant, . . . $p = .01$. Discriminant function weights showed that Classification was most strongly affected (coefficient = −.74), followed by Analogies (coefficient = −.68) and Omnibus (coefficient = −.35). Univariate F tests confirmed that the Piacceleration curriculum was significantly better than the existing curriculum for the

Table 1   *O-LSAT and SESAT Scores After Normal and Piacceleration Curricula*

Test component	Normal		Piacceleration	
	M	*SD*	*M*	*SD*
O-LSAT				
Full-scale SAI	87.7	15.1	98.0	13.2
Percentile SAI	31.1	27.5	48.3	26.6
Classification	6.5	3.2	9.2	2.8
Analogies	6.3	3.0	8.6	3.0
Omnibus	14.9	5.2	27.2	4.4
SESAT Percentiles				
Environment	22.1	22.2	28.4	21.0
Mathematics	29.2	19.5	38.8	16.3
Letter/Sounds	30.3	16.0	34.4	18.7
Words/Stories	22.9	21.4	32.4	21.3

Classification scale, . . . $p < .01$, and the Analogies scale, . . . $p < .01$, whereas the result for the Omnibus scale was not significant. Means and standard deviations for O-LSAT and SESAT scores for each group are given in Table 1. The direction of the differences favors the Piacceleration curriculum for all scales.

Discrimination with Mathematics Components

The overall effect of the curricula on the Mathematics scale components was significant (. . . $p < .05$). The discriminant weights indicated that Concepts was most affected (1.07) whereas Geometry/Measurement, Addition/Subtraction, and Problem Solving had much smaller coefficients (–.37, –.02, and –.26, respectively). Univariate F tests confirmed that the two curricula produced significantly different performances only on the Concepts part of the Mathematics scale, . . . $p < .01$. Piacceleration children averaged 61% correct on this subscale, whereas children in the normal curriculum averaged 47%.

Discrimination with Words and Stories Components

The Words and Stories test components were affected by the curricula (. . . $p < .05$). The discriminant function weights indicated that the Comprehension component was most affected (coefficient = 1.25), whereas Vocabulary was not affected (coefficient = −.52). Univariate F tests confirmed that the curricula were distinguished by performance on the Comprehension subscale, . . . $p < .01$. Children in the Piacceleration curriculum averaged 59% correct, whereas those in the normal curriculum averaged 47%.

Summary of Differences

. . . [A] range of evidence suggests that the piacceleration curriculum was significantly superior to the existing curriculum for these low-achieving kindergartners.

Discussion

. . . Pasnak previously reported that Piacceleration was a useful instructional program for improving the cognitive functioning of normal kindergarten children who were lagging behind their classmates. Our research confirms that finding for a larger sample from a different locale and with a different measure of ability. . . .

The question remains as to why the Piacceleration instruction would be especially effective, for classification is taught in virtually all school curricula, some form of conservation is taught in many school curricula, and seriation is taught in some curricula. Piaget's . . . answer is that the cognitive structures involved, because they are self-regulating and self-constructing, are remarkably resistant to change, so that ordinary instruction is relatively ineffective. . . . Piacceleration is based on the premise, derived from laboratory research, that the extent to which new cognitive operations can be learned so well that they generalize widely and can be applied to new contexts and situations is directly tied to the number and *variety* of concrete examples used in instruction. Thus, although classification, seriation, or conservation taught with a few excellent materials may fail to generalize broadly and have little impact on a child's cognitive operations, the use of a large variety of ordinary materials seems to ensure generalization. Further, Piacceleration's emphasis is on continuing instruction until the operations are firmly internalized and on involving the children's egos in each operation's expression. Also, all three operations critical to the transition from preoperational to concrete operational thought are taught.

. . . [T]he conclusion that the Piacceleration group blossomed more than those who received the normal curriculum rests on the assumption that the groups were intially equal. Our use of randomization is usually considered a sufficient guarantee that the groups were virtually equal in all respects at the outset of an experiment. Also, because the attrition that occurred was balanced, it is not likely that either group was favored.

The fact that children in the experimental group received the special attention of the classroom aide is a more important concern. . . . [T]hey had the attention of the aide for 15 min in a small group, while the rest of their class had the attention of their teacher in a large group (16 to 19 students). Control children had to share the attention of the aide and the teacher with all of their classmates during this part of their school day.

This confound would have been more serious if all the children in all classes had not been formed into small groups receiving the undivided attention of either an aide or a teacher at different times during the school day, so that being in a small group with one of these instructors was commonplace. Also, . . . the children were accustomed to being formed into small special groups and taught by . . . specialists. Another reason for attributing the effects on the O-LSAT and SESAT to the independent variable . . . is the lawfulness and nature of the effects. Changes were noted primarily on the scales that involved reasoning ability. The less conceptual achievement subscales, on which children who are motivated to extra effort by special attention might be expected to more easily improve their scores, showed only small differences. Presumably, confounds would have had effects on these scales—either primarily . . . or at least as much on these scales as on the others.

Thus, we concluded that mastery of key concrete operations led to a generalized cognitive gain that led to increased academic achievement in mathematics concepts and verbal comprehension. . . .

. . . The positive outcome of the present experimental intervention is probably best understood as resulting from early remediation of at least some aspects of a developmental lag, to the benefit of a group of children poised to gain from such cognitive opportunities as they became available.

The Piacceleration instructional method, which grew out of research projects with handicapped children, is doubtless only one way to produce cognitive gains for underachieving kindergartners. The distinguishing features of this method are that only three key transitional operations are taught, that they are taught with a wide range of exemplars, and . . . taught under the criterion of full mastery. Because the concrete operations are part of many programs of studies, one should not underestimate the importance of using numerous, widely varying kinds of materials to induce generalization to new examples and materials. . . . Finally, when well done, Piacceleration instruction involves constant efforts to boost children's self-esteem by emphasizing their increasing mastery of cognitive processes that are natural and recurrently useful for their age group. We estimate that any instructional method that incorporates all of these features would be successful, or even more successful, with the population studied.

CRITIQUE OF STUDY EXAMPLE 8.2

1. What was the rationale for the study?

2. What was the purpose of the study?

3. How were participants selected and assigned to the two groups?

4. Who were the participants?

5. Can the groups be considered equivalent?

6. What measures of ability and achievement were used?

7. Are there questions about reliability or validity of the tests?

8. What was the general procedure for both groups?

9. What were good features of the design?

10. What are questionable aspects of the design?

11. How many discriminant functions were determined?

12. Which subtests of the O-LSAT differentiated the two groups?

13. Which aspects of the SESAT differentiated the two groups?

14. Ignoring methodology, what do these results indicate?

15. What was the overall conclusion reached by the authors?

16. On what bases did they rule out the role of the confounds of increased attention and learning in a small group in the experimental subjects?

17. How reasonable are these arguments?

18. Overall, is Piacceleration training superior to traditional training?

ANSWERS

1. Cognitive functioning of 5-year-old children varies. Some think at what Piaget called a preoperational level. They cannot sort objects by form, size, and so on, or serially in graded fashion. Others have attained a level where they understand such concepts as conservation of numbers. Performance of kindergarten children on problems involving classification, seriation, and conservation predict later performance on standardized achievement tests. If preoperational children can be identified and given special training at this age, their later achievement performances might improve. Learning set methods have been most favored as ways of teaching deficient children to classify objects, seriate, and understand the principle of conservation. Many problems are presented with various objects, all of which can be solved by the same principle. The Piacceleration method has been tested in preliminary studies with handicapped and nonhandicapped children, but data are limited because measures of achievement were made just 2 weeks after training ended. No study has used a large sample and tests of achievement after more time has elapsed.

2. To evaluate the effectiveness of the Piacceleration method in improving academic achievement and performance of young children who are likely to profit from such training. Their achievement was to be compared with that of a comparable group taught traditional mathematical concepts in kindergarten.

3. All 17 kindergarten teachers selected 5 children who were likely to be the lowest achievers in their classes. These were from six schools that serviced low-income children. Each group of 5 children was randomly assigned to experimental or control conditions, with equal numbers from morning and afternoon classes of the same school and same teacher.

4. After attrition, there were 17 white and 11 minority children in the experimental group (average age was 6.01 years) and 15 white and 14 minority children in the control group (average age was 5.99 years).

5. Yes.

6. The Otis-Lennon School Ability Test was used to measure reasoning ability and the Stanford Early School Achievement Test was used to measure knowledge of the social and physical environment as well as mathematical and verbal achievements.

7. No. Reliability and validity have been established for both tests.

8. Control subjects remained in the class and were taught mathematical concepts by their teachers from December through February. Experimental children were brought to a corner of the room at the time that mathematical concepts were taught. Instruction occurred from November through January, except for slower children, who learned by February. Experimental children were taught by two aides who praised each success and gave positive or negative feedback for all to hear. When a child successfully learned, he or she joined the class and received further lessons on mathematical concepts. Tests were administered 3 months later.

9. The methods for selecting participants and assigning them to the two groups, the use of reliable and valid tests, the use of two (presumably somewhat naive) independent aides to teach the experimental children.

10. Experimental children were taught in the same room while class was in session and knew that they were receiving extra attention and praise; children who learned and could solve all problems joined their classmates and potentially had as much as a month of extra lessons; and the two tests may not have been given in counterbalanced order.

11. Two: one for subtests on the Otis-Lennon School Ability Test and one for subtests on the Stanford Early School Achievement Test.

12. Classification and analogies tests.

13. Mathematical concepts and comprehension of words and stories.

14. Piacceleration led to greater ability to classify objects, identify analogies, understand mathematical concepts, and understand the meaning of words and of stories than did traditional training.

15. Piacceleration training improved the cognitive abilities of kindergarten children from impoverished environments.

16. First, that the children were used to working in small, special groups, and second, that the increased attention they received would have facilitated performance on all subtests.

17. Somewhat. Small group format may not have made the children feel special, but special training is confounded by attention and lots of reinforcement for correct answers and those parts of the subtests on which the children excelled were directly related to the special training. Moreover, their explanation does not take into account the possibility that some of the children received additional training when they joined the rest of their class. (The fact that the tests may not have been administered in counterbalanced order would not be a big problem in this case because if there was an order effect it would affect experimental and control children alike.)

18. This study does not show this conclusively.

Supplementary Readings
on This Topic

- Diekhoff, G. (1992). *Statistics for the social and behavioral sciences: Univariate, bivariate, multivariate*. Dubuque, IA: Wm. C. Brown.
- Dunteman, G. H. (1984). *Introduction to multivariate analysis*. Beverly Hills, CA: Sage.
- Kachigan, S. K. (1986). *Statistical analysis: An interdisciplinary introduction to univariate & multivariate methods*. New York: Radius Press.

9

TWO-CONDITION EXPERIMENTAL STUDIES

Up to this point the focus of the critiques mainly has been on descriptive studies. Because no variable was actively manipulated, cause and effect conclusions could not be reached. (There were two exceptions in Chapter 8: One study manipulated time to take a test, and the other manipulated type of training.) The remainder of the evaluations focus on experiments: Independent groups are randomly assigned to levels of the independent variable(s), or the orders of the levels are assigned to participants who will be exposed to all these levels. We had two examples of the latter in Chapter 1.

Two-group designs are useful for answering one of two questions: Does a particular treatment work? Which of two treatments is relatively more effective? From a procedural point of view, the major concern is whether the two groups are initially equivalent with respect to the dependent variable. If they are, then differences in the response measure after treatment can be attributed to the treatment. This equivalence is more likely if participants are randomnly assigned to the groups or are matched on the dependent (or a related) variable and then randomly assigned to the two levels. Of course, caution still is required regarding similarity in testing conditions as well as testing by a naive experimenter. And if testing occurs on more than one occasion, attrition may present another threat to internal validity if the loss is selective; that is, remaining participants in each of the conditions may constitute two groups that are no longer equivalent.

From a statistical point of view, the precise test used to evaluate effectiveness of the independent variable depends on the dependent variable. If scores are at least part of an interval scale (e.g., scores on a standardized test) and are not terribly skewed, a t test is most appropriate. This involves determining the probability that a means difference of the magnitude obtained would be obtained if treatment were not effective. If that probability is ±.05, the obtained difference is attributed to the treatment. The df are determined by $n_1 + n_2 - 2$. In the event that a t test is inappropriate (e.g., when distributions are very skewed or variances are very different—both of which are likely to wash out any differences that might exist and lead to a Type II error) a nonparametric test can be used (e.g., Mann-Whitney U-test, median test). The following study that we will review together uses t tests.

STUDY EXAMPLE 9.1

This was actually a pilot study to establish validity of a (then) relatively new scale developed to measure the use of humor in coping with stress. This also represents a good example of a frequent use of the independent-groups design: two groups that differ initially are compared for differences on some dependent variable. Technically, then, this is not a true experimental design because participants are not randomly assigned to the two conditions. And it means that there is always the possibility that differences found after "exposure to the conditions" are due to nonequivalence. However, if participants are randomly selected, some of the "nonequivalence" may be eliminated.

The Study

- Trice, A. D., & Price-Greathouse, J. (1986). Joking under the drill: A validity study of the Coping Humor Scale. *Journal of Social Behavior and Personality, 1*(2), 265-266. Used with permission of Select Press.

As part of a series of studies of the moderating effects of humor on stressful life events, Martin and Lefcourt . . . developed the Coping Humor Scale (CHS), a seven-item 4-point Likert self-report scale indexing the use of humor in stressing situations. The use or non-use of humor as a means of dealing with stress may be an important individual difference variable. This note reports a pilot validity study of joking and laughing in what is generally regarded as a highly stressful situation.

1. What was the rationale for the study?

A humor coping scale was developed, which measured use of humor in stressful situations. An individual difference variable may be the use or non-use of humor to cope with stress.

2. What was the purpose of the study?

A pilot study to validate the scale in a stressful situation.

Method

Forty patients at a university dental clinic who had completed the CHS through a mail survey participated.

(The sample is select and consists of respondents who volunteered to complete the questionnaire. Moreover, they are probably poor, inasmuch as they are described as patients at a dental clinic.)

During a subsequent visit to the clinic for an amalgam restoration (silver filling) each was observed during the 10-15 minute period between the end of the dental student's examination and the approval of the procedure by a member of the dental faculty.

(Whereas obtaining a filling generally is not stressful—unless one is afraid of an injection, the fact that the procedure will be carried out by a dental student might be stressful.)

Two behaviors were observed: laughter and verbal joking. Six dental students and an independent observer made the observations.

(Observations by seven other people could be stressful—even without the procedure. Moreover, because they apparently knew they were being observed, reactive measures cannot be ruled out.)

Initially we had intended to quantify the number of episodes of each behavior, but the interrater agreement on the number of "laughs" or "joking statements" was low due to difficulty in determining the beginnings and ends of laughter and joking episodes. Instead, we coded patients for the presence or absence of joking and/or laughter.

(There is also "nervous laughter," which is not humor but behaviorally may not be distinguished from it. Moreover, patients have already completed the questionnaire and, because they were university students, may have seen some connection between the scale and their present situation.)

There was 100% agreement between raters on this classification.

(Some good features of the design: a check for interrater reliability and use of a naive observer.)

The dental students were instructed to refrain from joking, and no such joking was observed by the independent observer in this set of observations.

3. Who served as participants?

Forty patients at a university dental clinic who completed the scale in a mail survey. They required silver fillings.

4. Can the sample be considered as representative?

No. They were voluntary respondents and probably unable to afford a private dentist.

5. What was the general procedure?

During the time between the examination and approval of the dental procedure, six dental students and an independent observer rated each patient for presence or absence of laughter/joking by the patient. After the dental procedure, each participant rated the procedure for level of stress. (This is mentioned later.)

6. What are experimentally sound aspects of the study?

   (a) Establishment of interrater reliability
   (b) Use of an independent observer

7. What are some major weakness of the procedure?

The inability to distinguish between joking/laughter as humor and as a sign of nervousness, the fact that patients probably knew that they were being observed, and the fact that they had completed the questionnaire before being observed.

Results and Discussion

Twenty-one patients joked, all of whom laughed. Three additional patients also laughed, without joking. These 24 patients constitute the joking-laughter group, with the remaining 16 patients designated the non-laughing group. CHS scores were higher for the joking-laughter group (*M* = 22.6, *SD* = 6.0) than in the non-laughing group (*M* = 17.3, *SD* = 6.9), *t* = 2.51, *p* < .02 (high scores indicate high humor utilization). When patients were asked to rate the stressfulness of the procedure on a 10-point scale at the end of the appointment, those in the joking-laughter group rated the procedure less stressful (*M* = 6.5, *SD* = 2.1) than those in the non-laughing group (*M* = 7.8, *SD* = 2.5), *t* = 1.73, *p* < .10.

(The rating was retrospective, and p < .10 is not uniformly considered an acceptable level for significance. And, if you check a t table you will see that they performed a one-tailed test. This procedure, too, is questionable because the scale was being validated and they presented no evidence to substantiate their assumption that humor users would find a stressful situation less stressful.)

8. *What were the two main results of the study?*

   (a) Laughter group had higher scores on the coping scale than the non-laughter group.

   (b) Laughter group rated the procedure as less stressful than the non-laughter group (at *p* < .10).

These findings support the CHS as a valid predictor of the use of humor in a stressful situation.

(An obvious false conclusion. Most important, the groups were not equivalent on perception of stress, and results might have been obtained regardless of the use of humor on stress. Secondly, stress was measured after the procedure and after

*the scale had been completed, and other factors could have
accounted for the perception. For example, according to the
principle of cognitive dissonance, those who laughed might
have felt stressed but justified their laughter by the fact that
the situation was not as stressful as they had anticipated;
this would result in a lower rating of stress.)*

This study further suggests that the use of humor may
reduce the subjective experience of stress, although the
methodology employed doesn't rule out the possibility that
humor use and self-reports of stress may be influenced by
variables not taken into consideration. For example, although highly similar procedures were examined, those in
the non-laughing group may have actually had more stressful surgical procedures.

How one deals with stress is clearly an important individual characteristic, with implications for both clinical and
personality psychology. Humor, too, is an obvious individual
difference. While the Martin and Lefcourt scale was ration-
ally developed and the only psychometric data presented was
a modest internal consistency index of .6, its two aspects,
coping and humor, should provide impetus for further research. In the present study the internal consistency index
was .68, and the correlations between CHS scores and stress
ratings was significant ($r = -.39$, $p < .01$). Additionally, we
administered the scale to 64 undergraduates at 4 week
intervals and found a temporal stability index of $r = .92$.
Further development of the scale may be warranted.

?

9. *What was the major conclusion reached by the
   authors?*

The coping scale validly predicts the use of humor to cope
with stress.

10. Is the conclusion justified?

No. The groups were not equivalent with respect to perception of stress in a situation, and their perception may have had nothing to do with the use of humor to cope. Ratings of stress may have been a reactive measure to being measured on the humor scale and observed by seven observers. Finally, the rating came after the fact and this could have differentially affected their ratings.

Supplementary Readings
on This Topic

- Lehman, R. S. (1991). *Statistics and research design in the behavioral sciences.* Belmont, CA: Wadsworth.
- Neal, J. M., & Liebert, R. M. (1986). *Science and behavior: An introduction to methods of research* (3rd ed.). Englewood Cliffs, NJ: Prentice Hall.

10

SINGLE CLASSIFICATION STUDIES

The two-group or two-condition situations are limited. They inform you about whether an independent variable works or does not, or which of two effective treatments is more effective. If more than one level of the independent variable is introduced, then additional questions can be answered about relative effectiveness of each level. At a minimum, three levels can be studied. They can be two different therapies versus a control condition or two different drugs versus a control or even three different therapies or drugs. (If effectiveness of each has been established and relative effectiveness is being investigated, a control condition may not be necessary.) If the summary data are means, the type of analysis depends on whether separate groups have been tested at each level or the same group was tested at each level.

When separate groups are tested, participants are randomly assigned to the different levels of the independent variable. By this procedure we have some assurance that, before treatment, participants at each level initially are equivalent on the dependent variable and other characteristics related to it. Therefore, differences in performance after treatment can be attributed to the independent variable. If no mention is made about random assignment, nonequivalence among groups looms as a possible confound. (Another procedure, used with small *N*s, is to match the participants on the dependent variable, or on one related to it, and then assign the conditions to the matched groups.) Likewise, if testing occurs on more than one occasion, you need assurance that any loss of subjects is not a selective loss. Further, testing conditions should be uniform, experimenters should be naive regarding the purpose of the experiment, and the measuring instrument should be reliable and valid.

Final performance measures generally are summarized by means and standard deviations (or variances). In order to detect differences among the groups, an overall test first is performed to determine whether any differences exist among the means. The test is analysis of variance (ANOVA) and it indicates the extent to which all possible differences among the means (between-group variance) exceeds what is expected on the basis of random error or individual variations in performances (within-group variance). The ratio is *F* and has associated with it $J - 1$ *df* for the numerator and $N - J$ *df* for the denominator (error). If the *F* ratio is significantly greater than what is expected if all groups had been drawn from the same population, it indicates that at least the two extreme means differ.

Specific questions about which means differ (i.e., which treatment is more effective than another) are answered by post hoc analyses. (Sometimes, the researcher initially plans to make certain comparisons among the means. In this case, ANOVA is not performed; planned comparisons are performed.) The danger in simply performing each comparison between means is an increase in the risk of committing a Type I error: declaring a means difference to be significant when treatment was not differentially effective. Several methods reduce the overall probability (i.e., familywise error) of committing the Type I error. The most conservative Bonferroni test sets each comparison to .05/[# comparisons]. Remaining tests are less conservative (e.g., Scheffé, Dunnett, Tukey, Newman-Kuels) and will be described as we come to them in the separate articles.

When the same group is tested at all levels of the independent variable we have a within-group design. Because the same group is tested repeatedly, the levels have to be introduced in a counterbalanced order to rule out, as possible explanations of the results, the effects of practice, fatigue, and carryover. The procedure requires that each level appears at each stage of practice an equal number of times. Moreover, each level must precede and follow all other levels an equal number of times. Please note that any study that utilizes multiple (standardized) tests must meet the same requirements; the tests, too, must be administered in counterbalanced order.

Data emanating from a within-group design are analyzed by ANOVA for repeated measures. Statistically, this is a much more powerful design—more likely to reveal means differences— because two sources of variance can be isolated from random variability in addition to that due to the independent variable, namely, variability due to the participants and variability due to the interaction between the effects of treatment and the participants. The latter serves as the error term in the analysis. This results in a smaller error term than would be true if separate groups had been used. However, there is a statistical assumption whose violation can result in a Type I error: circularity. If all differences between all possible pairs of scores (e.g., A – B, A – C, B – C) are determined and variances computed of these differences, we have, here, three variances of differences. The circularity assumption is that all variances are the same. If they differ, it indicates that the effect of going from, say, A level to B level is not the same as the effect of going from, say, A level to C level or from B level to C level. The net result is that the calculated F ratio may be inflated and result in a Type I error. This is counteracted by reducing the degrees of freedom used to determine whether F is significant. Usually, $df = (J - 1)$ for the numerator and $(J-1)(S-1)$ [S = number of participants] for the denominator. If no mention is made about circularity, and especially if F is declared significant at $p < .05$, you can perform a check to determine whether the declaration is valid. Reduce the df to $1/(J-1)x(J-1) = 1$ and to $1/(J-1)x(J-1)(S-1) = S-1$. If F still is significant (check an F table), then the conclusion is valid. If F is not significant, then the conclusion *may not be* valid. The emphasis is on *may not be* because these reductions in dfs are the maximum. In reality, the appropriate dfs would be somewhere between $(J-1)$ and 1, and somewhere between $(J-1)$ $(S-1)$ and $S-1$ for error.

We'll review one study together, with independent groups, and we'll do the same with a study that used the same participants.

STUDY EXAMPLE 10.1: SINGLE CLASSIFICATION

This first study involves the use of three independent groups that participated in a study dealing with training to make diabetic patients aware of their blood glucose levels. Terms that might not be familiar to you are hyperglycemia (high blood glucose), hypoglycemia (low blood glucose), and glycosylated hemoglobin. The latter refers to a measure of glucose that becomes attached to hemoglobin in the blood and is an indication of relative blood glucose control over a period of about 2 months.

You will be asked to perform F tests on the data as well as post hoc analyses using the Tukey test. As a reminder, the Tukey test controls for a familywise Type I error by testing each statistic against the most conservative tabled value. The studentized range statistic is computed by dividing the difference between two means by error: $\sqrt{[MS_e/n]}$. Because the ns in each group are not equal but are highly similar, we can use the harmonic n: $[3]/[1/n_1 + 1/n_2 + 1/n_3]$. The final statistic is compared with the tabled value for, in this case, 3 (group means) and df of the error term from the original analysis of variance.

The Study

- Cox, D. J., Gonder-Frederick, L., Julian, D. M., & Clarke, W. (1994). Long-term follow-up evaluation of blood glucose awareness training. *Diabetes Care, 17*(1), 1-5. Used with permission of the American Diabetes Association.

Blood glucose awareness training (BGAT) is a patient education procedure designed to teach insulin-requiring diabetic patients to more accurately estimate their general blood glucose (BG) levels and specifically detect hypoglycemia. BGAT involves teaching patients how to identify symptoms sensitive and specific to their hypoglycemia and hyperglycemia. Additionally, it teaches patients how to accurately interpret information concerning types, amounts, and timing of insulin, food, and exercise to better anticipate extreme BG levels. BGAT typically requires seven weekly classes, reading the training manual, and daily homework exercises designed to apply and personalize the material presented in a particular chapter of the manual. Numerous studies have now demonstrated, in the short term, that BGAT is effective in improving patients' ability to estimate their BG levels and glycosylated hemoglobin. . . . Maintenance of such gains is critical in evaluating the cost-effectiveness of BGAT. No studies to date have evaluated the long-term benefits of BGAT. With the growing concern about the increased incidence of hypoglycemia with attempts to normalize BG . . . it is especially important to know whether BGAT leads to greater awareness of hypoglycemia and fewer severe hypoglycemic episodes in the long term.

?

1. What was the rationale for the study?

Blood glucose awareness training sensitizes patients to become aware of shifts in their blood glucose levels, especially hypoglycemia. Although short-term benefits of training have been demonstrated, long-term benefits have not been studied.

This study followed up subjects who had participated in BGAT and control subjects from our previous studies. . . . At follow-up, half (*n* = 14) of the BGAT subjects received a brief booster-training program intended to review BGAT procedures. The general question addressed was: Are BGAT participants better off at long-term follow-up compared with baseline or control subjects? The specific hypotheses tested were 1) at long-term follow-up, BGAT subjects in general would be more accurate at estimating their BG levels and more aware of their hypoglycemia in particular; 2) BGAT subjects would have fewer negative consequences caused by severe hypoglycemic episodes, as defined by lost work days and fewer automobile crashes; 3) BGAT subjects would maintain their improved glycosylated hemoglobin; and 4) a brief booster-training program would enhance overall accuracy of BG estimation and, specifically, sensitivity to hypoglycemia.

?

2. What was the purpose of the study?

To conduct a follow-up study on patients who were trained earlier; half were given booster training, and both groups were compared with a control group. Four hypotheses were tested regarding the benefits of training in estimating blood glucose, detecting hypoglycemia, preventing accidents, and maintaining glucose levels.

Research Design and Methods

We were able to locate 52 of 64 subjects from two previous studies, . . . 41 of whom were able and willing to participate.

> *(Note that 11 refused or were unable to participate. Therefore, a selection factor may be operating—for example, those 41 were most motivated.)*

Table 1   *Subject Characteristics for the Three Groups*

	Control group	BGAT group	BGAT plus booster
Final *n*	13	14	14
Age(years)	41.1 ± 3.1	40.3 ± 3.2	47.2 ± 4.3
Duration of disease (years)	17.6 ± 4.	14.2 ± 1.8	17.1 + 2.8
Follow-up (months)	47.0 + 5.3	51.2 + 3.6	55.5 + 4.0

Note. Data are means + *SD*.

(According to the first author [personal communication] what are reported as SDs were, in fact, SEs (standard errors). Analyses using SDs revealed no differences in participant characteristics, as reported.)

Twenty-eight of these subjects had undergone BGAT and 13 were past control subjects. Table 1 lists subject characteristics. No significant differences existed between groups on any of these variables. Incentives to participate included a free glycosylated hemoglobin determination

(an expensive test)

and a $75 payment at the conclusion of data collection.

(Note that the two previous studies were conducted at two different times [probably 1987 and 1990] and that [according to the references] one involved standard versus intensive BGAT. We don't know which training the present participants had received. Moreover, the months since follow-up differ for the 3 groups. In fact, the F ratio can be calculated from the three means and standard deviations. It is 12.98, p < .01 and a Tukey test reveals that all three months since follow-up differ. This suggests that control participants may have been from one study and that the two experimental groups from the two studies may not have been randomly assigned to the two training conditions. Therefore, group nonequivalence should be kept in mind as a potential confound. This is bolstered by the fact that if you calculate F ratios on age and duration, they, too, are significant.)

?

3. Who served as participants?

41 out of 52 participants located from two previous studies.

4. The authors' claim that the 3 groups did not differ significantly on participant characteristics can be checked. Using definitional formulas

$$(MS_b = \Sigma n_j[M_j - M_g]^2/df \text{ and } MS_e = \Sigma[n_j - 1\{SD\}]^2/df),$$

calculate F ratios for age, duration, and follow-up times.

Age: $M_g = [13(41.1) + 14(40.3) + 14(47.2)]/41 = 42.91$.

$MS_b = [13(41.1 - 42.91)^2 + 14(40.3 - 42.91)^2 + 14(47.2 - 42.91)^2]/2$
$= 395.616/2 = 197.808$.

$MS_e = [12(3.1)^2 + 13(3.2)^2 + 13(4.3)^2]/41-3 = 488.81/38 = 12.863$.

$F = 197.808/12.863 = 15.378$, $df = 2, 38, p < .01$.

Duration $M_g = [13(17.6) + 14(14.2) + 14(17.1)]/41 = 16.27$.

$MS_b = [13(17.6 - 16.27)^2 + \ldots + 14(17.1 - 16.27)^2]/2 = 46.31$.

$MS_e = [12(4)^2 + 13(1.8)^2 + 13(2.8)^2]/38 = 8.843$.

$F = 46.31/8.843 = 5.237$, $df = 2, 38, p < .01$.

Follow-up: $M_g = [13(47) + 14(51.2) + 14(55.5)]/41 = 51.34$.

$MS_b = [13(47 - 51.34)^2 + \ldots + 14(55.5 - 51.34)^2]/2 = 243.708$.

$MS_e = [12(5.3)^2 + 13(3.6)^2 + 13(4)^2]/38 = 18.778$.

$F = 243.708/18.778 = 12.978$, $df = 2, 38, p < .01$.

5. Perform the Tukey test on the mean ages. What can you conclude?

Harmonic $n = 3/[1/13 + 1/14 + 1/14] = 13.65$

Error $= \sqrt{12.863/13.65} = 0.9707$

$[47.2 - 41.1]/0.9707 = 6.284$, $p < .01$

$[47.2 - 40.3]/0.9707 = 7.108$, $p < .01$

$[41.1 - 40.3]/0.9707 = 0.824$

The group given booster training was older than the remaining two groups.

6. *Perform the Tukey test on duration means. What can you conclude?*

   Error = $\sqrt{8.843/13.65}$ = 0.8049

   [17.6 – 17.1]/0.8049 = 0.621

   [17.6 – 14.2]/0.8049 = 4.224, $p < .05$

   [17.1 – 14.2]/0.8049 = 3.603, $p < .05$

The BGAT group had diabetes for fewer years than the remaining two groups.

7. *Perform the Tukey test on the time since follow-up. What can you conclude?*

   Error = $\sqrt{18.778/13.65}$ = 1.1729

   [55.5 – 51.2]/1.1729 = 3.666, $p < .05$

   [55.5 – 47.0]/1.1729 = 7.247, $p < .01$

   [51.2 – 47.0]/1.1729 = 3.581, $p < .05$

The control group was retested after a fewer number of months than the two experimental groups. And the standard training group was retested after a fewer number of months than the group given booster training.

At an introductory meeting, subjects signed an informed consent, completed a questionnaire concerning past experiences with hypoglycemia and driving, and had blood drawn for glycosylated hemoglobin analysis. . . .

Past BGAT subjects were matched on posttreatment BG estimation accuracy and months of follow-up and then randomly assigned to either BGAT or BGAT plus booster training.

(Note that if matching on follow-up time had been successful, those two times would not have differed. But they do.)

Before use of the hand-held computer, BGAT plus booster subjects were given a 2-week diary. This diary was similar to those used in BGAT. Each time booster subjects measured their BG, they recorded in the diary any BG-relevant symptoms and relevant information about insulin, food, and/or exercise; estimated and recorded their BG; measured and logged their actual BG; and plotted their estimated-actual BG readings on an error grid. . . . Plotting the actual-estimated BG provided booster subjects feedback on the types of estimation errors being made . . . such as whether they were systematically overestimating their low BGs and/or underestimating their high BGs. After 2 weeks of completing diaries, booster subjects were given hand-held computers to collect follow-up data.

> *(Note that nothing is said about the BGAT group's activity during the 2 weeks. Either they were tested during those 2 weeks—so that testing times varied—or waited 2 weeks so that testing for all groups occurred at the same time.)*

All subjects . . . were instructed to use the computer-BG monitoring during routine measurements and whenever they thought their BG was either low or high. Each computer trial required subjects to enter their BG estimates, rate a variety of perceived autonomic and neuroglycopenic symptoms on a 0 = none to 6 = extreme scale, and measure and enter their actual BG results. Subjects were instructed to make a minimum of 50 such entries or continue until they had at least 10 actual BGs <3.9 mM to a maximum of 80 entries. This was accomplished during the subjects' daily routine over a 3- to 4-week interval. . . .

The computer tracked date and time of each entry and elapsed time between the computer's prompt to measure BG and the subjects' entry of their actual BG measurment. This allowed a check for compliance by examining whether at least 60 s elapsed between the prompt to measure BG and entry of actual BG. Because it requires at least 1 min to lance the finger, secure a blood sample, and get a BG reading, any BG readings entered in <60 s were considered unreliable and dropped from analysis. . . . Based on this compliance check, we dropped 5 subjects' hand-held computer data from analysis because they consistently entered actual BG values immediately after instructions to measure BGT. This resulted in the elimination of hand-held computer data from 2 subjects each in the control and BGAT groups and from 1 subject in the booster group.

?

8. What was the general procedure?

Participants first completed questionnaires regarding driving accidents and hypoglycemia occurrences. Experimental participants were matched on posttreatment BG and time since posttreatment and randomly assigned to BGAT or booster BGAT. The latter filled in a diary for 2 weeks regarding shifts in BG, estimated and actual levels and factors related to BG (insulin, exercise, etc.). They plotted actual and estimated BG to detect errors—over- or underestimations. All experimental participants used a hand computer to record a minimum of 50 or maximum of 80 BG episodes. They entered estimated and actual BG and rated physiological responses. Five participants were eliminated for inaccurate use of the computer (noncompliance).

9. What nonexperimental factors may have differentiated the two experimental groups?

BGAT group may not have been accurately matched with the booster group on time since last participation. And, the BGAT group either started earlier than the booster group or "did nothing" for 2 weeks while booster training occurred.

Data Analysis

The accuracy index is a general index of BG estimation accuracy . . . derived by calculating the percentage of accurate estimates (those within 20% of the measured BG or those estimates and actual BG readings, both <3.9 mM) and subtracting the number of dangerously erroneous estimates (failure to recognize either hypoglycemia or hyperglycemia).

A univariate analysis of variance (ANOVA) was performed comparing only the three groups' follow-up accuracy index because of the inequity between pre- and posttreatment data and follow-up data. . . .

Because our booster training occurred for only a 2-week period just before data collection, it did not have an impact on long-term variables, such as automobile crashes, lost work days, or glycosylated hemoglobin. Consequently, booster and nonbooster BGAT subjects were collapsed in comparison with control subjects for such variables. Additionally, although subjects whose hand-held computer data were unreliable were not analyzed for accuracy of BG estimation, these subjects were included when analyzing glycosylated hemoglobin and automobile crashes.

Results

Effects of BGAT and Booster
Training on BG Estimation Accuracy

A univariate ANOVA on the accuracy indexes for BGAT plus booster, BGAT, and control subjects (39, 30, and 26%, respectively) yielded significant results ($F = 7.02$, $p < .001$). Planned contrasts indicated that BGAT plus booster subjects were superior to both BGAT ($t = 2.49$, $p = .01$) and control ($t = 3.64$, $p = .000$) subjects. BGAT subjects exhibited a trend toward superior estimation of their BG levels compared with control subjects ($t = 1.13$, $p = 0.10$).

Of specific interest was whether BGAT improves subjects' ability to detect hypoglycemia over the long term. The percentage of low BGs (<2.8 mM) detected by BGAT plus booster, BGTAT, and control subjects was 85, 50, and 43%, respectively. Overall, this was significant ($F = 4.29$, $p < .02$), with BGAT plus booster better than either BGAT ($p < .02$) or control subjects ($p < .01$ . . .). This would suggest that, although a trend exists for the original BGAT subjects to be better at estimating their BG levels, subjects who received

BGAT with booster training were more accurate in general and specifically more aware of their hypoglycemia.

?

10. What did the significant F = 7.02 indicate?
There was at least one difference in accuracy in estimating BG among the three groups.

11. What were the results of the planned comparisons?
The booster group was more accurate than the remaining two groups in estimating their BG levels. The BGAT group was not more accurate than the controls.

12. What two factors might account for lack of difference in accuracy between the BGAT group and the control group?
   (a) The control group had diabetes for a longer period of time and may have been more sensitive to BG levels because of experience.
   (b) The BGAT group had a longer time span between post-treatment and follow-up than the control group and may have forgotten some of the original training.

13. What were the essential results regarding percentage of times that low BG was detected?
The booster group was more successful than the remaining two groups, which did not differ from each other.

Ancillary Long-Term Effects of BGAT

Although BGAT did not lead to fewer self-reported lost work days, BGAT was associated with significantly fewer automobile crashes. Respective crash rates per 1,000,000 miles driven were 6.8 vs. 29.8 ($U = 77.5$, $p = 0.01$).

(Note that U is the statistic for a Mann-Whitney test between two groups whose scores are not normally distributed. As such, it is one of the most popular nonparametric tests.)

Of the control subjects who drove (one subject did not drive), 42% had at least one automobile crash during follow-up. In contrast, only 15% of our BGAT subjects who drove had accidents. One subject in each group had two accidents. The remaining subjects in both groups had only a single accident during follow-up. The mean number of months between the last group treatment session and accidents, for those subjects who had accidents, was 14.0 months for control subjects and 28.3 months for BGAT subjects ($t = 1.02$, $p = 0.13$).

14. *What were the general results regarding automobile accidents?*

BGAT groups had fewer accidents—and suggestively after a longer period of time since training—than control subjects.

Conclusions

Although BGAT was not originally designed to produce long-term effects, these data indicate that BGAT led to sustained improvement in glycosylated hemoglobin and fewer automobile accidents. BGAT plus a low effort booster training led to greater general accuracy in estimating BG and detecting hypoglycemia in particular. Although improved metabolic control is important, it was not unique to BGAT. Our control subjects, who participated in general diabetes education classes, also showed a sustained metabolic improvement. This would suggest that both group programs were effective in sustaining improved self-care behaviors. However, because we did not have a no-treatment control group, we cannot rule out the possibility that the simple passage of time was responsible for this improvement.

One of the more interesting findings of this study is that BGAT may lead to fewer automobile accidents. . . . Our current data suggest that the effect of BGAT is to increase awareness of when not to drive. The potential of such an effect might be made more robust if periodic booster training were provided.

?

15. What were the major conclusions?

BGAT led to long-term improvement in estimating BG and in detecting hypoglycemia—as well as in fewer car accidents.

16. Are the conclusions valid? That is, are differences due to training?

Not necessarily. First, no differences in accuracy or in detecting hypoglycemia were found between BGAT and control groups and can be attributed to more years of experience of the latter and forgetting on the part of the former. Moreover, the booster plus training group was older and had diabetes longer than the BGAT group. These factors could have contributed to superior performance. Finally, because of apparent nonrandom assignment of participants to control and experimental groups, autombile accidents may be unrelated to training (i.e., due to individual factors).

17. From a practical point of view, if you had to provide advice to newly diagnosed diabetic patients regarding awareness training, what would it be?

On the basis of the results of this study and because of possible confounds, the best advice would be to undergo BGAT, followed by periodic booster training sessions (i.e., training is probably better than nothing).

STUDY EXAMPLE 10.2:
SINGLE FACTOR (REPEATED MEASURES)

This experiment represents the simplest instance of a within-subjects design: Three measures of behavior are made on the same group of participants. In this study, the independent variable was treatment. Therefore, the usual confounding variable of order effect had to be controlled.

Analysis of the data depends on the number of levels of the independent variable. With more than two levels, data can be analyzed by a trend analysis if the independent variable is time, trials, or different magnitudes (e.g., drug dosage, amount of reinforcement, etc.). For other types of independent variables ANOVA for repeated measures is appropriate. Another alternative, especially when circularity (sphericity) is grossly violated, is to perform a multivariate analysis of variance, which detects whether participants differed in their pattern of responses to the different levels of the independent variable.

The study we are about to review involves conditioning pigeons to press a foot treadle in order to produce a light (signal) that signals the availability of food. If they have to press a set number of times, this is called a fixed ratio. For example, if exactly five presses are required to produce the signal, this represents a 5:1 fixed ratio. If the number of required presses varies, then we have a variable ratio; sometimes three, sometimes seven, but on average five presses are required before the signal appears. One outcome of either arrangement (ratio schedule) is that when the signal appears, the pigeon begins to peck at it—even though it is not required to do so for the food to be available. This phenomenon is called autoshaping and the number of pecks to the signal is an indication of strength of the effect of the ratios of responses required for access to food.

In this study, the emphasis is on cost of food. The assumption is the higher the required ratio to produce the signal for food availability, the higher the cost of the food. Likewise, the greater the number of pecks to the signal, the harder the work to obtain food. The study examines the relationship between work and the cost of food.

The Study

- O'Connell, J. M. Several effects of behavioral cost on pigeons' reactivity to food and to Pavlovian signals for food. *Journal of Experimental Psychology: Animal Behavior Processes, 14(4)*, 339-348. Copyright © 1988 by the American Psychological Association. Adapted with permission.

The effects of the cost of food on operant behavior in free-feeding experiments have been studied extensively. . . . For instance, Collier et al. . . . manipulated the unit cost of food in two ways: (a) by varying the fixed ratio (FR) of bar presses per reinforcement and (b) by varying the size, or duration of access to, reinforcement. They found that . . . in both cases response rate was a direct function of cost. . . . [B]oth results seem to contradict general principles of conditioning. . . .

Rashotte and O'Connell . . . adapted Collier's general procedure to examine how pigeons would respond to a Pavlovian signal that was inserted between the operant response and the food reinforcement. Requiring pigeons to treadle-press on a FR 6 schedule, Rashotte and O'Connell varied, across phases, the duration of access to a food hopper given on each trial. They . . . found that the strength of responding to the reinforcement was reflected in the conditioned response to the signal; pecking at the keylight was greater when the hopper duration was short than when it was long.

. . . [T]he inverse relation between the rate of pecking at a keylight and hopper duration in Rashotte and O'Connell's study seems to contradict the Pavlovian principle of greater conditioning with larger unconditioned stimuli. . . . Rashotte and O'Connell proposed that the keypeck/hopper-duration relation represented differences in the unit cost of food. . . . Furthermore, it was proposed that the unit cost of food operated on keypecking by altering the value of the food;

reinforcement value is generally thought to be an important determinant of the strength of the conditioned response. . . .

The cost of food was manipulated in Rashotte and O'Connell's . . . study by varying the duration of access to food while using a fixed number of treadle presses per trial. In the present experiments the cost was manipulated by varying the number of treadle presses, leaving the duration of access to food unchanged. . . .

A prominent feature of the present work is that presentations of the keylight, a conditioned stimulus (CS), and the food, an unconditioned stimulus (US), occurred within a behavioral context. That is, each subject was instrumental in producing CS-US pairings. . . .

?

1. What was the overall rationale of the studies?

Studies on the effect of cost of food on operant conditioning, by Collier, manipulated cost by (a) varying FR per reinforcement (b) varying size or duration of access to reinforcement. Response rate varied with cost—it increased with FR and decreased as size (i.e., cost) went down. Rashotte and O'Connell used pigeons in a Pavlovian signal situation. When treadle pushes led to signal access to food with varying durations of access, they pecked more at the light when duration was short. Both studies contradict conditioning principles which state that size of reinforcement determines response strength. They proposed that unit cost of food determines operant strength by altering reinforcement value.

2. What was the purpose of Experiment 1?

To show that responses to a signal and eating behavior of pigeons is directly related to cost of the food as defined by number of treadle-press responses required to produce a signal that food is available.

• Experiment 1 •

The notion that signal- and food-directed behavior is directly related to the instrumental cost of producing the signal-food pairings was investigated in the first experiment. The experiment used a 24-hr free-feeding procedure in which the pigeons could obtain food at any time during the daily 10-hr light periods by stepping on a foot treadle. Completion of the required number of treadle presses was followed by a keylight-food sequence. The cost of food was varied across blocks of days by using four FR schedules to determine the number of treadle presses required; hopper duration did not vary. It was expected that rate of keypecking and the rate of eating would be directly related to the number of treadle presses required.

Method

Subjects. Six adult, experimentally naive pigeons (3 males and 3 females) were purchased from a local supplier. . . . The pigeons adjusted to living on a 10:14-hr light-dark cycle in individual cages in a colony room for at least 2 months before the experiment began.

?

3. Who were the participants?

Six pigeons, 3 males and 3 females, purchased from a breeder and that had not served as subjects in other experiments.

Apparatus.

(The experimental chamber is fully described. It contains an operating key that signals food availability after a foot treadle has been pressed the appropriate number of times.)

Procedure.

(The early pretraining is described, during which time the pigeons were habituated to the experimental chamber and trained to press the treadle for access to food, which occurred after the signal appeared.)

The experiment consisted of four 4-day blocks, for a total of 16 days. The number of treadle presses required on each trial was varied across blocks, but within a block that number was fixed. Four FR schedules were employed that required the pigeons to step on the treadle either 5, 10, 20, or 40 times. Half the birds received these schedules in ascending order (FR 5, FR 10, FR 20, and FR 40) and the remaining 3 birds received the schedules in descending order (FR 40, FR 20, FR 10, and FR 5). Completion of the fixed ratio resulted in a 10-s keylight, followed by access to food for 10 s. . . .

Dependent variables. The primary measurement of behavior was number of pecks made on the key during keylight presentations; keypecks were not required and had no programmed consequence, but, as in the autoshaping procedure, the pigeons came to peck at the signals for food. The amount of time in which the bird's head was in the hopper (detected by the photobeam) during food presentations was also recorded and used to compute the rate of eating. The number of trials completed, the pigeons' daily body weights, food and water intake, and the amount of food spilled each day were also recorded. No attempt was made to measure either the rate or pattern of treadle pressing.

?

4. What was the general procedure?

Following pretraining, each pigeon was trained to press the foot-treadle a fixed number of times to produce the signal. Then each pigeon received four blocks of 4 days of pressing the treadle on FRs of 5, 10, 20, 40 pressses or 40, 20, 10, 5 presses. Only one schedule was administered during the 4-day block.

5. The four fixed ratios were present in only two orders. Does the lack of counterbalancing present a problem?

No. The experimental question related to the effect of increasing or decreasing the cost of food, not of the effect of specific cost.

Results

There were no systematic differences in the results obtained from the birds that experienced the ascending series and those that experienced the descending series of fixed ratios. Therefore, the data for the 6 birds were combined. All of the data were averaged across the 4 days in each FR condition, and those averaged data were analyzed by performing one-way analyses of variance (ANOVAS) for repeated measures.

. . . [T]he mean rate of keypecking, and . . . the mean rate of eating, as functions of the size of the fixed ratio . . . indicate that responding was directly proportional to ratio size. The analyses of these data confirmed that the effect of the ratio size on both keypecking, $F(3, 15) = 7.30$, $p < .01$, and the rate of eating, $F(3, 15) = 13.58$, $p < .001$, were statistically significant.

. . . Because the hopper duration on each trial was fixed at 10 s, the inverse relation between FR and trials per day means that the pigeons had much less access to food on the high-FR conditions than when the FR was low.

The reduced availability of food in the high-cost conditions was offset by two changes in the pigeons' behavior: (a) As reported above, the pigeons ate faster when the cost was high, and (b) the pigeons made better use of the time during which the hopper was raised. The pigeons' heads were in the hopper, and presumably they were eating, for an average of 45.2%, 53.6%, 59.1%, and 64.9% of the time the hopper was raised during sessions in which 5, 10, 20, and 40 treadle presses were required, respectively. These differences were statistically significant, $F(3, 15) = 10.36$, $p < .001$. . . .

?

6. *What was found regarding rates of keypecking and eating as the cost of food increased?*

Both increased: the pigeons pecked faster and ate faster as cost (i.e., FR) increased.

7. *F ratios report 3, 15 df. Are these correct?*

Yes. There are four fixed ratios and $4 - 1 = 3$, and there are six pigeons and $(4 - 1)(6 - 1) = 15$.

8. *No test for circularity is mentioned. Using the most stringent criterion of 1 and 5 df, are the F ratios significant?*

$F(1, 5,).05 = 6.61$ and $F(1,5,).01 = 16.26$. Both of the obtained F ratios are significant, but at $p < .05$ rather than $p < .01$.

Discussion

Manipulation of the number of operant treadle presses required to produce keylight-food pairings resulted in widespread changes in the pigeons' behavior. First, the pigeons seemed to reach a compromise between amount of work performed and amount of access to food obtained each day. The actual number of treadle presses completed each day was much greater when the cost was high than when it was low. . . . Second, in order to compensate for the reduced access to food at the higher costs, the pigeons ate faster and spent more time eating per minute of access; those changes in behavior served to minimize the change in food intake. . . . Third, the change in the response to the food was also reflected in the response elicited by the signal for food. In general, the pigeons were much more responsive to signals for food when the cost of food was high, a result that supports Rashotte and O'Connell's . . . proposal that the rate of key-pecking reflects the current value of the food which is . . . determined by the behavioral cost of the food.

This experiment demonstrated that pigeons' reactivity to Pavlovian signals for food and to the food itself was directly related to the cost of producing the signal-food pairing. . . .

Finally, the faster rate of eating observed in the high-cost conditions is consistent with the idea that the value the bird places on the food is determined by the amount of work the bird must perform to gain access to that food. Reactivity to the keylights, then, may simply reflect the current value of the food signaled by those lights. One question that arises from this view concerns the time period over which the value of the food is assessed. On a more empirical level, over what time frame is the direct relation between cost and reactivity maintained? Cost may operate from trial to trial, so that reactivity to a signal is solely determined by the number of treadle presses that immediately preceded that signal. Alternatively, some type of averaging process may occur which necessitates that each cost be in effect for a certain length of time (or number of trials) if the keypeck rate (and eating rate) is to be a function of cost. An answer to this question is critical for an understanding of the mechanisms underlying the cost-reactivity relation. In the next experiment this question is addressed.

?

9. What were the conclusions from Experiment 1?
Increasing cost of food resulted in its higher value in terms of increased pecking and faster eating.

10. Are the conclusions justified?
Yes.

11. What was the rationale for Experiment 2?
Although cost affects reactivity to it, we don't know whether cost is evaluated trial by trial or is averaged over a series of trials.

• Experiment 2 •

The procedure for the second experiment was essentially the same as in Experiment 1 except that the behavioral cost was determined by variable ratio, rather than by fixed ratio schedules. The four VR schedules employed required an average of 5, 10, 20, or 40 treadle presses per trial, but each schedule consisted of actual ratios equal to 0.2, 0.6, 1.0, 1.4, and 1.8 times the average cost. With this procedure, cost was varied in two ways: (a) The average cost was varied across blocks of sessions, and (b) within a session, the actual cost varied from trial to trial. If the pigeon's reactivity to a particular signal is directly and immediately determined by the cost of producing that signal, then, within each VR condition, the rate of keypecking should be high on high-cost trials and low on low-cost trials. That is, reactivity to the signal should be directly related to the trial cost as well as to the average cost. However, if an estimate of the prevailing cost is obtained by averaging across a number of trials, then keypecking may be found to be related to the average cost but not to the cost on a particular trial.

12. What was the purpose of Experiment 2?
To determine which of two alternatives would occur. Variable ratios were introduced within a session which averaged 5, 10, 20, 40 presses. Again, averages varied across blocks of days. If cost is evaluated trial by trial, rate of responding should vary as cost increases within a session. If cost is evaluated by averaging, rate of responding should increase as the ratio increases.

Method

Subjects and apparatus. Six adult, experimentally naive pigeons were used. These pigeons were purchased at the same time and housed under identical conditions as those of Experiment 1. There were 3 female and 3 male pigeons. The apparatus was the same as was used in Experiment 1.
Procedure.

(Pretraining is essentially the same as in the first study, except that it ended with training on FR schedules.)

The experiment consisted of four 4-day blocks. The average number of treadle presses required was varied across blocks. Also, within a block, the number of presses required on each trial was varied. . . .

(As in the first study ascending and descending VR schedules were used for half the pigeons.)

Each variable ratio scheduled consisted of five different ratios. The VR 5 schedule required either 1, 3, 5, 7, or 9 treadle presses. The VR 10 schedule required 2, 6, 10, 14, or 18; VR 20 required 4, 12, 20, 28, or 36; and VR 40 required 8, 24, 40, 56, or 72 treadle presses on each trial. Thus, on each schedule, the actual ratios were equal to 0.2, 0.6, 1.0, 1.4, and 1.8 times the average ratio. The sequence of ratios was systematically arranged to ensure that a particular ratio was equally likely to follow each of the five ratios comprising the VR schedule.

?

13. What was the general procedure?

After pretraining—ending with fixed ratio training—6 naive pigeons had four blocks of 4-day testing. Within each block, they had to respond to a variable ratio schedule of 5, 10, 20, 40 presses. Each schedule was based on various ratios of the average. Half the pigeons had an ascending and half had a descending order of the ratio.

14. Was any counterbalancing involved in the schedules?

Yes. Within a session, the exact number of treadle-presses required was counterbalanced.

Results

The mean rates of keypecking and eating for each average cost . . . was directly related to the value of the VR schedule. ANOVAS performed on these data confirmed that the differential rates of keypecking, $F(3, 15) = 9.44$, $p < .01$, and of eating, $F(3, 15) = 9.12$, $p < .01$, were statistically significant.
. . . [K]eypecking was inversely related to the trial cost. That is, within a session the pigeons responded to the signal more on trials requiring the fewest number of treadle presses and responded less on trials requiring the most treadle presses. The . . . effects of average cost, $F(3, 15) = 9.48$, $p < .01$, and of trials cost, $F(4, 20) = 21.16$, were statistically significant. . . .

15. What were the results regarding rate of keypecking and eating and average size of the ratio?

As in Experiment 1, the higher the ratio (i.e., cost of food), the higher the rate of keypecking and eating.

16. What do the significant F ratios indicate?

All pigeons responded differentially to the four ratios. They responded at the highest rate to the largest average ratio and at the lowest rate to the lowest ratio.

17. What were the results regarding rate of keypecking to the size of the ratios within a session?

As the size of the ratios increased, the rate of keypecking declined: the higher the particular ratio, the lower the rate of responding.

. . . [T]he pigeons were able to minimize changes in food intake by eating faster (above) and utilizing more of the access time. Indeed, the pigeons had their heads in the food opening for an average of 57%, 64%, 68%, and 71% of the time that food was available, $F(3, 15) = 19.87$, $p < .001$, in the 5, 10, 20, and 40 VR schedules, respectively. Nevertheless, varying the VR schedule significantly affected the amount of food eaten each day, $F(3, 15) = 10.49$, $p < .001$, although the body weight of the pigeons was not affected, $F(3, 15) = 2.05$, $p > .05$. . . .

Discussion

Most of the results obtained by using variable ratio schedules in Experiment 2 confirmed and replicated the effect of fixed ratio schedules obtained in the first experiment. . . .

Interestingly, within a day, the pigeons' responsivity to the keylight was inversely related to the cost as the cost varied from trial to trial, the exact opposite of the effect produced by varying cost (or average cost) across days. This result indicates that the pigeon's reactions to the signal, and perhaps to the food as well, were not simply determined by the amount of work immediately preceding each signal-food pairing. Rather, the pigeons appeared to be sensitive to the cost prevailing over an extended period of time. One possibility is that the pigeons maintain a running estimate of the cost and that their responses to food are determined by this estimate of the average cost.

The supposition that the pigeon employs an averaging process to estimate the cost and that the estimated cost governs the response to signals for food cannot account for the inverse relation between keypecking and the cost on a specific trial. If the pigeons were simply responding on the basis of the average cost, they would have keypecked at the same rate on low- and high-cost trials within each session. The fact that they pecked more on the low-cost trials suggests that some type of comparative process operates under these conditions. In other words, when the cost varies from trial to trial, the primary determinant of reactivity may be the average cost, but a secondary determinant may involve a comparison between the actual cost on each trial and the average cost. . . .

This experiment demonstrated two effects of cost that are opposite in direction. That difference seems to depend on the degree to which the different costs are intermixed. Varying the VR schedules across blocks of sessions effectively segregated the different average costs and resulted in a positive relation, whereas varying the number of treadle presses required from trial to trial intermixed the different costs and led to a negative relation between keypecking and cost. Experiment 3 elucidates the empirical relation between cost and signal-directed responding by examining the importance of intermixing different costs.

?

18. What did the author conclude?

As average cost of food (size of VR) increases across sessions, responding increases. But as cost of food increases per trial, responding declines.

19. Was the conclusion justified?

Yes.

• Experiment 3 •

In the first two experiments it was found that the rate of keypecking and rate of eating were positively related to the cost of producing the signal-food pairings when each cost (or average cost) was in effect for an extended period of time. However, when the cost varied from trial to trial, rate of keypecking was negatively related to cost. Those results suggest that the effect of behavioral cost on signal-directed responding depends on the extent to which the different costs are intermixed. In Experiment 3, the degree to which different costs were intermixed was systematically varied. Pigeons were required to press the treadle either 4 or 36 times on each trial. In the initial condition, the two costs were in effect on separate, alternating days and, thus, were completely segregated. In another condition, a single alternation schedule was used, so that the two costs alternated from trial to trial. Other conditions had each of the two costs in effect for 2, 4, 8, 16, and 32 trials in a row. It was hypothesized that when two costs were highly intermixed, such as in the single and double alternation schedules, the pigeons would keypeck more on the low-cost trials, whereas when the two costs were relatively segregated, such as when they occurred in blocks of 32 trials or on alternating days, they would keypeck more on high-cost trials.

?

20. What was the rationale for the final experiment?

The conflicting results of Experiment 2 suggested that when the different costs of food are separated (e.g., variable ratios across sessions), responses depend on comparisons between sessions. When costs are intermixed (within a session), comparisons of costs are made within the session.

21. What was the purpose of Experiment 3?

To elucidate the relationships between cost of food and responses for food when costs are segregated and intermixed and to test two hypotheses: (a) When two costs are intermixed, there will be a higher rate of responses to the lower cost; (b) when two costs are segregated, there will be a high rate of responses to the higher cost.

Method

Subjects and apparatus. The 6 pigeons from Experiment 2 and 2 pigeons from Experiment 1 served as subjects ($N = 8$; 4 males and 4 females). Housing of the birds and the apparatus were the same as in Experiments 1 and 2.

Procedure. The general procedure was the same as in the first two experiments. . . .

Two response ratios were used in this experiment; the pigeons were required to step on the treadle either 4 or 36 times in order to produce the keylight-food pairings. These ratios are equivalent to the lowest and the highest ratios in the VR 20 schedule used in Experiment 2. On the first 4 days, the two ratios were scheduled on alternating days, with 4 birds experiencing the sequence FR 4, FR 36, FR 36, FR 4, and the remaining 4 birds experiencing the sequence FR 36, FR 4, FR 4, FR 36. Over the next 12 days, six different alternating schedules, each in effect for a block of 2 days, were used to program the treadle-press requirement. The alternating schedules programmed each ratio (4 or 36) to be in effect for either 1, 2, 4, 8, 16, or 32 consecutive trials. Within each 2-day block, one day began with the low ratio and the other began with the high ratio. Four pigeons experienced the alternating schedules in an ascending series, and the remaining 4 experienced a descending series.

22. Did it matter that previously trained pigeons were used in this study?

No. All pigeons served in all conditions and previous training would have the same effect on all of their performances.

23. What was the general procedure?

Two fixed ratios were used: F4 and F36. For the first 4 days these two ratios were presented on alternate days, one schedule per day. For the next 12 days, over two blocks, ratios were alternated after 1, 2, 4, 8, 16, or 32 presentations of the first ratio. For example, F4 was presented twice before F36 was presented (twice). Half the pigeons had the ascending series, and half had the descending series.

Results and Discussion

As predicted, the pigeons responded more strongly on low-cost trials when the single and double alternation schedules were in effect, but they responded more strongly on the high-cost trials when the two costs occurred on alternating days or in blocks of 32 trials. . . . [T]ests confirmed that keypecking on low-cost trials was greater than on high-cost trials in the 1-, 2-, and 4-trial conditions . . . but that the reverse was true in both the 32-trial . . . and the alternating days. . . .

?

24. What were the essential results?

As hypothesized, when the two schedules were alternated after one or two presentations of one, there were more responses after the lower ratio (low cost). But when alternation occurred after 16 or 32 presentation of one, there were more responses after the higher ratio (high cost).

General Discussion

. . . Experiments 1 and 2 showed that as average cost of obtaining access to food increased, the number of trials produced each day by the pigeons decreased. This decrease in number of trials per day occurred despite an increase in the actual amount of work (i.e., the total number of treadle presses per day) performed by the pigeons. That result suggests a compromise between time spent treadle pressing and time spent eating. . . . Second, the decrease in trials and consequent loss of food access was offset, to a great degree, by an increase in the percentage of food access time utilized by the pigeons and by an increase in the rate of eating. Those changes in behavior allowed the birds to defend their food intake at all but the highest cost. . . . Third, the pigeons were relatively successful in defending their body weight despite a drop in food intake by as much as 20%. . . . Rashotte and Henderson . . . have postulated that there is a hierarchy of defenses to protect against high food costs, with behavioral adjustments serving as a first line of defense and metabolic changes serving as a second line of defense.

An additional way that pigeons cope with reduced food availability is to become more responsive to signals for food. In these experiments the pigeons' rate of pecking on the Pavlovian signal for food bore a direct relation to the average cost of that food. . . . Rashotte and O'Connell . . . proposed that decreasing hopper access time increases the value of the food by making it more costly. The present experiments support that proposal by showing that a direct manipulation of cost yields the same result. . . .

. . . Rashotte and O'Connell . . . proposed—and this study has supported that proposal—that the value of the reinforcer is determined by behavioral cost.

An important contribution of the present study is the light shed on the process by which reinforcer value is determined by manipulation of behavioral cost. The failure to find a direct relation between keypecking and cost when cost varied from trial to trial suggests the operation of an averaging process by which the cost (or availability) of food is evaluated over a series of trials (or period of time). Experiment 3 provided evidence that the average is revised on each trial in such a way that over a series of low-cost trials following a shift from high cost, there is a progressive decrease in the value of food and a consequent decrease in responding directed toward the food signals. The opposite occurs during series of high-cost trials. When different costs are highly intermixed, however, changes in the value of food should be negligible, because the average cost should be relatively constant over a series of trials.

. . . [I]t appears that keypecking was modulated by a comparison between the actual cost on the trial and the average cost. The conditioned response was enhanced when actual cost was less than average, but depressed when actual cost was greater than average. . . .

?

25. What were the general conclusions reached by the author?

As cost of food increases, responses to a signal also increases. Although this results in less access to food, rate of ingestion increases and, on the whole, body weight is maintained. When costs are intermixed, an averaging effect occurs such that more responses occur with low costs and fewer responses occur with high costs, particularly when the two costs are alternated frequently. Overall, rate of responding to a signal for food depends on the value of the reinforcer.

26. Are the conclusions justified?

Yes. There are no threats to internal validity of the studies.

27. To what extent do the results generalize?

To pigeons, whose "work" involves pressing on a treadle a certain number of times before a food signal is presented, when value of food is defined by the number of responses to the signal.

Supplementary Readings on This Topic

- Girden, E. R. (1992). *ANOVA: Repeated measures.* Newbury Park, CA: Sage.
- Iverswen, G. R., & Norpoth, H. (1987). *Analysis of variance* (2nd ed.). Newbury Park, CA: Sage.
- Kirk, R. E. (1982). *Experimental design: Procedures for the behavioral sciences* (2nd ed.). Belmont, CA: Brooks/Cole.

11

FACTORIAL STUDIES

Experiments that introduce more than one independent variable (factor) are called factorial studies. Although they require many participants, depending on the number of levels of each factor, they are time-savers by virtue of the information they yield in a single experiment. Not only do we learn whether each separate factor has an effect, we also learn whether the effects differ when both factors are combined. Separate or unique effects of each variable are called main effects. These refer to the average effects of each independent variable. When main effects are significant, we generally can make blanket statements about the effectiveness of those variables—statements without qualification. Combined effects let us know whether the effects of each variable simply add together or whether the effect of one variable depends on the level of the second variable. When the latter occurs, the combined effect is called interaction and implies that a qualification or stipulation has to be added to the description of effectiveness. For example, suppose we introduce three levels of reinforcements for three tasks of increasing difficulty and measure correct responses. We require three F ratios: one to let us know whether there is an overall effect of magnitude of reinforcement on number of correct responses (main effect), one to let us know if there is an overall effect of task difficulty on number of correct responses (main effect), and one to let us know whether the combined effects of both variables differ from the separate effects (interaction). If interaction is significant, the ultimate conclusion we might reach, after performing multiple comparisons, is that the highest magnitude of reinforcement is most effective—but only for the simplest task.

The type of analysis performed on the data depends on the design of the study. We have several alternatives, although we will always rely on three F ratios (for a two-factor study) to learn about main and interaction effects. (With more than two factors the main effects and possible interactions increase in number and complexity.) If participants are independent groups, then a two-way (or three-way, etc.) analysis of variance is appropriate. Most often, each of the independent variables consists of deliberately selected levels (e.g., particular drugs, particular dosages), and a fixed-effects model of ANOVA applies to the data. In rare instances, the levels of the independent variables have been randomly selected (e.g., order of presenting Rorschach cards), and a random-effects model of ANOVA applies to the data. Finally, if the levels of one of the independent variables are deliberately selected and the levels of the other are randomly selected, then a mixed-effects model of ANOVA applies to the data. These are critical to know because the model determines the appropriate error term in the F ratio. And if you need to check accuracy of degrees of freedom, each main effect df (for a two-way ANOVA) equals $J - 1$ and $K - 1$, whereas that for interaction equals $(J - 1)(K - 1)$. Degrees of freedom for the error term for testing main and interaction effects with the fixed-effect model equals $N - JK$. With a random-effects model, error for testing both main effects is the interaction and its $df = (J - 1)(K - 1)$, whereas interaction is tested by random variability as the error term and *df* is $N - (J)(K)$. If a mixed-effect model applies, the error term for the fixed-effect variable is interaction and has $(J - 1)(K - 1)$ *df*, that for the random-effect variable is random variability and has $df = N - JK$ for error, and interaction is tested by random variability and has $df = N - JK$.

From the point of view of design, you need assurance that participants were randomly assigned to the various groups. Of course, this is not possible if one of the variables is an individual characteristic (e.g., gender, personality disorder, etc.); these individuals should be randomly selected and then randomly assigned to levels of the other variable. Because attrition almost always occurs, you need assurance that the loss is not selective. And, as with all studies, there should be guards against experimenter effects as well as some assessment of the independent variables; that is, you want assurance that manipulation of the independent variable was perceived by the participant.

In many instances, factorial studies employ the same participants in more than one condition, and some ANOVA for repeated measures is appropriate for determining main and interaction effects. In rare instances, the same participants serve in all conditions of the study. Most frequently, however, different groups of individuals (one of the independent variables) participate in all levels of the second independent variable (or more for a higher order factorial study). In this instance, a two-way ANOVA with repeated measures on one factor is appropriate. When you want to check on validity of results, degrees of freedom for each effect depends on whether the circularity assumption has been met (cf. Chapter 10). The assumption does not apply to the variable that consists of separate groups. Therefore, $df =$ number of groups $(K) - 1$, for the group factor, and number of participants $(S) - K$ for the error term. The circularity assumption does apply to the within-group factor: for each group and for the pooled matrix of variances and covariances. If the assumptions are met, *df* for the within-group factor and its error term equals $J - 1$ and $(J - 1)(S - K)$, and interaction effects of both factors has $df = (J - 1)(K - 1)$ and $(J - 1)(S - K)$. However, the assumptions are seldom met, and you should be alerted to some statement about adjusting degrees of freedom to guard against a Type I error. With no indication and F ratios declared significant at $p <$ .05, you can evaluate the conclusions by comparing the F ratios against tabled values associated with $df = (1/J - 1)(J - 1) = 1$ (for the numerator) and $(1/J - 1)(J - 1)(S - K) = S - K$ (error) for the within-group, repeated measures, factor and $(1/J - 1)(J - 1)$ $(K - 1) = K - 1$ (for the numerator) and $S - K$ (error) for interaction. If F ratios are no longer significant, a Type I error looms as a possibility.

In terms of design, you need some assurance that participants were randomly assigned to the various groups or were randomly selected if the group variable is an individual characteristic, and that there was not a selective loss. Moreover, unless the repeated measures factor is some progressive event, such as trials or time, there should be an indication that levels of that factor were presented in counterbalanced order.

We begin here by evaluating a separate groups factorial study together and then do the same for a mixed-design study with repeated measures on one factor.

STUDY EXAMPLE 11.1

This experiment represents the simplest extension of a between-groups design, a 2 × 2 design. It introduces two levels of each variable. In the present study, babies were first classified as being criers or calm. This is the first independent variable. Then, each type of baby was randomly assigned to one of two conditions: They heard a recording of themselves crying or of another infant crying. This was the second independent variable. The infants were measured for amount of crying to each recording. The purpose of random assignment to each condition is that we have some assurance that criers and calm babies in each recording condition would show the same amount of crying before the records were played (i.e., they are equivalent).

The Study

There is a tendency for individuals to respond to others who are in a clear and unambiguous distress state in ways that are rapid, impulsive, and noncalculative. . . . These quick reaction times argue in favor of a basic helping tendency that is triggered by the awareness of affect or distress in another individual.

If such a capacity is inborn, it might be evident in children. . . . [R]esearchers have clearly demonstrated that children of ages 10 months to 4 years appear to become distressed in the presence of distress in others. Between the ages of 10 months and 16 months, the most common response is the distress cry. . . .

Even more suggestive of an inborn capacity to experience arousal as a result of exposure to distress cues from another individual is . . . that newborn infants cry in response to the cries of other infants. . . .

More recently, Simner . . . conducted a series of four exploratory studies to determine whether responsive crying actually occurs in newborns. . . . [H]e found that infants who were exposed to the tape-recorded cry of a 5-day-old female cried significantly more than those who heard either a silent control, white noise, a computer-generated synthetic cry, or the cry of a 5½-month-old female. . . .

Sagi and Hoffman . . . replicated the work of Simner . . . , using Simner's tapes with a younger population of infants. . . . The results clearly supported the earlier studies: Newborn infants cried significantly more in response to the cry of another infant than to a synthetic cry or to silence.

. . . It was the purpose of the present two experiments to conceptually replicate the findings of Simner . . . and Sagi and Hoffman . . . and to present further evidence of an in-born distress response to peer-generated, distressful stimuli.

There are two important research questions that were addressed in Experiment 1. The first question, perhaps the most critical, was can the apparent responsive crying in newborns be produced using tape-recorded cry stimuli other than the one employed by Simner . . . and Sagi and Hoffman . . . ? All five of these studies were based on the same tape of the cry of a 5-day-old infant. It could be that the response of the infants in these investigations was simply due to an artifact of that particular stimulus. . . . The present study used different tape recordings of the distress cry of several newborn male infants.

The second question of Experiment 1 resulted from a serendipitous finding obtained in a pilot study. Five crying male infants stopped crying when they heard a recording of their own cry. Apparently, the sound of their own cry did not provoke or increase distress. . . .

?

1. What prior literature findings provided the impetus for the first study (i.e., what was the rationale)?

Earlier studies found evidence for distress crying in infants, suggesting that there is an innate distress response. However, two of the best studies used the same tape of an infant crying, and their results might be due to an artifact, not a distress response.

2. What was the reason for conducting the first study (i.e., what was its purpose)?

To replicate the two studies using other tapes of male infants crying and to check an observation made in a pilot study that infants stop crying when they hear a tape of their own cry.

• Experiment 1 •

Method

Subjects

Forty-seven clinically normal, . . . full-term infants were pre-tested and selected from the newborn nursery population. . . . Seven infants were eliminated from the subject pool due to interruptions during the test period. The final sample consisted of 21 females and 19 males. The mean age of the infants in the study was 18.3 hours, and the mean birth weight was 7.5 pounds.

> *(Note that infants could not be randomly assigned to the two groups defining one of the independent variables because assignment depended on the pretest results. Nor could they be randomly selected after the pretest because of the limited number of babies available at one time.)*

?

3. What was the initial and final participant pool?

Forty-seven healthy newborns were initially included. Seven were excluded, leaving 21 females and 19 males, approximately 18.3 hours old, weighing about 7.5 pounds.

Apparatus

Each infant remained in his or her assigned hospital crib. The auditory stimuli were administered from a cassette player-recorder. . . . The tests were conducted in an 18 ft. × 16 ft. . . . sound-insulated nursery facility. . . . In the own-cry conditions, infants heard a tape of their own continuous crying. In the other-cry conditions, infants heard one of two tape recordings of the continuous cry of a newborn male infant (each less than 40 hours old) that had been obtained in a preliminary study. Durations of vocalizing were recorded using a computer stopwatch.

(Note that no mention is made of who brought the infants to the testing room, nor who timed the duration of crying. If, in fact, these tasks were performed by one of the authors, expectancy may play a role in the results.)

Procedure

This design crossed state of infant (crying or calm) with cry stimulus (own or other). All infants were pretested to determine the presence of the desired state. The calm-state pretest consisted of a 4-min. observation of an infant who was awake, alert, and not engaged in gross motor activity with at least one eye open. . . . If the total amount of vocalizing exceeded a maximum of 60 sec. the infant was not classified as calm. . . . [A]ll subjects in the calm conditions were totally silent for at least 3 min. of the 4-min. pretest. The crying-state pretest consisted of a 4-min. observation of an infant who was awake, grimacing, engaged in motor activity, and emitting intermittant cry sounds. . . . [A]ll subjects in the crying conditions were actively crying for at least 3 min. of the 4-min. pretest. . . . Following the pretest, the calm or crying infants were randomly assigned to own or other cry stimulus conditions. The order in which the test observations were made was randomly determined. . . .

(The general procedure involved exposing the crying or calm infant to a tape recording of his or her own cry or that of another infant crying. These exposures were conducted soon after the pretest.)

?

4. What was the design and general procedure of the study?

The 2 × 2 study used crying and calm infants who were randomly assigned to hear their own cry or the cry of another infant. All were first pretested to determine their status. Then, each was exposed to the appropriate tape for 4 minutes. Duration of crying and number of infants who cried in each condition were measured.

5. Would there be any problem in interpreting results if one of the authors served as experimenter?

Yes. Expectancy could operate to delay stopping the timer for crying infants and speed it up for calm infants—unintentionally.

Results

The number of infants who vocalized and the mean amount of vocalizations, in seconds, under each test condition are shown in Table 1. The results of a 2 × 2 analysis of variance . . . revealed a main effect of state of infant, $F(1, 36) = 26.82$, $p < .01$, a main effect for cry stimulus, $F(1, 36) = 65.32$, $p < .01$, and an interaction effect for State × Cry Stimulus, $F(1, 36) = 12.67$, $p < .01$. . . . A Newman-Keuls test applied to the test means indicated that all cells differed significantly from each other ($p < .05$) with the exception of the crying/own and calm/own comparison.

> *(The Newman-Keuls test is like the Tukey test but less conservative. However, only adjacent means are compared, so results are the same.)*

Table 1 *Mean Amount of Vocalizations (in sec) and Number of Infants Who Vocalized for Each Test Condition*

| | Cry stimulus | |
State of infant	Own	Other
Crying		
M	23.4a	149.3b
No. who vocalize	9	9
Calm		
M	5.36a	54.8c
No. who vocalize	4	10

Note. Means that do not share a common subscript differ significantly from each other (*p* < .05).

6. *Analysis of variance on mean time crying revealed two main effects. What is their meaning?*

The State main effect suggested that, on the whole, infants who were classified as criers consistently cried more than those classified as calm. The Stimulus main effect suggested that on the whole infants who heard another infant's cry consistently cried more than infants who heard their own cry.

7. *Why are degrees of freedom 1 and 36?*

There are two levels of each variable (2 − 1 = 1), and there are 10 scores within each of the four cells (40 − 4 = 36).

8. *What is the meaning of the State × Stimulus interaction?*

The interaction indicated that amount of crying to another infant's cry or to one's own cry depended on the state of the infant, whether it was a calm or crying baby.

9. Why are degrees of freedom 1 and 36?

There are two levels of each variable [$(2 - 1)(2 - 1) = 1$], and there are 10 scores within each of the four cells ($40 - 4 = 36$).

10. In what way does the results of Newman-Keuls test modify statements about the main effects?

Although infants cried consistently more to another infant's cry than to their own, regardless of state, the State main effect was modified. Crying babies cried more than calm babies only when (i.e., provided that) they heard another infant's cry; there was no differential crying between crying and calm babies when they heard their own cry.

11. How many babies did not vocalize at all during this period? From which group were they most likely to be?

Eight babies did not vocalize—most likely calm infants who had listened to their own cry. (This can be seen by assuming that each cell in Table 1 originally contained an *n* of 10.)

12. What factor(s) other than distress recognition might account for more crying to another infant's cry and less crying to the infant's own cry?

Aside from a possible experimenter effect of expectancy, there are three factors that rival a distress response that can account for the results: The crying infants may have been in actual distress, and that is why they cried more (this is a weak alternative because they cried more only when they heard another infant cry); the tape of the crying infant aroused fear, and infants exposed to it cried more; there was less crying to the infant's own crying because the sound aroused curiosity (our own voice sounds different on tape because we hear our own voice via bone conduction).

• Experiment 2 •

. . . [T]here is evidence from animal studies that the capacity to differentiate vocal sounds may be an inborn trait. . . . This strongly suggests that there is an inborn responsivity to certain social stimuli, at least in animals.

Such a capacity in humans was investigated by examining the ways in which infants respond to peer and other distress sounds. Responses of infants to the cries of another infant, a nonhuman primate, and an older child were compared. . . . [T]he cry of the infant chimp should be similar but clearly distinguishable from that of the human neonate. If responsive crying is species-specific, infants should cry less in response to the cry of a chimp than to another infant. Similarly, peer-specificity could be demonstrated by less responding to the cry of a child older than 6 months. . . .

13. What was the purpose of the second study?

To determine whether distress crying is species and peer specific.

Method

Subjects

Thirty-four clinically normal, full-term infants were pre-tested and selected from the same hospital nursery. Four infants were eliminated from the experiment because of interruptions during the test. The pretested infants were randomly assigned to one of the three experimental conditions. The final sample consisted of 13 females and 17 males.

(Note that because eliminations occurred during a test, there should have been some mention of the groups to which these infants belonged after random assignment.)

The mean age of infants in this experiment was 28.8 hours and the average birth weight was 7.3 pounds.

?

14. What were the initial and final pools of participants?

The initial pool consisted of 34 full-term, healthy babies. Four were excluded, leaving a final pool of 13 females and 17 males, about 28.8 hours old, and weighing about 7.3 pounds.

Apparatus

. . . The human neonate cry stimulus was that of a full-term infant, aged less than 40 hours, who had just received a painful injection to his right thigh. The nonhuman cry stimulus was that of a male chimpanzee, aged 16 days, who was removed from his mother and suspended from a rod for a short time. . . . The older child cry stimulus was obtained in a pediatrician's office; the 11-month-old male was suffering from a painful earache and had just received an antibiotic injection at the time of the recording.

Procedure

The infant subjects in a calm state . . . were exposed to one of the three distress stimuli for a period of 4 minutes. Upon

Table 4 *Mean Amount of Vocalization (in sec) and Number of Infants Who Vocalized for Each Test Condition*

	Condition		
Variable human	Neonate	Chimp	Older child
M	74.5a	.9b	3.3b
No. of infants who vocalize	9	1	3

Note. Means that do not share a common subscript differ significantly from each other ($p < .05$).

termination of the test phase, an additional posttest observation lasted for another 4 minutes. Otherwise, the procedure was very similar to that of Experiment 1.

15. What were the test conditions and general procedure?
All infants were tested while in a calm state. The infants were randomly assigned to hear a tape of an infant crying (peer), an older baby crying, or a baby chimpanzee crying (species).

Results

The number of infants who vocalized and the mean amount of vocalizations, in seconds, under each test condition are shown in Table 4. The results of a one-way ANOVA revealed a main effect for cry stimulus, $F(2, 27) = 14.22$, $p < .01$. A Newman-Keuls test applied to the test means indicated that the human neonate condition differed significantly from the other two conditions ($p < .05$), which did not differ from each other. . . .

?

16. What were the results of the test period, that is, essential results?

The initially calm infants cried more to the cries of their peer than they did to the cries of the older baby and the chimpanzees, with no difference in amount of crying to the tapes of the last two stimuli.

Discussion

The main findings of these investigations firmly support the results of Simner . . . and Sagi and Hoffman. . . . In both experiments calm infants who heard the cry sounds of another neonate began crying. These data offer strong evidence that the results of the earlier studies can be replicated using different tape recordings of human neonates. It can be stated with a fair amount of certainty that an infant's cry in response to hearing the cry of another infant is an identifiable behavior and that it is present at a very young age. . . . Whereas crying infants continued to cry when they heard the cries of another neonate, crying infants stopped crying when they heard their own cry, and calm infants who heard their own cry did very little crying. These results indicate that infants do respond differently to the cries of other newborns than to their own cries. . . .

The second experiment also provides helpful information. . . . Infants who heard the cry of a male newborn vocalized, and infants who heard either the cry of an infant chimpanzee or an 11-month-old boy gave almost no response. Clearly, the cries emitted by the infant subjects are in response to the newborn cry and not to an aversive sound. . . .

?

*17. What factor(s), identified in #12 as alternative expla-
nations of the results, can be ruled out as accounting
for these results and those of the first experiment?*

Arousal of fear can be ruled out because if this were a factor
there would be more crying to the older infant's and chimp's
cry, not less.

18. What factor cannot be ruled out?

Curiosity about the sound of one's own cry cannot be ruled
out as accounting for the results of the first study because
that condition was not presented here. Nor can expectancy
be ruled out.

*19. On the whole, are the conclusions reached by the
authors justified? Why?*

Generally, the evidence for a distress response (not for its
innateness) may be justified, if the role of expectancy can be
ruled out. The study was fairly well designed in that infants
were randomly assigned, although nothing was mentioned
about the infants who were dropped from the study. But the
findings, taken along with earlier findings, are in agreement.
Although, in both experiments, the taped vocalizations of the
infants were that of male infants, similar results were obtained in the reviewed studies when female vocalizations
were used.

STUDY EXAMPLE 11.2

The study reviewed so far employed independent groups of participants who were randomly assigned to their treatment conditions. The study we are about to review employs two groups that
are repeatedly measured on four levels. Therefore, data are ana-

lyzed by a two-way analysis of variance with repeated measures on one factor. The analysis includes a between-subjects component, to reveal whether any overall difference exists between the groups, and a within-subjects component, to reveal whether any overall difference exists among the four measures and whether there is interaction between the effects of the group and the measures. This study involves a survey conducted on college students. Here we will evaluate only a few of the many analyses conducted.

The Study

- Stacy, B. G., Singer, M. S., & Ritchie, G. (1989). The perception of poverty and wealth among teenage university students. *Adolescence, 24*(93), 193-206. Used with permission of Libra Publishers, Inc.

. . . [I]nequalities of wealth . . . have been a major concern of social scientists and figure prominently . . . in their theories of society. . . . Empirical research in different countries has consistently shown that economic inequalities impact on the social development of the young. Of particular significance, during the first two decades of life there is a general developmental trend towards acceptance of economic inequalities as both legitimate and preferential on grounds of distributive justice. Further, during the second decade many youngsters come to believe that poverty is the responsibility or fault of the poor and that they can overcome it by their own efforts. . . .

The empirical literature on the perception of poverty (poor people) and wealth (rich people) has been very briefly reviewed by Stacey and Singer . . . . They emphasized the developmental changes that occur in childhood and adolescence, the considerable uniformity of developmental trends . . . and the highly favorable views of the rich and the highly unfavorable views of the poor held by adolescents. . . . [F]our categories of attribution are important in adolescent explanations of poverty and wealth. These are external-social, internal-individual, family background, and luck-risk variables. . . .

The empirical content of the Stacy and Singer . . . paper dealt with the perception of poverty and wealth among high school teenagers in New Zealand. It was found that these youth stressed the significance of family and downplayed luck when dealing with poverty and wealth, and they did not rate the psychological consequences as being of much importance. The aim of the research reported here was to explore the perception of poverty and wealth among teenage university students.

?

1. What was the rationale for this study?

Sociologists are concerned about inequalities of wealth within all nations because it has an impact on social development. Research with adolescent teens shows that they have favorable attitudes toward the rich and unfavorable attitudes toward the poor. Moreover, they attribute wealth or poverty to one of four factors: "external-social, internal-individual, family background, and luck-risk." The most recent study of teen perception of wealth and poverty surveyed high school students in New Zealand, but there are no data on older teens.

. . . The present study was designed to investigate, among university students, explanations of poverty and wealth, perceived consequences of poverty and wealth, estimates of the incomes of poor and rich people, and estimates of the average teenager's chance of getting a job with and without a certificate qualification. It also investigated the association of sex, economic orientation, religious beliefs, and family financial position with attributions for poverty and wealth and the perceived consequences of poverty and wealth . . . estimates of the incomes of poor and rich persons and perceptions of employment prospects for youth among the sample.

2. What was the purpose of the study?

To survey perceptions of wealth and poverty by older teen-agers in a university in New Zealand. Specifically, the study intended to determine the students' explanation of wealth and poverty, their perception of the result of being wealthy or poor, their estimation of the income of the wealthy or poor, and their estimation of the chances of obtaining a job with or without certificate qualifications. These perceptions also were to be related to certain demographic characteristics.

Method

Subjects

Subjects were 220 teenaged undergraduates at the University of Canterbury . . . from several faculties (or schools), and were a heterogeneous volunteer sample who agreed to participate in the study. None received any sort of academic credit for participation.

3. Who served as participants?

220 university undergraduates who volunteered to take part without compensation.

4. What information is lacking in the description?

Number (and their characteristics) who refused to participate.

Questionnaire

Subjects completed a questionnaire . . . that directed them to rate, on a 7-point scale, the importance of 16 explanations for the existence of poor persons, 16 explanations for the existence of rich persons, 12 possible consequences of being poor, 12 possible consequences of being rich, and the average teenager's chance of getting a suitable job both with and without a standard school certificate qualification (usually obtained at age 15 or 16). The "explanations" items represented internal (individualistic), external (societal), familial, and luck (fatalistic) categories. The "consequences" items represented economic, social, psychological, and familial categories. These items were derived from the empirical findings. . . .

In addition, subjects estimated what they considered to be the income for both a poor man and a rich man supporting a wife and two children. They also provided demographic information (age and sex).

(They also rated their economic preference, religion observance, and family financial position.)

5. What was the general nature of the questionnaire?

An equal number of possible explanations of poverty and wealth, and of possible consequences of being poor or rich were rated on a 7-point scale, along with an average teenager's chances of getting a good job with or without a standard school certificate. Explanations were in the four categories found in the past research. Other information was sought.

Procedure

Potential subjects within the university were requested to take part in the survey on the basis of a general description of the purpose of the study. All student volunteers were presented with the questionnaire for completion within the university setting. It engaged the interest of the subjects and was well received. There was no time limit on completing the questionnaire, but it was typically completed within thirty minutes. . . . Every questionnaire was returned to the researchers anonymously, and no deception was involved.

?

6. What was the procedure?
Volunteers completed the questionnaire within the university—presumably anywhere they chose—with no time limit. They were returned anonymously, and no deception was involved.

7. What do you anticipate could have resulted from the described procedure?
If students were unsupervised, they could have collaborated; if places of completing the questionnaire varied, this could increase variability in ratings.

Results

For each subject the mean ratings was calculated for the bunches of items in each of the four categories of causal attributions and the four categories of consequences. . . . All data were then analyzed with reference to differences associated with sex, economic preference, religious position, and family financial position. The analysis of variance (**ANOVA**) technique was used extensively in the data analyses to

Table 1 *Poverty: Means of Causal Attribution Ratings*

	Causal attribution category*			
Sex	Internal	Societal	Familial	Luck
Male	4.82	3.45	3.39	4.81
Female	4.57	3.81	3.40	4.68

*Ratings: 1 = extremely important; to 7 = not important at all. Thus, low numbers indicate high importance, and high numbers low importance, with 4 indicating moderate importance.

ascertain whether any differences that emerged were statistically significant. Only those significant at the .05 level or better are reported here.

Table 1 **(in part)** presents the mean ratings for explanations of poverty. A 2 (Sex) × 4 (Attributions) ANOVA with repeated measures on the second factor was carried out on the causal attributions data. The main effect of attributions was significant, $F(3, 648) = 86.99$, $p < .001$. The Sex × Attributions interaction was also significant, $F(3, 648) = 4.89$, $p < .01$. Both sexes rated familial and societal causes as most important in determining poverty, but males rated societal causes as significantly more important than did females, $F(1, 217) = 4.29$, $p < .05$.

(The remaining analyses dealing with perceived causes of poverty have been omitted.)

8. *The results, of reasons attributed to poverty as a function of sex of the student, was analyzed by a two-way ANOVA with repeated measures on attributes. If all 220 students answered all items, how many dfs are associated with the test to determine whether there is a difference in attribute ratings between sexes?*

Sex = 2 − 1 = 1, and subjects within group = 220 − 2 = 218.

9. *How many dfs are associated with attribute ratings and with interaction between effects of sex and attributes?*

Attributes = 4 − 1 = 3, and error = (3)(218) = 654.
Interaction = (1)(3) = 3, and error = (3)(218) = 654.

10. *Reported dfs differ from what we expect. What are two possible reasons for the discrepancies?*

They are simply wrong; some data were missing.

11. *What is the meaning of the significant effect of attribution?*

There were differences, overall, in the extent to which the four attributes played a role (as perceived by the students) in causing poverty.

12. *What is the meaning of the interaction?*

Males and females differed in attributing certain factors as important causes of poverty. Whereas both sexes considered family and social factors as important causes of poverty, males perceived societal factors as more important than did females.

13. *No mention is made of correcting for failure to meet the circularity assumption. Suppose you wanted to make the most stringent correction as a test to determine whether the two relevant F ratios declared significant are significant. What would be the corrected dfs?*

Attributes: [1/3] × 3 = 1 and ([1/3] × 3)(218) = 218.

14. *Using the corrected df (again, as the most stringent test), do any of the conclusions change?*

No.

Table 2   *Poverty: Means of Consequence Ratings*

	Consequences*			
Sex	Economic	Psychological	Social	Familial
Male	2.96	4.56	4.38	3.51
Female	2.98	4.79	4.09	4.04

*Ratings: 1 = extremely important; to 7 = not important at all.

Table 2 **(in part)** indicates the mean ratings for consequences of poverty. A 2 (Sex) × 4 (Consequences) **ANOVA** with repeated measures on the second factor was carried out. The main effect of consequences was significant, $F(3, 645) = 104.21$, $p < .001$. The Sex × Consequences interaction was also significant, $F(3, 645) = 6.10$, $p < .01$. Both sexes rated the economic consequences as most important and the psychological consequences as least important. But the males rated the familial consequences higher than did the females, $F(1, 217) = 7.91$, $p < .01$.

(Remaining analyses dealing with consequences of poverty have been omitted.)

15. *Interpret the ratings of the relative importance of the four consequences of being poor.*

Economic consequences, overall, were considered most important. Also, males considered familial consequences as more important than did females.

Table 3   *Wealth: Means of Causal Attribution Ratings*

	Causal attribution category*			
Sex	Internal	Societal	Familial	Luck
Male	4.06	3.68	3.02	4.94
Female	3.85	3.96	3.42	4.88

*Ratings: 1 = extremely important; to 7 = not important at all.

Table 3 **(in part)** shows the mean ratings for explanations of wealth. The same type of analysis was carried out on this wealth data as on the poverty data. For the Sex × Attributions **ANOVA** the main effect of attributions, $F(3, 648) = 113.92$, $p < .001$, and the Sex × Attributions interaction, $F(3, 648) = 5.30$, $p < .01$, were statistically significant. Both sexes rated familial causes as most important and luck as least important in determining wealth, but males rated familial causes as significantly more important than did females.

(Remaining analyses dealing with attributes of wealth have been omitted.)

The mean ratings for consequences of wealth are set out in Table 4 **(in part)**. The Sex × Consequences ANOVA produced a significant main effect of consequences, $F(3, 648) = 167.11$, $p < .001$. . . .

(Remaining analyses have been omitted.)

?

16. *Interpret the ratings of importance of the four attributes in accounting for wealth.*

Both sexes considered familial factors as most important in accounting for wealth and luck as least important; males

Table 4 *Wealth: Means of Consequences Ratings*

Sex	Consequences*			
	Economic	Psychological	Social	Familial
Male	2.96	5.10	4.12	4.62
Female	2.94	5.03	3.95	4.99

*Ratings: 1 = extremely important; to 7 = not important at all.

again considered familial factors more important than did females.

17. What is the meaning of the significant main effect of consequences of wealth?

Overall, both sexes considered the economic results of wealth as most important and the psychological consequences least important.

Discussion

In their explanations of poverty and wealth, the New Zealand university students sampled placed most importance on familial factors, followed by societal or external factors, then internal or individualistic factors, with luck factors considered least important. Emphasis was placed on the internal category with reference to wealth more than poverty. This general pattern of attribution results is the same as the pattern previously obtained from . . . high school students. . . . Further, these results again indicate the significance of family factors in teenage thinking about poverty and wealth, contrary to . . . emphasis upon internal factors. . . .

In their ratings of the consequences of poverty and wealth, the students placed most importance on economic consequences and least on psychological consequences. The familial consequences were rated much higher for poverty than for wealth, and ahead of social consequences for poverty but not for wealth. The pattern of these results again replicates that of the earlier study. . . .

For the total sample, our findings suggest that students operate primarily with social-psychological notions of poverty and wealth rather than with political or individual psychological notions. But this does not apply uniformly to all sections of the sample. . . .

One limitation of the present study concerns the use of single rating scales in the identification of the subgroups on the three key variables of economic preference, religious beliefs, and family financial position. However, this modest empirical study has extended some of the significant findings concerning high school teenagers' perceptions of poverty and wealth . . . to a sample of young university students. Further, this study identified certain significant associations between the economic preference, religious beliefs, and family financial position of these young students and their perceptions of poverty and wealth. It also demonstrated the value of focusing on subjects in their late teens in that it extended the scope of economic socialization.

?

18. What were the major findings of this survey?

University students attribute poverty and wealth to family factors first, then societal (external) factors, followed by internal factors and luck as the least important cause.

19. Given that attributes are a function of economic preference, religious observance, and family financial position, what other factors might account for these results?

Select nature of the volunteers, wording of the explanations, explanations selected per se, where and with whom the questionnaire was completed.

20. To whom do the results apply?

School-age (including university) students who live in New Zealand, with the same type of economic structure and governmental policies.

Supplementary Readings
on This Topic

- Girden, E. R. (1992). *ANOVA: Repeated measures*. Newbury Park, CA: Sage.
- Iverswen, G. R., & Norpoth, H. (1987). *Analysis of variance* (2nd ed.). Newbury Park, CA: Sage.
- Kirk, R. E. (1982). *Experimental design: Procedures for the behavioral sciences* (2nd ed.). Belmont, CA: Brooks/Cole.

12

QUASI-EXPERIMENTAL STUDIES

The major characteristics of a true experimental design, such as have been considered in the preceding chapters, include random assignment of participants to the various conditions of the study and control groups to eliminate alternate explanations of results. In many instances, random assignment is not possible or not permitted by an administrator. For example, if learning rate of alcoholics is to be determined with results attributed to alcoholism per se, you cannot randomly assign participants to an alcoholic and nonalcoholic group. However, investigators will attempt to design the study in such a way that confounds are minimized so that a cause-effect conclusion may be feasible. Such designs are seemingly experimental or quasi-experimental. There are two basic categories of these designs. Repeated measures types obtain a number of measures of the dependent variable before and after the intervention (independent variable) on the same group of participants. Separate groups types introduce control groups that have not been randomly assigned to the control conditions; hence, they are called nonequivalent control groups.

Although the factor of initial nonequivalence on the dependent variable cannot be controlled experimentally, it is sometimes possible to achieve equivalence statistically, by means of analysis of covariance. With this technique, an initial measure of the dependent variable, or a variable correlated with it, is made. This is the covariate. Then, that part of variability of the posttreatment dependent variable associated with the covariate is removed. The final analysis is performed on the remaining part of variability to determine how much is due to treatment and how much to experimental or random error. The statistical procedure is not a cure-all for a poorly designed study. Instead, it is introduced after careful consideration. As in any statistical procedure, there are certain assumptions made before the final analysis is performed. One of the most glaring is that the relationship between the covariate and dependent variable is about the same in all groups. Therefore, there should be some indication that a test of "homogeneity of regression slopes" has been performed. And in checking for accuracy of the statistical test, df = number of groups − 1 for the numerator and total N − number of groups − 1 for the error term. We'll evaluate two quasi-experimental studies together. The first involved some random assignment and the second was a definite nonequivalent control group study.

STUDY EXAMPLE 12.1

The present experiment involves a between-groups design of a special kind. It combines random assignment of participants and the use of an intact control group; hence, it is basically a nonequivalent control group quasi-experimental design. In particular, the experiment concerns recovery of a learning ability among patients being treated for alcohol abuse.

The Study

- Sharp, J. R., Rosenbaum, G., Goldman, M. S., & Whitman, R. D. Recoverability of psychological functioning following alcohol abuse: Acquisition of meaningful synonyms. *Journal of Consulting and Clinical Psychology, 45*(6), 1023-1028. Copyright © 1977 by the American Psychological Association. Adapted with permission.

  Footnote: This study was in part based on a master's thesis submitted to Wayne State University by the first author.

  (Note that the information is very important. Most data for master's theses are collected by the candidate.)

Recent reviews . . . present substantial evidence that neuro-psychological deficits are associated with chronic alcohol abuse. Research on recoverability of these deficits . . . has been relatively sparse . . . and is essential for treatment planning that currently presumes psychological functioning to be adequate immediately following detoxification.

Using verbal learning tasks to assess cognitive deficits . . . **several investigators** . . . found some recovery of short-term memory and new learning ability over a 3-week period after detoxification. Intellectual test scores have also been reported to increase over a 1-week span, . . . a 6-week span . . . and a 1-year span.

In studies of recovery of perceptual and motor deficits, improvement in performance has been demonstrated over 8 weeks using the Purdue Pegboard, . . . over 80 days on the Bender-Gestalt, . . . and over 1 year on a number of Halstead-Reitan visual-motor tests. . . .

Interpretation of much of the available research on recovery parameters, however, appears limited by methodological considerations. The derivation of a recovery parameter requires multiple independent assessments of psychological functioning following cessation of drinking. Most studies used only two data points for assessment, precluding the possibility of generating a complete recovery function and of specifying exactly when recovery occurs. In addition, many studies used a test-retest design with the same subjects, allowing for the possibility that improvements in performance may have resulted from practice with tasks rather than recovery of functioning. . . . There remains a need for generating . . . a recovery function for the learning of meaningful verbal material, since this ability reflects high-level cerebral processing. . . .

?

1. *What previous findings provided the rationale for the study?*

Literature suggests that alcoholics undergoing detoxification begin to recover some verbal and perceptual motor skills. However, most of the studies used two data points (measures at the beginning and some point after recovery began), not allowing for a functional relationship between performance and the time since recovery began. Other studies used a test-retest method and no control for a practice effect in accounting for "improvement."

2. *What was the purpose of the study (i.e., why was it conducted)?*

To arrive at a recovery function for a verbal (intellectual) skill by alcoholics undergoing detoxification, while controlling for the effects of practice.

The Synonym Learning Test (SLT) . . . was selected for the assessment of complex verbal learning ability because (a) it has been shown to be sensitive to neuropsychological deterioration in the aged and is likely to be sensitive to a similar sort of deterioration in alcoholics; (b) it incorporates a typical "hold" test of neuropsychological function (a test that usually does not show deterioration after brain damage) as an estimate of prior intelligence, in the form of the Mill Hill Vocabulary Scale; (c) it assesses the learning of meaningful verbal items; and (d) it provides an individualized control for the difficulty level of the vocabulary items to be learned. . . .

?

3. What was the rationale for selecting the Synonym Learning Test as the learning task?

It is sensitive to neurological impairment, has a "hold" test, measures learning of verbal items (synonyms) and adjusts for difficulty of to-be-learned items.

The current study assessed the recovery of detoxified alcoholics' ability to learn meaningful verbal items in accord with the aforementioned methodological considerations. . . .

Method

Design

The SLT was administered so as to ascertain a three-point recovery curve while controlling for practice effects. Group 1 was tested three times, as close as possible to Days 5, 15, and 25 of the program. Group 2 subjects only received the Day 15 and Day 25 administrations, and Group 3 only received the Day 25 administration. The control group was tested only once during hospitalization to provide a nonalcoholic reference point . . . Comparisons across the first testing of each group provided a recovery curve uncontaminated by practice. The effects of practice were discernible in comparisons across groups on Day 25. The combined effects of practice and recovery appeared within the three testings of Group 1.

Subjects

Three groups of 11 male alcoholics, matched on age, years of education, and drinking history, were tested during a 28-day inpatient treatment program conducted in the Alcohol Unit of Detroit Memorial Hospital.

(Note that the groups can be considered equivalent only with respect to these three matching variables.)

Eleven male nonalcoholic control subjects, matched with the three alcoholic groups as to age and years of education, were obtained from the general medical wards of the Allen Park, Michigan, Veterans Administration Hospital.

(Note that the experimental patients were not reported to be veterans and could have differed from these control patients on a number of possibly relevant variables.)

Subjects with any psychiatric or neurological diagnosis were excluded from the study. The 44 subjects remaining in the four matched groups were derived from an original sample of 64 subjects participating in a larger study of psychological recoverability. . . .

4. What populations of participants were sampled?

Patients were selected from a larger pool of 64 participants, part of a large project being conducted at an alcoholic center and a nearby veteran's hospital.

5. On what bases were the groups formed?

The 33 alcoholics were matched on age, years of education, and years of drinking to form three groups. The 11 veterans were matched with the experimental groups on the bases of age and education.

6. Could the three alcoholic groups be considered equivalent?

They are equivalent on the matched variables. However, the authors do not report the method used to assign groups (or patients) to the three conditions, and therefore they may not be equivalent on other important variables.

Table 2 *Group Means for Demographic Variables*

Group	Age	Years of education	Years of alcohol abuse
1	41.55	11.64	9.73
2	45.45	11.64	12.18
3	43.36	11.00	10.55
Control	37.55	11.82	—

7. Could the control and experimental groups be considered equivalent?

It is not likely that controls and experimental groups are equivalent. The controls were veterans and could have differed on such variables as SES (socioeconomic status).

Table 2 presents the group means for the demographic variables on which the four groups were matched. No significant differences were found among the four groups on the mean age and number of years of education, and the three alcoholic groups did not differ on the reported number of years of alcohol abuse. . . .

Procedure

. . . [T]he SLT procedure measures new word acquisition by teaching the subjects the meanings of 10 words immediately beyond their initial Mill Hill Vocabulary levels. . . . [Group 1, tested 3 times, was given 3 alternate forms of synonyms on each of the tests. Group 2, tested 2 times, was given 2 alternate forms of the synonyms.]

At the first testing, each subject was given the synonym section of the Mill Hill, and his vocabulary level was determined. . . .

The experimenter . . . read aloud to the subject the 10 words and their meanings immediately beyond the subject's vocabularly level on the . . . word list. If the subject failed to recall the meanings of at least 6 of the words in one trial, the same words and their meanings were read to him again, and this continued for a maximum of 10 trials. . . .

(Note that no mention is made about the experimenter. Because the footnote of the article indicates that this study was a master's thesis, it is likely that the first author was the experimenter. Therefore, expectancy may be an additional contaminator. Also, there is no indication of where testing occurred. If both hospitals were used, there is an additional source of confound with experimental patients tested in one place and controls tested in another.)

8. What four testing conditions were introduced?

Group 1 was tested on Day 5, Day 15, and Day 25 after detoxification began; Group 2 was tested after 15 days and 25 days; Group 3 was tested after 25 days; and the control group tested once.

9. What was the purpose of having three experimental groups?

By staggering the time of the first test in each of the three groups, the effect of practice on synonym learning was controlled, and course of recovery could be determined.

10. What was the general procedure (i.e., what were the subjects required to do)?

After initial vocabularly level was determined, the next higher level of synonyms was presented individually. A list of 10 words and their meaning was read to the subject. He was required to remember the meaning of at least 6 words. If this criterion was not met, the words and meanings were repeated for a maximum of 10 times. Group 1 went through the procedure three times with equivalent forms of the synonyms, Group 2 went through the procedure twice, and Group 3 once.

Table 3 *Mean Vocabulary Level, SLT, and Adjusted SLT Score of Each Group at Their First Testing*

Group	Vocabulary level	SLT score	Adjusted SLT score
1 (Day 5)	25.64	56.00	55.02
2 (Day 15)	27.27	79.09	74.33
3 (Day 25)	24.00	70.54	76.28
Control	22.27	73.73	76.81

Note. SLT = Synonym Learning Test.

Table 4 *Correlation Coefficients Among SLT Scores, Vocabulary Levels, and Matching Variables for the Three Alcoholic Groups*

Variable	SLT	1	2	3	4
1. Vocabulary	.58**				
2. SES[a]	.32	.43*			
3. Age	.23	.28	.07		
4. Education	.42*	.20	.59**	.12	
5. Alcohol abuse	.11	.01	−.28	.41*	−.40*

Note. SLT = Synonym Learning Test. $N = 33$.
[a]Socioeconomic status (SES) was computed by summing the ranks for educational and occupational level.
*$p < .01$; **$p < .001$.

11. Who was the experimenter most likely to be?

The experimenter was most likely the first author, who was working on his master's thesis. There is a possibility of an experimenter effect affecting the outcome.

Results

The mean vocabulary and synonym learning scores for the *first* testing of each group are presented in Table 3. . . . The intercorrelations among these scores and all relevant demographic variables are presented in Table 4.

Inspection of Table 3 shows that the scores on the Mill Hill Vocabulary Scale are quite comparable in the four groups. A simple analysis of variance of these vocabulary scores was nonsignificant as anticipated. Thus . . . in the earliest stages of alcohol recovery . . . vocabulary knowledge was not impaired. . . [T]he correlation between years of alcoholism and vocabularly score was .01 and nonsignificant, consistent with . . . previous findings that vocabulary level is unaffected by drinking history.

?

12. *What two findings suggest that vocabulary level is not impaired by alcohol abuse?*

Analysis of variance performed on the four mean vocabulary scores revealed no differences among the means, and there was no correlation between vocabulary score and years of alcohol abuse.

. . . Examination of the relationship between the vocabulary and SLT means in Table 3 and, more particularly, their intercorrelation in Table 4 ($r = .58$) clearly indicates that subjects' ability to learn new items was not independent of initial vocabulary level. . . . To control for possible differential effects of vocabulary level in the four groups, an analysis of covariance with SLT scores adjusted for initial vocabulary level **(the covariate)** was performed. These adjusted SLT scores, which also appear in Table 3, show the performance of Group 1 at Day 5 to be significantly below that of the other alcoholic groups tested later in the treatment program, $F(2, 29) = 3.571$, $p < .05$.

(Note that the dfs are correct. There are three experimental groups and numerator df = 3 − 1 = 2. And the error df = 33 − 3 − 1 = 29.)

This finding indicates that alcoholics' ability to learn new word meanings was impaired shortly after detoxification, but it recovered to normal levels within 2 weeks postdetoxification.

?

13. *Analysis of covariance was performed on the syno-nym learning scores of the three experimental groups (for first-time testing). (a) Why?*

There was a correlation between vocabulary score and SLT score. The analysis removed the effect of vocabulary on SLT by introducing vocabulary as a covariate. The final SLT measure (i.e., its variability) was uncontaminated by vocabulary.

(b) *Degrees of freedom are reported as 2 and 29. Why is the error df 29 and not 30?*

An additional *df* is lost from the error term because of the estimation of the regression coefficient in the analysis.

(c) *What did the results reveal?*

Analysis of covariance revealed that SLT scores are significantly lower after 5 days of detoxification than after 15 and 25 days.

No significant practice effects were obtained by analysis of covariance comparisons of adjusted means across all groups on their final testing. . . .

(If there had been a practice effect, Group I, tested three times, would have obtained the highest mean and the F ratio would have been significant.)

. . . Hence, it was possible to cross-validate the previous findings via a repeated measures analysis of variance within Group 1 across the three testing intervals. . . . [A]ny improvement observed within Group 1 was apparently attributable solely to psychological recovery. This analysis confirmed the earlier findings by showing that at Day 5 ($M = 56.00$) the performance of Group 1 was significantly below subsequent testings (M for Day 15 = 82.36, M for Day 25 = 71.18), $F(2, 30) = 9.219$, $p < .001$. . . .

(The df for the repeated measures should be 3 – 1 = 2, and [3 – 1] [11 – 1] = 20.)

?

14. *Because of no evidence for a practice on the scores of Group 1, a repeated measures ANOVA was performed on their 3 sets of scores. The F ratio reported 2 and 30 df. What are the correct values?*

$df = (3 - 1) = 2$ and $(3 - 1)(11 - 1) = 20$.

15. *Assuming that 30 df indeed had been used to calculate MS_{error}, the F ratio reported may very well be wrong, as may be the conclusions reached about the three means. We have sufficient information to check these.*

   (a) *Calculate MS_b using the three reported means of Group 1. (Hint: You need the definitional formula for MS_b.)*

$M_g = (56 + 82.36 + 71.18)/3 = 69.85$; $MS_b \ \Sigma[n(M_j - M_g)^2]/2$
$\quad = 11[(56 - 69.85)^2 + (82.36 - 69.85)^2 + (71.18 - 69.85)^2]/2$
$\quad = 1925.50$.

   (b) *Based on $F = MS_b/MS_{error}$, the MS_b that you just calculated, and the F value that was reported, determine the value of MS_{error} that was used, based on 30 df.*

$F = 9.219$; $F = MS_b/MS_{error}$; $MS_{error} = MS_b/F = 1925.50/9.219$
$\quad = 208.86$.

(c) *Now, based on* $MS_{error} = SS_{error}/df_{error}$, *calculate* SS_{error}.

$MS_{error} = SS_{error}/df$; $SS_{error} = MS_{error} \times df = 208.86 \times 30$
$= 6265.874$.

(d) *Using* SS_{error} *and the correct df, recalculate* MS_{error}

$MS_{error} = 6265.874/20 = 313.294$.

(e) *Using the new* MS_{error}, *calculate the appropriate F ratio and determine whether it is still significant.*

$F = 1925.50/313.294 = 6.146$, $p < .01$.

(f) *A basic assumption of repeated measures analysis is that of circularity. One quick check on the validity of the F ratio is to determine whether the ratio would be significant with 1 df for the numerator and* $n - 1 = 10$ *(here) df for the denominator. Does the new F ratio pass the test?*

The $F_{(.05)}$ for 1 and 10 $df = 4.96$. The new value is significant.

(g) *Although the Scheffé test is not the best post hoc test for a repeated measures situation, it is conservative and will yield the information we need. Use the Scheffé test to compare the three means of Group 1.*

56 versus 82.36: $SS = 11(56 - 82.36)^2/2 = 3821.67$;
                                   $F = 3821.67/313.294 = 12.198^*$

56 versus 71.18: $SS = 11(56 - 71.18)^2/2 = 1267.38$;
                                   $F = 1267.38/313.294 = 4.045$.

82.36 versus 71.18: $SS = 11(82.36 - 71.18)^2/2 = 687.46$.
                                   $F = 687.46/313.294 = 2.194$
                             $S^2 = (J - 1)(F_{(05,2,20)}) = 2(4.35) = 8.70$.

16. *On the basis of the reanalyzed data, what can be concluded regarding recovery of synonym learning ability after cessation of drinking?*

Although SLT scores were significantly lower after 5 than 15 days of detoxification, they were not lower than scores after

25 days of detoxification. This suggests that there is some recovery of this verbal ability after 15 days of detoxification, but that recovery either levels off thereafter or may even begin to decline.

Discussion

. . . [A]s expected, a well-practiced verbal habit, vocabulary knowledge, was relatively unimpaired by chronic alcohol abuse; and . . . the capability of assimilating new vocabulary was impaired shortly after drinking ceased but recovered to normal levels within 2 weeks postdetoxification. No permanent neurological effects of a lengthy drinking history were noted on this test. . . . The current experimental design eliminated the possibility that task practice rather than psychological recovery was responsible for improvement. Also, the use of three data points permitted the specification of the recovery as occurring during the first 2 weeks of postdetoxification. . . .

?

17. What was the major conclusion reached by the author?

That recovery of a verbal skill, after alcohol abuse, begins within the first 2 weeks of detoxification.

18. Is the conclusion valid on statistical grounds?

It may not be. Assuming that the numbers reported are accurate, there is only a difference in SLT scores between the first and second data point tests.

19. *What factor(s), other than a genuine recovery of func-*
   tioning, might account for the results?

Because the experimenter was likely to be the first author,
whose task it was to score items as correct or incorrect, and
because he did anticipate certain results, an expectancy
effect cannot be ruled out. And the three experimental
groups were formed on the basis of three matching variables,
so another subject variable confound also might have operated. Finally, if testing occurred at the respective hospitals,
conditions may have been more favorable for one of the
groups.

STUDY EXAMPLE 12.2

This is a second example of a quasi-experimental design; a classic
example of a nonequivalent control group design. Two fourth
grade classes were selected, with one designated as the experimental group and the other as the control group. Because the
experiment was conducted during school hours it would have
been almost impossible to randomly assign the children to the
two groups. However, while reading the report, you might begin
to think about ways in which tighter control conditions could
have been introduced to render the conclusion more plausible.
This study, however, does introduce some control procedures. It
makes use of pretests and posttests, allowing for within-group
comparisons via correlated *t* tests, initial between-group comparisons on pretest measures via independent *t* tests and posttreatment comparisons via analyses of covariance. An alternative
way of analyzing the data could have been analyses of gain scores
(i.e., differences between pre- and posttest scores). Still another
alternative, because multiple dependent variables were made on
each child, is to analyze the data by multivariate analysis of
variance. This allows experimenters to detect group differences
in patterns of means of the various measures.

The study was an attempt to demonstrate that relaxation training will reduce stress among fourth-grade children.

The Study

- Zaichkowsky, L. B., & Zaichkowsky, L. D. (1984). The effects of a school-based relaxation training program on fourth grade children. *Journal of Clinical Child Psychology, 13(D)*, 81-85. Used with permission.

We live in a society where statistics suggest that stress-induced disease in adults has reached almost epidemic proportion. . . .

Like adults, children today have to deal with the realities of a rapidly moving, high pressure world. . . . [A] recent review estimated that 20% of the child population is negatively affected by biological (e.g., chronic disease) and psychological stressors (e.g., parental divorce), but a much greater number by stressors which might be termed social, economic and cultural (e.g., disadvantaged families and disadvantaged or high pressure schools). Regardless of the stressor involved, the "fight or flight" response (Cannon . . . is activated in the child, . . . thus preventing many youngsters from performing optimally in school, and enjoying optimal health.

. . . [H]ealth care professionals should be focusing their efforts on preventing stress-induced disorders, rather than treating them. Further, it seems that any preventive program should focus on the *young child.* . . .

The efficacy of stress management training programs with children has been evaluated infrequently. . . .

. . . Lowenstein . . . has proposed a stress management program for children which employs an adaptation of the Jacobsonian progressive relaxation, guided imagery, and temperature biofeedback. This program also has not been formally evaluated.

Two Swedish educational researchers recently reported preliminary findings from a study conducted on 294 high school students in Sweden. . . . Preliminary analysis showed the majority of the students favored the program, learned relaxation, and found it useful. Additionally the students felt their school work was better, their sleep had improved, and they felt less stressed.

Perhaps the most popular, but as yet unevaluated, program for children has been developed by Stroebel et al. . . . . [N]o formal evaluation of its short-term efficacy has been published to date. . . .

. . . [T]hese studies indicate that school based stress management programs have the *potential* to effect a number of health, life style, and performance changes. The purpose of this study was to investigate the effects of a six week relaxation training program on selected physiological and psychological measures of fourth grade children.

?

1. What was the rationale for the study?

Evidence suggests that a sizable number of children as well as adults are affected by social, psychological, and biological stressors. A reasonable solution to reducing their effects is by means of early intervention. Whereas a number of stress management programs have been tried with children, very few of the programs have been scientifically evaluated.

2. What was the purpose of the study?

The study intended to test a stress reduction program, relaxation training, on fourth-grade students to determine whether it would effectively reduce stress in this young age group.

Method

Subjects included two fourth grade classes that were randomly selected from a group of fourth grade teachers who volunteered to participate in the study.

> *(Note the implication that some teachers did not volunteer. Perhaps those who did had students who were most stressed. Moreover, each class had a different teacher, so we have to consider the possibility that the two groups are not equivalent on variables that are related to stress.)*

There were 19 subjects in the control group (13 females, 6 males) and 24 in the experimental group (12 males, 12 females).

?

3. Who were the participants? How were the groups formed?

Participants were fourth-grade children who were part of two classes in a particular school. The classes were randomly selected from a group of classes whose teachers had volunteered to take part in the study. One class served as the experimental group ($n = 24$, 12 females and 12 males), and the other served as the control group ($n = 19$, 13 females and 6 males).

4. Could the groups be considered equivalent with respect to initial levels of stress?

If the teachers volunteered to take part in the stress study, they may have had the most stressed classes. However, unless fourth graders are randomly assigned to different teachers, there may have been some reason for one teacher to have what became the experimental group and the other teacher to have what became the control group. Also, there is no indication of the basis for designating one class as experimental, so a selection factor may have been operating.

Dependent Measures

Measurements were taken on five tension related dependent variables; three physiological and two psychological.

Heart Rate. Heart rate was measured using the "insta-Pulse," a . . . hand-held instrument. . . . The experimentors recorded three consecutive measures of heart rate and used the mean as the indicator of heart rate.

Skin Temperature. Skin temperature was measured using a Cyborg P42 temperature unit. . . . The thermistor was attached to the student's first finger, of the dominant (writing) hand. When the instrument was stable (2-3 minutes) that value was used as the measure of skin temperature.

Respiration Rate. Respiration rate was measured by placing a folded 3 × 5 card on the abdomen of the subject and counting the number of respirations in 30 seconds and multiplying by two. . . . All of the above measures were taken with the children lying quietly on matted floors. Testing conditions were standard for both groups during pre- and post-tests. . . .

State and Trait Anxiety. State and trait anxiety were assessed using Spielberger's Scale for Children, a self-report measure. . . .

(Note that there is no mention about the order in which these measures were taken. If anxiety scales were administered last, their measures might be affected by the previous ones.)

5. *What measures of stress/relaxation were used? In what order were they applied? Does it matter?*

In essence, five measures were used: physiological measures of heart rate, respiration, and skin temperature and psychological measures of state and of trait anxiety. There is no indication that any attempt was made to counterbalance order of the measurements, especially because measurements were made when the entire group was present rather than on an individual basis. Yes, it does matter; responses may be a function of order effects, instead of or in addition to stress.

Research Design

The research design followed a pre-test, post-test control group format. The groups were measured on the five dependent measures prior to and at the conclusion of the six week program. The experimental group received the relaxation training program which consisted of a 20 minute theoretical lesson and seventeen, 10 minute lessons using progressive muscular relaxation, mental imagery, and breathing techniques. Three lessons were taught per week, two in the gymnasium, with subjects lying on gymnastics mats, and one in the classroom with the subjects sitting in chairs. All lessons, as well as the pre- and post-testing, were conducted by the experimenters. . . .

> *(Note that nothing is said about control children. If nothing was done, they had less attention than experimental children—a possible confound. Moreover, experimenters did the training and testing and certainly expected positive effects, so expectancy, too, cannot be ruled out.)*

. . . [T]he theoretical structure of the training curriculum is derived from the principles of progressive muscular relaxation, mental imagery and breathing. . . .

Even though there were only seventeen 10 minute lessons, which did not allow a great amount of time for practice, a cassette tape was made and given to each child to use at home following the third week. . . . Children were encouraged to share and use this tape with parents and siblings, and practice using the relaxation strategies under conditions of stress.

> *(Although home practice is part of training, these children may also have received more attention at home.)*

6. What was the general procedure?

Both groups were pretested on the five measures. The physiological measures were made with the children on a matted floor. The experimental group underwent a 20-minute lesson followed by seventeen 10-minute sessions of relaxation training, two in the gymnasium and one in the classroom, for 6 weeks. They also were given a cassette to practice their exercises at home and encouraged to share it with their families. Afterward, both groups were posttested.

7. Who tested and trained the children?

The children were all pretested, trained, and posttested by the experimenters themselves.

Results

T tests for independent means were performed on all dependent measures on the pre-test data by group and sex. The results indicated that the groups were not significantly different at the start of the program nor were there statistically significant differences between the sexes. Since no significant sex differences were found the male and female data were collapsed.

8. What was the purpose of conducting the initial series of independent t tests?

Independent *t* tests were performed on the pretest scores to determine that both groups did not differ on the measures initially, as well as to determine that there were no gender differences within groups. This allowed the experimenters to consider males and females together as single groups.

Table 1   *Means and Standard Deviations for Experimental and Control Groups (pre- and post-testing)*

| Variable | Experimental (n = 24) | | | | Control (n = 19) | | | |
| | Pre | | Post | | Pre | | Post | |
	M	SD	M	SD	M	SD	M	SD
Heart rate	96.20	12.26	81.38	9.81*	94.21	14.85	97.84	11.73
Respiration	22.50	5.73	17.58	4.37*	21.16	2.69	21.26	3.96
Temperature	80.30	5.43	87.97	2.71*	80.11	5.71	90.30	1.74*
State Anxiety	38.46	4.99	35.42	7.61	37.95	6.41	35.74	5.46
Trait Anxiety	27.88	5.10	26.54	5.81	30.26	7.37	29.42	6.26

*Significant pre- to post-test change ($p < .01$).

Table 1 contains the means and standard deviations for both groups, pre- and post-test, on all five dependent measures. *T* tests for correlated means were used to analyze changes pre- to post-test. The experimental subjects experienced significant pre- to post-test gains ($p < .01$) in a positive direction for heart rate, respiration rate, skin temperature, and state anxiety. The control subjects experienced a significant increase in their ability to raise skin temperature ($p < .01$).

9. Why were correlated t-tests performed?

Correlated *t* tests were performed within each group to determine the change in measures from pre- to post-test.

Analysis of covariance (pre-test used as covariate) for determining between group differences revealed the following: The experimental subjects differed significantly from the control subjects on the adjusted post-test means on heart rate, . . . respiration rate, . . . [and] temperature. . . . No significant differences were obtained for state and trait anxiety.

?

10. *Why were pretest scores used as covariates in the between-groups comparisons?*

The pretest scores were used as covariates, when comparing experimental and control groups, to control for initial levels of each of the measures in accounting for posttreatment measures.

11. *What were the essential results of training?*

All pretest measures were found to be statistically alike, as were measures for males and females. Significant pre- to posttest changes were found for all physiological measures of the experimental group, as well as in state anxiety, which decreased. The control group showed a positive change in skin temperature from pre- to posttest. Finally, analysis of covariance revealed that the experimental group had lower heart rate, respiration rate, and lower skin temperature than the control group. No differences were found between groups in the psychological measures of anxiety.

Discussion

The findings of this study confirms the . . . findings . . . that children can in fact learn tension/stress control in a period as short as six weeks. Heart rate and respiration rate are traditional measures of physiological arousal and it appears that children can learn to control these parameters by focusing on breathing, relaxing their musculature and imagining warm relaxing scenes. Skin temperature as a measure of physiological arousal is a more recent criterion measure which has evolved from research in biofeedback.

. . . [T]he control subjects also demonstrated a significant increase in skin temperature which was greater than the experimental subjects. A probable explanation for this finding is that the control group was post-tested on a day in which the room temperature was five degrees higher than during the pre-testing and the humidity was extremely high; both room temperature and humidity can have a significant effect on vasoconstriction/dilation.

?

12. What did the experimenters conclude?

The experimenters concluded that young children could learn relaxation techniques to reduce their level of stress.

13. What factors other than or in addition to training could have equally accounted for the results or invalidated the conclusion?

Extra attention might have been given to the experimental group which presumably was not given to the control group in school and especially at home. The pretest scores may be a reflection of the order in which the tests were given rather than a function of stress. The experimenters, who anticipated beneficial effects of training, did the measuring and training. Posttest scores may be a reflection of expectancy effects rather than training. Control group may well have learned about the special treatment the experimental subjects were receiving and may have resented not getting the same treatment (resentful demoralization). However, this factor might not play a role. Their pre- and posttest scores would have differed significantly and they did only for the temperature measure. Given that the groups were not equivalent, there could have been a difference in rate of maturation for the two groups (i.e., faster for the experimental group), leading to a selection x maturation threat to internal validity. There might have been a selection bias, especially because the teachers volunteered.

14. *What factors are least likely to have confounded the results of training in this study?*

(a) History, because both groups attended the same school and were likely to be exposed to the same potentially confounding events. (b) Instrumentation, because the same measurements were made by the same experimenters. (c) Initial (repeated) testing, because three of the measures were physiological and the children were not very likely to remember earlier responses to test questions asked 6 weeks earlier. (d) Regression toward the mean, because the two classes were randomly selected from what would seem to be the most stressed classes and no pretest differences were found between groups. (e) Selective loss, because they report no loss of participants from either group.

15. *How might the study be designed, within the confines of the school setting, to eliminate some of these confounds?*

Given that intact classes are the most feasible groups to use in the school setting, match the classes on age, IQ, and stress. Randomly assign the classes to experimental or control conditions. The control group has to receive equal (placebo) attention to that of the experimental group. Because home practice is part of relaxation training, this aspect would have to be retained. However, the children should not be encouraged to share the tape with family members. Relaxation exercises could be presented by videotape because anyone who is trained in the technique will have a positive expectancy. Finally, a "blind" experimenter should take the pre- and post-test measures.

Supplementary Readings
on This Topic

- Cook, T. D., & Campbell, D. T. (1979). *Quasi-experimentation: Design and analysis issues for field settings.* Chicago: Rand McNally College Publishing.
- Kazdin, A. E. (1992). *Research design in clinical psychology* (2nd ed.). Boston: Allyn & Bacon.
- Kirk, R. E. (1982). *Experimental design: Procedures for the behavioral sciences* (2nd ed.). Belmont, CA: Brooks/Cole.
- Neale, J. M., & Liebert, R. M. (1986). *Science and behavior: An introduction to methods of research* (3rd ed.). Englewood Cliffs, NJ: Prentice Hall.

ABOUT THE AUTHOR

Ellen R. Girden received her bachelor's degree from Brooklyn College (1956), with a major in biology and minors in education and psychology. She earned her master's degree in general psychology (1958) also from Brooklyn College and studied at Northwestern University for the doctorate in physiological psychology (1962). She taught at Hobart and William Smith Colleges in Geneva, New York, for two years, where she completed her dissertation. In 1963, she joined the faculty of Yeshiva University in Manhattan, New York. After a joint appointment with the graduate and undergraduate schools (Stern College for Women), she was able to confine her teaching to the female undergraduates and reached the professional rank of Associate Professor. During these years she conducted studies related to the physiological basis of fear-motivated behavior of rats, time estimation by students, and a series on the effects of crowding and litter size on various behaviors of rats.

In 1977, she married and moved to Florida. A year later she was one of the original faculty of the School of Professional Psychology of Florida, conducting courses in research design, statistics, learning, and the history of psychology. In 1981, the School merged with Nova University. Within a few years she was promoted to Professor and focused on research design and intermediate and advanced statistics. She remained in that position until 1993, when she retired.

Besides research, she supervised over 15 dissertation projects, coauthored a chapter with her husband, and wrote a monograph for Sage on repeated measures analysis of variance.